Creative Writing

DeMYSTiFieD®

DeMYSTiFieD® Series

Accounting Demystified
Advanced Statistics Demystified
Algebra Demystified
Alternative Energy Demystified
ASP.NET 2.0 Demystified
Biology Demystified
Biotechnology Demystified
Business Calculus Demystified
Business Math Demystified
Business Statistics Demystified
C++ Demystified
Calculus Demystified
Chemistry Demystified
Commodities Demystified
Corporate Finance Demystified, 2e
Data Structures Demystified
Databases Demystified, 2e
Differential Equations Demystified
Digital Electronics Demystified
Electricity Demystified
Electronics Demystified
Environmental Science Demystified
Everyday Math Demystified
Financial Accounting Demystified
Financial Planning Demystified
Financial Statements Demystified
Forensics Demystified
Genetics Demystified
Grant Writing Demystified
Hedge Funds Demystified
Human Resource Management Demystified
Intermediate Accounting Demystified
Investing Demystified, 2e
Java Demystified
JavaScript Demystified
Lean Six Sigma Demystified
Linear Algebra Demystified

Macroeconomics Demystified
Management Accounting Demystified
Marketing Demystified
Math Proofs Demystified
Math Word Problems Demystified
Mathematica Demystified
Matlab Demystified
Microbiology Demystified
Microeconomics Demystified
Nanotechnology Demystified
OOP Demystified
Operating Systems Demystified
Options Demystified
Organic Chemistry Demystified
Pharmacology Demystified
Physics Demystified
Physiology Demystified
Pre-Algebra Demystified
Precalculus Demystified
Probability Demystified
Project Management Demystified
Public Speaking and Presentations Demystified
Quality Management Demystified
Real Estate Math Demystified
Robotics Demystified
Sales Management Demystified
Six Sigma Demystified, 2e
SQL Demystified
Statistical Process Control Demystified
Statistics Demystified
Technical Analysis Demystified
Technical Math Demystified
Trigonometry Demystified
UML Demystified
Visual Basic 2005 Demystified
Visual C# 2005 Demystified
XML Demystified

The Demystified Series publishes over 125 titles in all areas of academic study. For a complete list of titles, please visit www.mhprofessional.com.

I write to find out...
what I didn't know I knew...
until I wrote about it.

Creative Writing
DeMYSTiFieD®

Sheila Bender

McGraw
Hill

New York   Chicago   San Francisco   Lisbon   London   Madrid   Mexico City
Milan   New Delhi   San Juan   Seoul   Singapore   Sydney   Toronto

ISBN 978-0-07-173699-2
MHID 0-07-173699-9

LIBRARY OF CONGRESS CONTROL NUMBER: 2010935976

This publication is designed to provide accurate and authoritative information in regard to the subject matter covered. It is sold with the understanding that neither the author nor the publisher is engaged in rendering legal, accounting, securities trading, or other professional services. If legal advice or other expert assistance is required, the services of a competent professional person should be sought.
— *From a Declaration of Principles Jointly Adopted by a Committee of the American Bar Association and a Committee of Publishers and Associations*

Trademarks: McGraw-Hill, the McGraw-Hill Publishing logo, DeMystified® and related trade dress are trademarks or registered trademarks of The McGraw-Hill Companies and/or its affiliates in the United States and other countries and may not be used without written permission. All other trademarks are the property of their respective owners. The McGraw-Hill Companies is not associated with any product or vendor mentioned in this book.

McGraw-Hill books are available at special quantity discounts to use as premiums and sales promotions, or for use in corporate training programs. To contact a representative, please e-mail us at bulksales@mcgraw-hill.com.

This book is printed on acid-free paper.

With thanks and love to my husband, Kurt VanderSluis,
for the hours of attention he has given each section of this book,
asking me the questions that helped me find the answers.

About the Author

Sheila Bender has been teaching writing since 1980. In 1991, she published her first book about writing, *Writing in a Convertible with the Top Down*, co-authored with Christi Killien. A new edition is available now electronically and in print through Libertary.com (www.libertary.com). She went on to publish many more books, including a memoir, *Turning to Poetry in a Time of Grief*, Imago Press; *Writing and Publishing Personal Essays*, Silver Threads; *Perfect Phrases for College Application Essays*, McGraw-Hill; and *A Day in the Life: Journaling for Self-Discovery*, initially from Writer's Digest Books and now available through the International Association of Journal Writing (www.IAJW.com). She has also written content for LifeJournal for Writers journaling software (writers.lifejournal.com).

Her essays and poems appear online and in numerous North American literary magazines and anthologies, including *Poetry Northwest*, *The Seattle Review*, *The Bellingham Review*, and *Tiny Lights*, among others.

A presenter, instructor, and panel member at writing conferences and teacher-training venues, as well as an occasional feature writer for *The Writer* and *Writer's Digest* magazines, she also publishes *Writing It Real*, a weekly online magazine for those who write from personal experience. To view sample articles and resources, subscribe, or learn about her books, visit www.writingitreal.com.

Contents

Preface

Clearing the Fog, Savoring the Mystery

> *Things are not all so comprehensible and expressible as one would mostly have us believe; most events are inexpressible, taking place in a realm which no word has ever entered, and more inexpressible than all else are works of art, mysterious existences, the life of which, while ours passes away endures.*
> —Rainer Maria Rilke, *Letters to a Young Poet*, translated by M. D. Herter

> *I have forced myself to begin writing when I've been utterly exhausted, when I've felt my soul as thin as a playing card, when nothing has seemed worth enduring for another five minutes… and somehow the activity of writing changes everything.*
> —Joyce Carol Oates, *Paris Review interview*, Fall-Winter, 1978

Creative writing is an art form that tackles the "mysterious existences" Maria Rainier Rilke writes about and encompasses and helps us write our way through the mood swings Joyce Carol Oates describes. For some of us, producing our writing is important for our sanity and self-actualization. For those who read it, it provides companionship, acknowledgment of life's quandaries and quests, and, often, answers to life questions. When we begin each piece of creative writing, however, we start from not knowing; creative writing is a process in which individual writers stumble upon answers to questions they may or may not have known they had until they started writing. Creative writing is for those who like to find out what they want to know about and what they do know about but didn't know they did. It is an art form motivated by an intense desire to articulate what doesn't yet have words and to think what isn't possible to think without an exploration through writing.

So what is it I can demystify about creative writing when those of us who write in the creative writing field trust that we'll have I-don't-know-how-it-happened-but-I-was-in-flow-as-I-wrote-and-suddenly-everything-fell-together experiences? We honor and expect the synchronicity that seems to be at work when just the right thing happens in our outer life to trigger a scene or connection for our writing. It is a form of magic, we believe, that brings our writing alive.

But we also know that we pick up new writing strategies when we hang around writers and read their writing on writing; that we learn more about our craft from other writers, living and dead.

I know I can help you feel comfortable with the idea that once you start, you will learn more as you continue to write. I know that I can help you understand that you never have to feel you don't know enough to get started in creative writing. With the explosion in creative writing degree programs, creative writing subgenres, and creative writing publications, especially online, many new to the field have the sensation they are jumping into the middle of things; they do not know where their writing fits or if they are "doing it right." By describing the range of genres in the field of creative writing and providing a wealth of exercises aimed at helping you begin to write in each of them, I can demystify how to cut through the inertia of not writing, so you can start writing; I can demystify a system for evaluating what your writing is up to and provide guidance on how to stay committed to and engaged in the rewarding process of creative writing.

After doing the exercises in this book, I think you will understand what the poet William Wordsworth meant when he said that poetry (and many of us take that to mean all writing from the heart and imagination) is one person's insides speaking to another's (he said "one man's" insides, but that was a long time ago—certainly today he'd agree with us that both sexes write!). Creative writers want, above all, to understand themselves and to understand others. I hope that as you write from the exercises in this book, you will experience how your words build intimacy not only between you and your readers, but also between your own outer and inner selves.

In *Creative Writing Demystified*, I have worked to construct an environment in which you come to value creative writing as an important life tool for yourself and others and value your own work-in-progress as part of that important process. Doing exercises in all the genres will prove important, as skills of the craft cross genre boundaries. My book includes thoughts from many writers as well as exercises I've solicited from some to supplement my own. By offering discussions and exercises for you to consider in poetry, creative nonfiction, and fiction, we help you cultivate writing that informs, entertains, and, most importantly, opens hearts and minds.

Though I can't demystify the miracle of inspiration and creativity, I can teach you to recognize treasures you put into your writing and treasures your writing delivers to you.

Acknowledgments

I am grateful for the many writers who write on writing, sharing their expertise online and in books. I have included these mentors' work in my references, bibliography, and lists of resources. I am particularly grateful to the writers who have contributed exercises to this book. Their biographical information is at the back of the book. A special thank you to writer David Reich for his help in finessing many of my points in the book's fiction chapter.

Parts of my discussions and exercises have appeared over the last eight years in *Writing It Real*, my online magazine at www.writingitreal.com for those who write from personal experience. I have also reprinted poems and other writing of mine that have appeared in earlier books, noted on the About the Author page.

Introduction

About Creative Writing

On What Beginning Feels Like

In the weeks before my husband and I traveled to Turkey in 2009, on a trip we had longed to take, we were overwhelmed with information we found online. Understanding the ferry system and options for a trip we wanted to take on public transportation through the waterways of the country proved more than we could figure out, as did building a three-week itinerary that would make us happy exploring a country so rich in history and culture. So, I found myself typing phrases like "vaccines needed for travelers to Turkey" into my browser, hoping to start somewhere where the answers were simple and accessible.

As I thought about organizing this book for those new to creative writing, I vividly remembered how, when I started to write seriously, I didn't know where to get information that I wanted. Often, I didn't know what information would be useful. Other times, I didn't know what to do with information I received. I didn't know writers' jargon or the steps in the journey of developing into an accomplished writer. I didn't know how to work with and assess the impact on me of those involved in the field. I didn't know if I had the stamina or the talent necessary to write well or how to inoculate myself from others' judgments and snubs. All I had was the feeling that I wanted to write, poetry in particular at that time, because it was going to make my life feel grounded and real. So, despite feelings of being overwhelmed and despite considering myself a foreigner to the field, I decided to trust that once I started somewhere, things would become easier. For me, that somewhere was the University of Washington, both in their Experimental College low-cost extracurricular classes and in their Creative Writing Department.

Thirty-four years later, I am convinced that anyone can begin any time under any circumstances. Those creating a writing life may find success taking different steps of different lengths at different times and even in different directions. Sometimes classes help. Sometimes a writing peer is most significant; sometimes attending readings stokes the fire; sometimes reading authors on the craft is inspiring; but always writing, writing, writing makes the difference. There is no one right way to take this trip, but each step, no matter how big or how small, can be a step in the "write" direction, if you keep writing and keep learning.

After visiting Turkey, my husband and I know a lot more about how to approach our next visit, where to find the information we need, and what not to worry about finding because it will be there when we get there. That's how I'd like you to approach writing. In this book, I've provided the lay of the creative writing land, and I've given you the highlights of what you can visit and participate in. You will definitely learn much and learn to feel more comfortable with what you have yet to learn. You will find surprises along the way and navigate them successfully. On your journey, you can use the book straight from beginning to end or by dipping into different sections at different times. Doing exercises in all genres will help you write more fully in any that you ultimately choose as your own.

Learning about what sparks stories, memoir, and poems, about what hooks writers and will not let them go until they have tenaciously crafted words, helps new writers begin. Learning writing strategies and about what writers value in their writing lives helps new writers pay attention to their own processes and gain confidence that they are moving in the "write" direction. I hope you enjoy your visit to the country of creative writing and make it one you want to visit again and again.

Checklist of Attributes to Bring with You

If you wonder what it takes for this journey, here is a short checklist of helpful attributes:

- You enjoy sitting (or at least *do* sit) with a notebook or computer to experience the magic of images, details, and metaphor for evoking the world and how you feel about it.

- You like to read what writers you admire say about writing and/or go to lectures where they describe the writing life.
- You join with others in writing groups, workshops and classes to find an audience of trusted listeners.
- You plan to read from your work at literary or other gatherings.
- You have, or plan to have, patience and fortitude concerning your drafting process and submitting your work to journals, magazines, and websites.
- You don't "feel right" when you haven't been writing.

We are a meaning-making, story-telling, wishing-to-discover-and-influence-others species. As creative writers, we fill the blueprints of established genres with contemporary experiences, and we invent hybrid subgenres along the way to help us express the experience of being alive today. Just how creative writing comes about and offers its readers and writers entertainment and wisdom will always be full of mystery, but the information and exercises in this book offer much to anyone who wants to feel at home where mystery resides.

Bon voyage!

What Is Creative Writing?

To most of us, the term "creative writing" probably means writing we are not using to impart factual, objectively supported arguments and points of view in reports, case histories, technical manuals, interviews, instruction, and academic papers and articles. In reality, though, all writing is creative because all writing is a made thing; in the artifice of the making, we reveal who we are, slightly or more fully, depending on the level of subjectivity we involve. And subjectivity creeps into everything written (whether that's in creative writing or journalism), from the way authors leave out, include, and prioritize facts, as well as how they choose words with particular connotations and denotations.

Despite the fact that all writing is a made up way of sharing information, what we mean when we say "creative" writing is writing that isn't trying to appear objective. It is writing that embraces subjectivity. Even when we write about fact-based subjects, we find a way to declare that it is our individual way of selecting facts and telling the story that is important in the writing. In journalism, history, and science writing, research takes center stage, but in creative nonfiction and poetry, although there may be factual information included, reflection takes center stage.

The label "creative writing" is one adopted by schools. It generally includes the genres of fiction, poetry, and creative nonfiction. And each of these genres includes multiple subgenres and/or styles. Playwriting and screenwriting are branches of creative writing most usually taught in drama and film departments, outside of the Bachelor's and Master's of Fine Arts in Creative Writing programs. This is so despite the fact that poets have a long history of writing in those genres. Shakespeare and William Butler Yeats are among those whose work was well produced, and Dorothy Parker and Dylan Thomas were among those writers Hollywood studios hired to turn out screenplays. Fiction writers, of course, such as Rebecca Miller, Nora Ephron, Nick Hornby, and Stephen King regularly write screenplays.

Journalism may include creative writing in what is referred to as New Journalism, but there is a big distinction on college campuses in the training of journalists and the training of creative writers. The former observe and report on events with an eye toward others and not toward the response of the observer/author, while the creative writer is always looking for the interior story and writes about events as avenues for self-reflection.

Even though we make distinctions, the line between what's taught in the traditional noncreative writing programs and creative writing programs is blurring, and inside the standard creative writing programs themselves, the lines between fiction, poetry, and creative nonfiction blur even more, yielding hybrid work like lyric essays and partly fictionalized stories.

Whatever the subgenre or hybrid a creative writer is working in, most of the time, the author attempts, as Marilynne Robinson writes in *The Death of Adam: Essays on Modern Thought*, "to reclaim human civilization by returning to the idea that people have souls, and that they have certain obligations to them, and certain pleasures in them." One of the obligations is trusting that our souls will find and/or create structures that best help us express and recognize ourselves.

History of the Term Creative Writing

Ralph Waldo Emerson may have coined the term *creative writing* in an 1837 address he made to the Phi Beta Kappa Society, entitled "The American Scholar." (www.emersoncentral.com/amscholar.htm), Emerson wrote:

The world—this shadow of the soul, *or other me*, lies wide around. Its attractions are the keys, which unlock my thoughts and make me acquainted with myself. I run eagerly into this resounding tumult...

...the best books...impress us with the conviction that one nature wrote and the same reads. We read the verses of one of the great English poets, of Chaucer, of Marvell, of Dryden, with the most modern joy—with a pleasure, I mean, which is in great part caused by the abstraction of all *time* from their verses. There is some awe mixed with the joy of our surprise, when this poet, who lived in some past world, two or three hundred years ago, says that which lies close to my own soul, that which I also had well-nigh thought and said...we should suppose some pre-established harmony, some foresight of souls that were to be, and some preparation of stores for their future wants, like the fact observed in insects, who lay up food before death for the young grub they shall never see.

There is then creative reading as well as creative writing.

The actions and events of our childhood and youth, are now matters of calmest observation. They lie like fair pictures in the air. Not so with our recent actions—with the business which we now have in hand. On this we are quite unable to speculate. Our affections as yet circulate through it. We no more feel or know it, than we feel the feet, or the hand, or the brain of our body. The new deed is yet a part of life—remains for a time immersed in our unconscious life. In some contemplative hour, it detaches itself from the life like a ripe fruit, to become a thought of the mind. Instantly, it is raised, transfigured; the corruptible has put on incorruption. Henceforth it is an object of beauty, however base its origin and neighborhood. Observe, too, the impossibility of antedating this act. In its grub state, it cannot fly, it cannot shine, it is a dull grub. But suddenly, without observation, the selfsame thing unfurls beautiful wings, and is an angel of wisdom.

So is there no fact, no event, in our private history, which shall not, sooner or later, lose its adhesive, inert form, and astonish us by soaring from our body into the empyrean. Cradle and infancy, school and playground, the fear of boys, and dogs, and ferules, the love of little maids and berries, and many another fact that once filled the whole sky, are gone already; friend and relative profession and party, town and country, nation and world, must also soar and sing.

Emerson presented something essential about creative writing authors: When we write, we relish the fact that kernels and images arise, and we know we'll work from them. We relish the fact that authors, even those who came centuries before us, had this experience, too, and reading their creative writing illuminates our experience as we hope to illuminate the experience of others. Often creative writing authors introduce their work with epigraphs made from the words of other authors or offer thanks to authors whose works and words inspired them. In this way, creative writing is a conversation, a very long one that has and will go on through the ages.

More Recently

If Emerson may be credited with coining the term creative writing, The University of Iowa may be credited with establishing creative writing as an area of expertise worthy of study. The school offered creative writing coursework (verse-making) as early as 1897, 60 years after Emerson's speech to eastern academia. In 1922, Iowa became the first U.S. university to accept creative projects as theses for advanced degrees. This meant that collections of poems, musical compositions, or series of paintings could be presented to the Graduate College, which led to the creation of the Master of Fine Arts degree and to a larger place for writers and artists in the academy.

The writing workshop method for the study of writing emerged at Iowa: In writing workshops, senior writers lead discussions about work by class members; all the workshop students share impressions, advice, and analysis; and writers benefit from listening to a variety of responses and thoughts on their writing. Many of today's famous poets and novelists have gathered at the Iowa Writers' Workshop since its founding in 1936. In 1987, The English Department at Iowa approved the "M.A. in English With Emphasis on Expository Writing," which later became the Nonfiction Writing Program.

How did the term *nonfiction writing* change to *creative nonfiction*? Lee Gutkind, founder of the influential journal *Creative Nonfiction*, explains on the journal's website (www.creativenonfiction.org/thejournal/whatiscnf.htm) that creative nonfiction became an official term in 1983 at a meeting convened by the National Endowment for the Arts to deal with the question of what to call writing outside the realm of fiction, poetry, and plays that uses the craft of those genres to elevate its quality, whether the piece be memoir, personal essay, travel writing, nature writing, or investigative journalism that mixes the personal experience of the investigator with the story under investigation. George Orwell's *Down and Out in Paris and London*, James Baldwin's *Notes of a Native Son*, Ernest Hemingway's *Death in the Afternoon*, and Tom Wolfe's *The Right Stuff* are, according to Gutkind, "classic creative nonfiction efforts—books that communicate information (reportage) in a scenic, dramatic fashion," thus dividing creative nonfiction from traditional nonfiction (journalism and scholarship), which is mostly information.

In the realm of creative writing today, subgenres and names for them keep popping up in literary and writing circles: flash fiction, drabble, 69-er, sudden nonfiction, and lyric essays, among them. But whatever you call a particular piece of creative writing, what is most important to remember is that writers write, and as they write, they discover new strategies and rediscover older ones for researching themselves and moving others. Eventually, editors, school programs, and grant-giving organizations find a name to distinguish what they are printing, teaching, and funding. Creative writing is creative through and through, and by the time you are reading this book, scores of online journals, print journals, and performance pieces may have new names for work in this expanding field. *Narrative Magazine*, an online venture, publishes traditional creative writing as well as six-word and iPhone stories! As the Internet has given all of us access to the equivalent of the printing press, more writers, using more and more publishers, are joining the creative writing conversation.

I write to find out...
what I didn't know I knew...
until I wrote about it...

Part I

Building Your Creative Writing Muscle

chapter 1

What Are the Elements of Good Creative Writing?

The novelist Andre Dubus III said in an online interview with Random House (www.randomhouse.com/boldtype/0300/dubus/interview.html):

> I think what I love most [about writing] is that feeling that you really nailed something. I rarely feel it with a whole piece, but sometimes with a line you feel that it really captured what it is that you had inside you and you got it out for a stranger to read, someone who may never love you or meet you, but he or she is going to get that experience from that line.

Although as Andre Dubus III admits, every line you write won't achieve perfection, there are simple things you must do in your writing "to get something out" in a way that a stranger reading it will have the experience you are writing about and engage in reading it, whether it be a happy or a sad experience.

Show, Show, Show

When you offer readers information they can take in through their senses, you offer them a world they can enter and experience. That is true whether you are writing from your imagination, your memory, or what is in front of you right now. Replace language that tells readers how to feel or how to judge something—words like beautiful, ugly, wonderful, and frustrating—with sensory images that offer them the experience to feel for themselves. Describe a couch as the color of mud pies, for instance, or a morning you awake happy as one with song birds on every branch of the tree outside your window.

Avoid Using Clichés

Most of the time, avoiding clichés improves writing because clichés are overused phrases that form a kind of shorthand communication that once again tells readers what they *should be* experiencing without allowing them to do the actual experiencing. Clichéd phrases are the words in our vernacular so overused that readers no longer picture the content in them (it's raining cats and dogs, for instance) but instead quickly jump to supplying an editorializing word or phrase (the weather's lousy) that sums things up instead of evoking feeling (what it is like to be in heavy rain).

In 1946, George Orwell wrote about "dying metaphors" in his essay "Politics and the English Language." "A newly invented metaphor," he wrote:

> …assists thought by evoking a visual image, while on the other hand a metaphor which is technically "dead" (e.g. *iron resolution*) has in effect reverted to being an ordinary word and can generally be used without loss of vividness. But in between these two classes there is a huge dump of worn-out metaphors which have lost all evocative power and are merely used because they save people the trouble of inventing phrases for themselves. Examples are: *Ring the changes on, take up the cudgel for, toe the line, ride roughshod over, stand shoulder to shoulder with, play into the hands of, no axe to grind, grist to the mill, fishing in troubled waters, on the order of the day, Achilles' heel, swan song, hotbed.*

The phrases Orwell notes and others writers today use without thinking, such as "gotta have it" and "that's another story," replace particulars that provide vividness. When you come across this kind of cliché in your writing, consider it a placeholder, language that comes easily but sits on top of something much more interesting. Your job as writer is to lift this kind of cliché off of your writing, like a layer of frost over ice cream, and reveal the full flavor beneath it.

In "Politics and the English Language," George Orwell also wrote about "verbal false limbs." These, he said:

> ...save the trouble of picking out appropriate verbs and nouns, and at the same time pad each sentence with extra syllables which give it an appearance of symmetry. Characteristic phrases are *render inoperative, militate against, make contact with, be subjected to, give rise to, give grounds for, have the effect of, play a leading part (role) in, make itself felt, take effect, exhibit a tendency to, serve the purpose of, etc., etc.* The keynote is the elimination of simple verbs. Instead of being a single word, such as *break, stop, spoil, mend, kill,* a verb becomes a *phrase,* made up of a noun or adjective tacked on to some general-purpose verb such as *prove, serve, form, play, render.* In addition, the passive voice is wherever possible used in preference to the active, and noun constructions are used instead of gerunds (*by examination of* instead of *by examining*). The range of verbs is further cut down by means of the *-ize* and *de-* formations, and the banal statements are given an appearance of profundity by means of the *not un-* formation. Simple conjunctions and prepositions are replaced by such phrases as *with respect to, having regard to, the fact that, by dint of, in view of, in the interests of, on the hypothesis that;* and the ends of sentences are saved by anticlimax by such resounding commonplaces as *greatly to be desired, cannot be left out of account, a development to be expected in the near future, deserving of serious consideration, brought to a satisfactory conclusion,* and so on and so forth.

Write clean. Don't use more words than you have to but make sure the words you use are lively and do the work you want them to do. "To" is usually better than "in order to." "Unique" does not require "very" in front of it.

Figure Out What Has Urged the Speaker to Speech

Every "made" piece of writing comes into being because someone, either the writer or a character, has something to say NOW. And that something is not because the writer has a writing assignment or feels like writing. That something must reside in the moment of the poem, the essay, or the story. A poet may come to the page knowing only that she was struck seeing the outline of her husband's wet bathing suit through the jeans he wore for driving. The poet is urged to speech by her emotional reaction to seeing the wet outline of the swim trunks through heavy jeans. In her writing, she uses the literal occasion of looking at that outline until the emotional occasion of seeing the sadness and anger her husband is covering up begin to come through.

While teaching at Loyola Marymount University in Los Angeles, I assigned my students a description essay about a place for which they had strong feelings. One chose Dodger Stadium as his topic because he loved baseball. He associated many images with the topic, including the voice of Vin Scully, the game announcer he had listened to for years on TV when he watched games at home with his father. "But where do I start?" he said, "I have so many memories and thoughts about baseball."

You might sometimes get the feeling that your own writing is something like morning glory vines spread everywhere instead of having a shape and filling a succinct space. Herein lies the magic of occasion! As we talked, my student told me that he had recently gone to Dodger Stadium for the first time after years of listening to the games at home. At the ballpark, he searched for a glimpse of Vin Scully and could almost make out where he was sitting. He suddenly realized, though, that he wouldn't be able to hear Scully like his father would at home because Scully's voice was being broadcast over radio and TV, not over the playing field. He experienced a moment of shock when he realized that this game, the first live one he had ever attended, would not be narrated for him by Scully's familiar voice.

As I listened to my student, I realized that one occasion he could write from would be going to Dodger Stadium for the first time and missing the voice of the adored and familiar sportscaster. Not being able to hear Scully made this game emotionally different from others for this young man. I asked him to describe the moment when he went to Dodger Stadium and looked for Scully and saw him. What did he think at that very moment? He said he wondered about his dad, listening at home, who had turned his son on to baseball, but had never gone to the stadium himself and now refused to go. And yet, unlike his father, the son wanted to see the game live. The realization that he would miss hearing Scully's voice led him to explore what it felt like going to Dodger Stadium without his father. This was sounding like an essay about having learned from one's dad, going beyond what he taught, and then not being able to share a new experience with him.

The journey to this emotional information ultimately occurred through descriptions of the event at Dodger Stadium, comparisons to watching games at home, and stories of what the student's dad had taught him about baseball and how he played baseball to impress his father. His father's refusal to attend a live game made the student aware not only of his father's support but also the need to grow beyond what his father could offer.

Make Sure Something Is at Stake

Making sure something is at stake is closely associated with identifying the writing's occasion. The writer in poetry and creative nonfiction, or the main character (the protagonist) or his or her opponent (the antagonist) in a story, must have a need to find an answer to a recognizable question. Readers read not only to find out what that answer is but also to enjoy knowing how the writer or character finds the answer. If the question isn't one that requires a journey or isn't clear or doesn't really exist because the writer or character already knows the answer, the reader will soon tire of reading since there will be no suspense, no caring about how things will all work out.

Listen to Your Writing to Make It Sound Good

Writing that sounds good sounds that way because the writer was able to identify what was working well in the first drafts and facilitate it. When we trust what we are writing, we are likely to put words down that convey feeling accurately. We can then "work" our sentences to improve the sound we are making, taking away or replacing those sounds that are distracting. Writing with good sound involves knowing some of the tricks of the trade, like the tools we call rhyme and alliteration, but most of all it involves trust in ourselves that we (or our characters) are choosing words that allow the writing to be emotionally true to the situations we are portraying. We need to know the terms of the craft enough to be comfortable with what they help us name, even if we rarely write by trying to meet craft labels.

Remember the Key Definition: Writers Are People Who Write (And Read)

Novelist Elizabeth Evans, whose books include the award-winning novel *Carter Clay*, contributes this reminder and a good suggestion for making sure you fulfill the definition:

> *Longing* to write isn't writing. If you need to put a belt around your waist to keep you in your desk chair, then get out the belt. Write something most days, even if it's just for five minutes. The fitness experts tell us to aim for exercise six days a week, and that's probably a good goal for writing, too (it will keep you fit and in

writing-form). Write regularly and then you can legitimately call yourself a writer. Do not say, *"Oh, well, I'll tell myself that I am going to write for five minutes, but I bet that I'll end up writing for at least half an hour. Maybe I'll even write all day!"* No. Be disciplined. And kind to yourself. Stop when you have written for five minutes. If you imagine that you'll certainly end up writing longer—that you won't be successful at getting back to your writing unless you write for much more than five minutes—it's likely you'll wind up intimidated. Up ahead, you may well see the dragon of that obligation to write something big and so the exercise will start scaring you off even before you begin. Do five minutes a day for two weeks, or three if you still feel ill or your heart hammers at the process of sitting down with pencil and paper (and I do think that pencil/pen and paper are best for this exercise; for me, they feel closer to the heart, more intimate). The next two or three weeks, edge up to eight minutes. Don't feel rushed. Usually, it takes people a while to get blocked—though I've known of it happening quite quickly to people who've had a major success with one book and now are afraid that the next book won't be as well-received. If you're serious about getting out of the dark hole of the block, be patient. Again: Don't try to trick yourself. Honor yourself. Try twelve or fifteen minutes for the next two weeks. In about a month in a half, you've made real progress! You're writing regularly. Add a little more until you get up to half an hour a day and stay there for a while. Don't rush it. It will come.

When I was in graduate school, I found that many of my classmates felt that it would be presumptuous to call themselves writers, even though they were turning out stories and poems. A lot of my classmates didn't keep on with their writing after we earned our degrees, and I suspect that had something to do with the fact that they didn't "presume" to call themselves writers. Don't be shy about calling yourself a writer, but make sure that you earn the title by writing! Honor your desire. *And read a lot.* You'll never stop learning new things from the great fiction writers. It is good to read work by your peers AND to read the works that have stood the test of time. By reading the very best work, we learn to recognize when our own work is whole and successful because we've already experienced the feeling of a successful whole in, say, Dickens or Chekhov. Be ambitious. You can be as sloppy and wild as you like in free writes—I use them all the time—but when you give your work to others to read, make sure you've taken it as far as you possibly can. Believe that you are writing for the ages.

Training Is Key

How do writers ensure that their writing includes the wanted elements and excludes the unwanted so it engagingly offers experience? By spending time working to 1) use the five senses; 2) trust details above generalizations; 3) employ metaphors, which refresh experience by likening things to other things not usually used in comparison; 4) notice clichés and use them only to strong effect; 5) create scenes where the outcome matters, so readers feel as if they are right there making choices and moving toward insight, surprising themselves with their feelings; and, 6) find the best sound they can in their sentences while keeping clarity.

Exercises to Build Your "Good Writing" Muscles

Practice with Sensory Images

To build convincing and engaging experience on the page, to make their created worlds vivid, writers employ all five senses in their writing, rather than summarize or editorialize. Using images from childhood speeds the process of learning to use sensory information in writing because our senses store what we remember from childhood, since we didn't "cerebralize" what we experienced at that time. That's the kind of memory we have to cultivate as writers.

Your Turn

To get started encouraging the use of the five senses in your writing, think of an image from your childhood, an object you saw and could touch like rubber boots, a backyard puddle, the couch in your living room, the fur of a pet, or the wooden chairs at the kitchen table. Now, write a paragraph about this object using five sentences, one sentence to capture the way you experienced this object with each of the senses. Sight: What color and shape was the object? Touch: What was the object's texture and temperature when you touched it? Was it hot or cold, warm or room temperature? Did it make your arm itch? Was it furry or rough? Smell: What did the object (or being near it) smell like? Perhaps the smell is coming from the next room—cookies baking while you sit on the couch watching your favorite TV program. Sound: What is the sound you remember? Did the boots squeak when you pulled them on? Was the telephone ringing as you tied the laces? Was there something some one always said when you were with this object? Taste: If you were putting the boots on, did you hold a wool mitten in your mouth until you were done? Was there something you'd just finished eating, the taste of which lingered for you? Did the air have a taste?

Your job is to create an experience of this object so that you, as well as anyone reading what you have written, is transported to the place and time you are writing about.

Caroline Arnold, author of more than 140 books for children, suggests her students choose an object, place, person, or animal, and write five sentences about it, one sentence (or two) for each sense—*sight, sound, touch, taste* and *smell*. Examples of how she does this simply in her children's books, *A Walrus' World* and *A Killer Whale's World*, are:

Sight: The baby walrus' plump body is covered with short fur.

Smell: The mother walrus sniffs her baby and rubs his back with her whiskers.

Sound: Splash! He tumbles into the water. Splash! His mother dives in too.

Touch: Using her whiskers, she feels a clam. Then she grabs the shell with her lips and sucks out the meat.

Taste: Their sleek bodies slide through the cool, salty water.

Whether your descriptions are simple or complex, "The important thing," Arnold says, "is to immerse yourself in the scene and use all your senses to convey the essence of that scene to your reader. To find out if you are using sensory descriptions in your writing, go through one of your stories with a highlighter, and mark each time you use one of your senses. Note which sense you use most often."

Now that you've shown that you can stick to your senses, let's work further on employing them in writing.

Sound

To practice with sound imagery, I think of a noisy place—like the street I used to live on in Los Angeles on garbage collection day—and then set about describing it. Here's an example:

> On garbage collection days, the disposal company my husband calls Loud and Early slams and smashes its way into our sleep. We hear garbage cans scrape the top of the thick rusty truck, then clatter across the asphalt and cement of street and curb. When we hear the garbage truck grind the dregs of our existence to a pulp, we slide our feet to the floor. A police helicopter hurls its hello from overhead, shaking the walls and shattering any memory of our dreams.

Your Turn

Choose a place or time of day you know well and write how it sounds. You'll find yourself using words in a row that start with the same letter (alliteration like "cans colliding" and "helicopter hurls") and words that sound like what they are describing (onomatopoeia like "clattering" and "slams").

Taste

When I want to get started writing from my sense of taste, I put something in my mouth and describe the taste of it. It makes it easier to go on to describe remembered tastes:

Soybean

I roll you around with my tongue and you are wet from the rinsing I gave you and you are cold from the refrigerator so you taste a little like a glass of water. I bite into you and I taste the smallest flavor of salt, as if there were a single tear on my tongue. When I chew you up good, I am surprised by the taste of something just a bit like the smell in the stagnant puddle gardeners' hoses leave at the foot of my apartment's driveway. It is so vague, though, that it is not at all unpleasant. I swallow, and you leave the taste of grass I remember from when, as a child, I sucked on green blades in summer.

Your Turn

What might you write the taste of in your writing that will enhance your sensory approach? The taste of school glue or a new pen? To practice with writing taste, put something edible in your mouth—beet greens, vitamin C, or chewing gum, for instance. Don't chew. What does it taste like so far? Now bite into it and write what it tastes like a little more dispersed in your mouth. Now chew it and describe the taste. Now swallow or spit it out and describe the taste left in your mouth. Compare the taste to other tastes if you'd like.

Smell

Oftentimes we smell something and a flood of memories come back—marinara sauce or pot roast cooking on the stove may bring us back to our childhood home or our grandmother's house. The smell of pies baking in the oven may remind us of a bakery we worked in during high school. The smell of janitors' floor-cleaning substances might remind us of our dorm cafeteria in college. The smell of tobacco or coffee on someone's breath or the smell of fresh-mown grass or coconut oil on sunbathers takes us back years to other times and places we've experienced. Our sense of smell should never be overlooked in writing.

Here's an example of a warm-up I wrote:

I sit here and I smell the pages and binding glue on my new book. This smell brings me back to flour paste and papier-mâché days in my Brownie troop and grade school. That's when I made maracas by coating burned out light bulbs with strips of newsprint soaked in non-toxic paste made of flour and water. Strip by strip we covered the bulbs, layer upon layer of newsprint, until none of the glass we'd started with shown through. I think we must have waited for layers to dry before we added more wet newsprint, smell of wet dog. Somehow our teachers knew when it was time for us declare the musical instruments done. Somehow the glass got smashed without our damaging the papier-mâché casing we'd painstakingly created. Then we painted our instruments bright colors. They began to smell like new patent leather shoes. I think we must have used them, broken glass both hitting and missing the beat.

Your Turn

Write down three smells you are aware of right now—for example, your own perfume, something cooking, burning oil from a car going by, the smell of water from a hose, charcoal in the grill, baby powder on a toddler after bath time, sunlight on a cat's fur, the new plastic smell of casings on electronic components or shower curtain liners. Think of what the smell reminds you of. Write about your memory by beginning like this, "I sit here and smell _____. This smell brings me back to _____. That's when I _____.... Keep writing for 10 or 15 minutes, remembering to include more smells from that time.

Touch

Our skin soaks in information all the time. Our fingers go out to greet the world by holding objects, stroking pets and loved ones, and shaking hands with strangers. We touch the fabrics of anything we sit on, open, close, carry, or use.

I wrote about dishwater to practice writing from the sense of touch:

> I plunge my hands into the soapy dishwater in the white Rubbermaid tub in my sink. It is warm as the morning coffee I sip and swallow. It slides over my skin like my cat's moist tongue when she is licking me. It feels buoyant around my hands like risen dough. I keep my hands in the soapy water before I pull the first dish out. I like feeling like a goldfish might, swimming in bowl full of sunlight from a nearby window.

I am surprised by how much I like part of the act of washing dishes! Perhaps if I chose something else, I would be surprised by dislike:

> When I put my hands inside my pantyhose, gathering it so I can slip my toe inside, my fingers snag the fiber like rough little emery boards. I pull the hose up along my ankle, calf, and thigh, feel its pressure grip my skin. At first, I like the way the hose seems to hold my skin together like the bread of an orange under the peel. But when my two hose covered legs brush against each other, I feel each one begin to itch. I want to take the hose off then as if it were a bandage I didn't need. Later when it sags at my ankles, I feel the downward pull, a sensation like I have in my stomach when the elevator goes up.

Your Turn

Make yourself aware of your sense of touch and how to incorporate it into your writing by thinking of something you are very familiar with touching—an article of clothing, a pot scrubber, your cat, a garden rake, the steering wheel of your car. Write about the feel of it in detail. Describe touching it by comparing how it feels to how something else feels. The images you use and the comparisons you make evoke the sensory information.

Sight

You may think that you cannot possibly get down accurately and interestingly in words what you observe through your eyes. You may worry that you will include too many details and be boring. Don't be intimidated. By adhering to the following ideas, with a little practice, you will be writing fluently and with momentum.

Instead of saying something is beautiful, show its beauty. "The birds were beautiful that day" is not as rich in experience or emotion as, "The bright red cardinal visited my bird feeder, while I watched two goldfinches sitting in the Canadian thistle, eager for their turn at the feeder."

Every time you are tempted to sum things up visually with words like beautiful or ugly, take the time to use specific sight words to show, show the quality you notice. When you are using adjectives to describe something, like "wooden" before desk, think if there is more visual detail you can use.

Your Turn

Look at an object in the room or place you inhabit right now. Describe what this object—say a desk—looks like without relying on adjectives. Instead of saying the rectangular wooden desk, say, "The desk is made of pine, with 10 boards about 6 feet in length joined side-by-side to the width of a canoe's belly." Do the same for a scene or object you might otherwise too quickly just label beautiful, ugly, awkward, or useless.

More Practice with Details

When we offer names and details, we are making our subjects real and showing rather than telling our readers about our experiences. Specifics, along with the sensory information, allow us to create experience on the page rather than just tell others we've had the experience. If you are writing about walking to school, put in the names of streets you walked. If there are other people with you, name them (even if only first names). If you are using equipment, put in its brand name to make the experience more immediate. Writers are often amazed at the way specifics carry connotations. When I wrote about my childhood schooling, I smiled as I remembered and wrote the name of my second grade teacher, Mrs. Bore. When I wrote an essay about knowing I had to learn a lot to recover from grieving, I wrote in the name of the bay I was overlooking: Discovery Bay. There are so many examples of the way specifics enhance the tone and meaning of what we are writing.

Here's a sample of scene with sensory information that evokes feelings in a tough situation:

Weekend at the Père Marquette   *by Deborah Gaal*

He sat down next to me and placed his hand on my knee. "I need to talk to you," he said. "I've been wanting to tell you this for a long time. I've been in a relationship with another woman for 11 years. She's also happily married. Having this relationship with her makes me realize how much I love you. You have always been my priority, and you always will be. I'm so lucky to have you."

I looked around the room at the evidence of our romantic weekend. There were a dozen red roses on the table (sent courtesy of YPO), starting to fade slightly. A couple of the stems were bent at the head, bowing, like the roses were embarrassed to witness the scene in front of them. The half-consumed bottle of champagne and two fluted crystal glasses were standing at attention. The bed sheets were crumpled, no longer crisp and fresh. There were wads of Kleenex strewn on the carpeted floor next to his side of the bed. Remnants of his latest allergy attack in the middle of the night. I studied him. I had never noticed before how Steven was looking every bit of his age. His skin looked slightly yellowish and was beginning to sag around his face. His chin looked almost receded, not completely yet, but you could see the direction where his face was headed. He wasn't going to be a distinguished looking man with a strong face and graying temples. He would have deep folds around a thinning face with no strength or solid line to it. No character. His blue eyes were too gentle and they were imitating innocence, staring at me waiting for the response; waiting for kind words of forgiveness and absolution. "Forgive me father for I have sinned," those eyes were saying. They were asking forgiveness but not really from me, from someone or something else. He needed to blow his nose again. It was starting to drip.

I looked down at his hand on my knee. How delicate his hands were. Small, slender, no calluses, no evidence of hard work. They were a woman's manicured, weak hands. I didn't want them touching me anymore.

> There was no air in the room. The thick red velvet drapes were still closed over the windows, making the room dimly lit and creating a feeling of heaviness. It felt muggy, which was odd in February. I needed air and sunlight. I wanted to get out of that space.
>
> I looked back at my husband. "If I'm your priority, then you will end it," I said. "Now, let's go home. I miss my kids."

What was supposed to be a romantic weekend soured, as had the husband's skin.

Your Turn

Write about a time you learned something new from someone. Even someone you didn't like much but who taught you something you needed to learn. Start your writing in the thick of the lesson with a snippet of dialog. Then describe things so readers know where you are standing or sitting, who is there with you, what you are holding or touching, what your task is. Use sensory images and the names of locations, people, events, and products. End with another snippet of dialog from one or the other of you. Your specifics will let the reader (and you!) know more about how you felt in that situation.

Practice with Metaphor and Simile

In a metaphor, the writer compares two unalike things to refresh our experience of the first. "My desk is my spaceship," a grade-schooler says, and we know something about his imagination and spirit. "When I soak in the bathtub at night, I am a larvae in a cocoon," a single woman breadwinner says, and we understand the way in which soaking in the tub is a respite from expectations and stresses.

Simile employs "like" or "as" to make comparisons. "When my teacher is angry, she looks like a horse with the reins pulled back," a young boy once told me. "The fluorescent lights on that ceiling look like parallel train tracks at the downtown station," an architect might say of inelegant fixtures.

Simile is valuable in writing, but emotionally, metaphor is stronger than simile because it says one thing *is* another thing: An angry parent is a broken chair; the empty page is a frozen lake. Metaphor creates a stronger jolt in the reader than when a "like" or "as" is inserted: An angry parent is like a broken chair; the empty page is like a frozen lake. Most writers prefer metaphor to simile, but there are times when the insertion of like or as is necessary for the word construction: He was as quick to take the money as a Lamborghini Gallardo on a German highway.

Practice with both metaphor and simile strengthens your ability to use both.

Your Turn

There is a short couplet form named Abantu, which you can read about in *Technicians of the Sacred* by Jerome Rothenberg. It comes from an oral tradition in Africa and is useful for developing dexterity with metaphorical thinking. In this oral tradition, one person offers an image and another person, as the rhythm of the work allows, offers an image in response. The participants are seizing an opportunity to use figurative language and refresh experience through association: The sound of an elephant's tusk cracking / The voice of an angry man. Whether you have never heard the sound of an elephant's tusk cracking or have heard it, the comparison allows you to experience something of the sound.

Creating Abantu will help you practice the associational thinking required for creating metaphor and simile. To do this, propose a first line, using a common image from your environment that appeals to one of the five senses. State the image in different ways to make several comparisons:

> Clothes fresh from the dryer
> Clothes tumbling in the dryer
> Clothes going into the dryer

Next, "answer back" to these lines with an image that makes you experience a physical sensation:

> Clothes fresh from the dryer
> A patch of carpet where my cat lies in sunshine
>
> Clothes tumbling in the dryer
> Leaves and paper in a windstorm
>
> Clothes going into the dryer
> Tangles of seaweed on the beach

To continually exercise and grow the metaphor/simile-making muscle, collect first lines throughout the day and answer them when you get a chance:

> The cornflakes in my bowl
> Waiting for the bus
>
> Students eating in the cafeteria
> Sitting at my desk

Later you might finish the couplets:

> The cornflakes in my bowl
> Sand bars in a bay
>
> Waiting for the bus
> A jellybean out of the bag
>
> Students eating in the cafeteria
> Undulating kelp
>
> Sitting at my desk
> A marionette with no one holding the strings

Think about forcing yourself to use all the senses:

> **Sound:**
> My mother's voice
> Water in a fountain
>
> My baby brother's voice
> Sirens behind our car
>
> **Smell:**
> The star jasmine at night
> Smell of my grandmother's dress as I clung to the folds
>
> Bubble gum out of the wrapper
> Plastic skin of a new Barbie doll

Taste:

A cracker with no butter

Brown paper bag in my mouth

The rubber bands on my braces

Tofu

Touch:

Wool hat on my head

Blades of dry grass

Touching the skin of a dolphin

The smooth peel under an eggshell

Developing facility with associational and figurative language will greatly enhance your writing. Remember to insert the Abantu construction into sentences:

When I woke up this morning, I went downstairs for breakfast. My mother had put cornflakes in a bowl for me. When I poured milk in, the brown flakes became sand bars in a bay, like the one where my father always took me fishing.

The more you use sensory images, details, and metaphor and simile, the less you will lean on abstract, intangible words that tell readers how they should feel rather than allowing them to experience the feeling you have created. When intangible words make appearances in your writing where you'd be better off with tangible words, figure out how to replace them with specific, sensory information.

"When she is angry, my teacher looks like a horse with the reins pulled back" evokes something much more immediate than, "When she is angry, my teacher is gross," which is what the student said before trying to create a simile. With the summarizing word "gross," we don't experience how big the teacher seems to the child and how closely the child observes her; we don't shrink from the child's proximity to his teacher's big teeth.

Practice Using Clichés to Good Effect (To Better Recognize When They Don't Work)

If you play with clichés, you will be alert to the ways in which they creep into your writing and into the speech of those around you. Paying attention, you'll be able to use clichés appropriately for characters as idiosyncratic tag lines, but comb them out of your writing when they operate like placeholders instead of enhancing the vividness of your writing.

I created an exercise that uses clichés to advantage after I experienced a conversation filled with clichés at an airport gate before the agent arrived to give out boarding passes. I was standing behind an elderly man and a middle aged man, both dressed in tight jeans, cowboy boots, and cowboy hats, their belt buckles sparkling under the florescent lighting. They may have been father and son.

Older man: There sure were a lot people downstairs at the check in.

Younger man: Yup, these days, you can never give yourself enough time.

Older man: They sure wanted us here early, and there's no one ready to see us.

Younger man: Yup, that's how it is, hurry up and wait.

Older man: I guess we could've gotten all jammed up at that place where they check the carry-ons and the people for weapons.

Younger man: Yup, these days you can't have enough security.

The clichés hadn't really allowed either party to say very much. Each clichéd answer in response to the older man's comments seemed to shut things down. "What if we apply a strategy like this to a situation where there are higher stakes?" I wondered. What might I have answered people who warned me not to become a writer, if I were using only clichés?

Talking to Those Who Don't Believe in My Writing

That's not bad for a first try, but why are you calling it a final draft?

A bird in the hand is worth two in the bush.

This little part isn't historically accurate.

Historical, schmorical.

People aren't going to like it.

You can't please everyone.

You may think you can write, but how do you know other people will think so?

Bite me.

Why would you want to write literature when there are plenty of good books to read by other people?

Stick it where the sun don't shine.

Your ego is getting in the way of your writing.

Takes one to know one.

Your style is too uninventive, not colorful enough.

I'm saving my pennies for a rainy day.

You shouldn't show this to anyone; it isn't ready.

And who made you the boss?

You could be spending your time productively.

Penny wise and pound foolish.

You aren't listening to me.

Whatever.

Your Turn

1. Think of a place or situation in which someone has power over you that you find annoying.

2. Name your writing after this place or situation: "In the Dean's Office," "Talking to My Boss," "At Lunch with My Mother-in-Law," "The Conversation I Imagine with My Ex," "When My Teenage Son Comes Down from His Room," "Talking to My Parents About My Plans."

3. Write a dialogue in which the annoyingly powerful person speaks the way he or she normally does. After every line of that person's, reply with a tired cliché (or something similar like an overused aphorism or expression). Don't worry about how it fits as a response. Just write down what pops into your mind.

To further explore and understand how clichés can help rather than hinder your writing try this variation: Take each cliché that you came up with in the dialogue you wrote and do a freewrite from it, exploring the meaning the cliché has for you, not only vis-à-vis the person you were responding to in the dialogue, but in other life situations and with other people, past and present.

This is something you can stop and do whenever you find an unwanted cliché has strayed into your writing. You'll most likely unearth much more to write, and you'll be able to easily take the cliché out.

Practice Identifying Occasion

Poet Stanley Plumly said to his classes that poems must certainly weigh more at the end than at the beginning. What matters to us has emotional weight, and as with poetry, all creative writing supplies vehicles for writers to seek out what matters and to feel the weight of it. As writers, we take ourselves, and ultimately our readers, on a journey during which we learn from our experience as we relive it on the page but maintain solid footing as we go. This solid footing comes partly as a consequence of the speaker of the writing revealing the reason he or she is urged to speech right now. Although as a writer, you may have been interested in your topic for a while, the speaker inside the writing must have an occasion upon which to start talking.

A journalist and technical writer approached me to coach her on personal essay writing. She wanted to describe her mother, an Italian immigrant who raised her daughter with gestures and words about the evil eye. She knew that her mother's old country superstitions had made a great impact on her, and she wanted to write about them as a way of exploring who she is as a mother raising her own children. The topic encompasses so much, however. It's that question again: Where to start? Well, what is the speaker's occasion? What prompts her to speech as the essay starts? Has she had an interaction with her son and responded in a way that reminds her of her mother? Is she facing a situation with her son that she doesn't know how to handle but thinks her mother would have handled by invoking fear of the evil eye? If this is so, she could start her essay with that situation and describe her hesitation about handling it and her knowledge about how her mother would have acted. Then she can write about what her mother taught her about the evil eye and what it takes to discourage it. She can write about the resulting effect on her thinking and feeling. Finally, she can return to the interaction with her son, ready to either do as her mother did or do something else she has figured out from thinking about her mother and her upbringing.

If you know the topic you want to write about or the subject you want to explore, and yet feel unable to make what is at the bottom of your heart and mind come into being on the page despite details, images, anecdotes and dialog, you might be confused about your occasion. Ask yourself this: "Why am I writing this essay now?" "Because I missed hearing Vin Scully at Dodger Park, and I missed having my dad there, too." "Because I caught myself in the act of doing something my mother had done in raising me, and I wanted to explore how her actions affected me so I might choose a different way of behaving as a parent."

Remember, your writing is a "made" thing. Once you realize why you are making it right now, you will find a way to start and end your writing. You can't know at the start what you or your characters will find out, but you can know by identifying the occasion for your writing what you or they are trying to find out about.

Your Turn

List five places you have visited—they can be local (as close as the rooms in your house or houses in your neighborhood), national, or international. Go back, and for each item on the list, write when you visited. List the most memorable moment you experienced there. Now, pick one item on the list and ask yourself what about it could urge you to speech right now (other than that you are doing an exercise!). Make that a first line, "It was in Madison, Wisconsin, that I learned just how much my father had sacrificed to raise a family." Then explain where you are in the locale as you experience the urge to speech:

> We had driven for two days from northern New Jersey, my sister, my mother, my father and I, and we'd unpacked my suitcases of clothes and my portable type-writer. In those days, you really didn't furnish your dorm room with anything much; you just accepted the sparse furniture, and lack of a microwave and TV, and hoped your roommate might bring a phonograph or posters to hang. Now my father and I walked two abreast down the street leading from the dorm to nearby restaurants, my mother and sister behind us.
>
> My dad turned to me, "These are the best years of your life. Enjoy them."

Remembering something in a particular place at a particular time begins to deliver an occasion for my writing. Here, my physical occasion is moving into my freshman dorm room. The emotional occasion is realizing, from what he told me, what becoming a dad when he was only 20 may have meant for my father about his longings.

Practice Writing in Persona

It is true that even the most autobiographical writing creates its own persona from the material of one's life. The persona created for the page is always more cohesive than you, the one living the events. When we refer to persona writing, though, we usually mean the creation of a voice for something or someone very different than the writer. In first-person poetry or prose, that voice may be one of an historical figure, an appliance, or an animal. It can utilize the words and worldview of a teenager, a prison inmate or escapee, a celebrity, a detective, a car repairman, or a slacker, as long as that persona is not one the author can attribute to him or herself.

In viewing the world through the impressions of another or an inanimate object, the writer seeks insight and evocation otherwise not as freshly or convincingly stated. It's a transferable lesson: Practicing this kind of writing helps you develop your skill in inventing characters as well as in creating cohesive first-person speakers.

Your Turn

Believe you are your toaster. Believe you have gone out to find the perfect soul mate for yourself or to find a lover or a good companion. This might be a person who you believe will have just the right touch on the lever that gets you hot or an appliance that works the same hours as you do. Write what is going on inside the toaster's head as he/she searches and perhaps finds someone or something. Remember to think specifically about where the toaster is—a grocery store, a state fair, on a counter in the employees' lunch room; anything is possible. If you'd like to imagine yourself as a different appliance, go ahead.

Here's another idea: Select someone prominent in national, world, or local events. Have that persona hiding from the public and thinking about a situation, while eating a specific food. For instance, golf star Tiger Woods might be ripping pieces of a pizza and feeding seagulls in a picnic area while he reflects on the impacts of his unwanted 2009 notoriety for having affairs. President Obama might be eating roasted chestnuts on the steps of the Hayden Planetarium in New York and thinking about his historic election. What is important is that you can fully imagine the persona's actions, observations, and questions, as well as the place you have him or her thinking and eating. Write until the persona you have chosen says something that surprises you and/or seems to resolve or come to grips with his or her topic.

Practice Dialog in Conjunction with Persona

There is a full discussion of dialog in Part Four, but it is valuable to learn to use commands and questions to evoke feelings and thoughts on topics you are writing about in any genre.

Let's look at the strategies of authors Jamaica Kincaid and Bruce Holland Rogers. In her short story "Girl" (www.turksheadreview.com/library/texts/kincaid-girl.html), Jamaica Kincaid uses commands throughout. They are snatches of dialog that have become inscribed in the character's consciousness:

> Wash the white clothes on Monday and put them on the stone heap; wash the color clothes on Tuesday and put them on the clothesline to dry; don't walk barehead in the hot sun; cook pumpkin fritters in very hot sweet oil; soak your little cloths right after you take them off; when buying cotton to make yourself a nice blouse, be sure that it doesn't have gum on it, because that way it won't hold up well after a wash; soak salt fish overnight before you cook it; is it true that you sing benna in Sunday school? Always eat your food in such a way that it won't turn someone else's stomach…

As the story continues with the words the character's Caribbean mother spoke to her daughter, the phrase "slut you are so bent on becoming" is repeated several times. At the very end, when the daughter finally asks a question ("What if the baker won't let me feel the bread?") the answer is, "…you mean to say that after all you are really going to be the kind of woman who the baker won't let near that bread?" The lines in the story evoke the stifling fear and lack of freedom in this girl's upbringing, as well as maddening gender-related oppression.

Bruce Holland Rogers' story "How Could a Mother?" (www.vestalreview.net/howcould.htm) is written all in questions. The effect is horrifying and haunting. Though there is no answer supplied to any of the questions, the content of each question builds the readers' understanding of the situation:

> When was it that your daughter—when was it that Josie started to cry? What was your state of mind when you punished her? What were you thinking when she wouldn't stop crying? Did your boyfriend say anything about Josie's crying…
> What time did you wake up? How soon after you woke up did you check on your daughter? You could tell right away?

At this story's end, the focus shifts and draws the reader closer to the underlying subject of the story, which is that if we are honest, we realize that we, too, have experienced an urge to disastrous violence:

> Do you have any thoughts about the question no one can answer? Not the one everyone asks, but the one only a mother who has felt her own hands shake with a rage that is bigger than she is can ask?

Your Turn

To practice using dialog, write a story all in commands. Think about ways you have been taught to behave in specific roles, places, or jobs. Choose the voice of someone who irritates you or has trapped you into doing something their way or behaving as they want you to. Next, write a piece entirely in questions. Fully imagine to whom you are asking the questions. Perhaps you are a mom who found her 18-year-old drunk and throwing up, or perhaps you work under someone who has very strict rules. Perhaps you are disappointed in how your behavior in a particular situation affected others. Alternatively, choose the voice of someone you admire. See how the feelings evoked by the same method are completely different.

Practice Building Scenes

It's nearly impossible to write without at least some scene building. Even so, too often we don't do enough scene building and that leads to telling rather than showing. In Part Four, there is more discussion about writing scenes, but here is an exercise to get you started seeing how recording the details in a scene helps you grow your writing.

For this exercise, I write descriptions of places I've been to recently:

> Dr. Ottoman's office is not crowded this morning. One of the office assistants is playing with a toddler in a designated play area, with a sunken square of floor and large plastic primary-colored toys. The little girl is giggling and running out into the main waiting room. The office assistant lures her back with a blue truck. The waiting room chairs are made of blond wood and pink upholstered cushions. Magazines for adults and children rest neatly against a far wall, held in wooden-slatted racks. Medical records hang with brightly colored tabs in file carts behind the receptionist's counter. When the nurse swings into the room from a door beside the magazines, she calls, "Penny Sharp? The doctor is ready for you." Three people look up, two women and one man. The younger and heavier of the two women gets up and walks toward the nurse, using a cane, and her large black purse swings near her hip, its silver buckle catching the sunlight through the window. Just as she and the nurse are headed through the door, a young woman approaches the door from the exam room side. She waits a moment while Penny and the nurse slowly walk through the doorway. When she steps into the waiting room, the young mother hurries to scoop up the toddler and then stands at the receptionist's counter to make her next appointment. The toddler pulls at her mother's hair and her mother gently takes the little girl's fingers away. As the little girl rides out of the office on her mother's hip, an elderly man enters the office using a walker. His back is curled over it like the hump in the young mother's ponytail. For a moment, it looks like he is headed to the play area, but he takes a seat, his walker parked just on the edge of the sunken area, standing like a guard railing to keep the blue and yellow plastic vehicles from entering the pedestrian-only area of the waiting room.

Then for fun, I drop a character into the scene, myself or someone I know or someone I have invented. In this case that someone, the she, is a composite of several people I know:

> She was so relieved that Dr. Ottoman's office was not crowded. She had no idea, really, why she had said yes to accompanying her mother to this appointment. But doing this would give her a chance to show that she had gone out of her way, staying over a night after a Sunday afternoon visit with her mother. She hadn't wanted to stay over. She was much too busy to not wake up in her own bed and get going, long vacations she blocked out months ahead excluded.

Seeing her mother for an afternoon once every quarter, now that it took two hours to drive there, she could keep to her schedule and not have to miss her social and community service activities. It was hard enough to squeeze them all in around the regular trips she and her husband made to visit their daughter who lived across the country. And she also liked taking trips abroad every year, real trips like she'd always admired her father for planning. She liked doing impressive things like he had.

As she sat waiting, she thought about the calls she'd make to figure out one more stretch of lodging for the trip to Australia only a few months away. One of the office assistants was playing with a toddler at the back of the room in a small sunken square of floor with large plastic primary-colored toys. The little girl's giggling and running were very distracting. Thank God the office assistant lured her back into the center of the play area with a blue truck. She didn't need a toddler coming over to start her mother reaching into her purse for some treat or other to engage the child's interest. She glanced over at her mother sitting quietly in the waiting room chair beside her, a square-ish blond wood and pink upholstered affair, not nearly as modern as the stainless steel and leather chairs in the city doctor's office. When she saw the magazines stored neatly in racks against the far wall, she got up to find one that might have articles about traveling. She'd been thinking of the Caribbean or Fiji or maybe some islands off Spain for a next trip after Australia. As she passed the receptionist's counter with carts and carts of medical records behind it, she raised her head slightly up and to the right, comparing things. This little town did seem to have its act together, she had to admit, but it sure would have been easier for her if her mother had stayed in the city. It was more fun, if you could call it that, to bring her books from Costco and cans of seltzer and Diet Coke on her way back from doing her own shopping, than it was to make the trip out here.

The nurse swung into the room. "Penny Sharp? The doctor is ready for you." Penny walked toward the nurse using a cane, her large black purse swinging near her hip, its silver buckle catching the sunlight through the window, spilling coins of light on the walls and upholstery. Fifty bucks, that's what she calculated the trip out here cost between ferry fares and gas.

An elderly man with a walker entered the office. He took a seat at the back of the room and parked his walker on the edge of the sunken area. From where she sat, the walker looked like it was keeping the blue and yellow plastic vehicles where they belonged. She looked again at her mother. She had no idea why she was needed here.

As I dropped my character into this scene, I wrote without stopping and then went back and did a little revising to make sure I had the scene as much from the character's point of view as I could manage. I went from 300 or so words to more than double that almost effortlessly. It's a good idea to give yourself a chance to write, write, write without wondering how you are going to shape something. In this way, you can gain confidence that starting with where you are or what you remember brings material you can have fun developing.

Your Turn

Think of a place you can describe in detail. Write a description of 250–350 words. Put the description away for a few hours or a day. Take it out and think of a character to drop into the scene and write from that character's viewpoint and life situation. As you do this exercise, pay attention to how you alter the scene to make it work from the dropped-in character's point of view. Some details might become important, while others are no longer important. More details might come to mind.

Lyric Techniques in Your Language

Paying attention to the music in your poetry and prose helps you build the emotional content and meaning of your writing:

> *An essential element for good writing is a good ear: one must listen to the sound of one's prose.*
>
> —Barbara Tuchman

> *Sound itself... is surely a signifier of mood, and thus of message...*
>
> —Mary Oliver

Use Repetition, But Artfully

As writers, we must be aware that repeating words without thinking about whether that helps or diminishes our writing can lead to avoiding the work of mining ourselves to write what we truly feel and know. Recently, I read a high school student's draft for an essay addressing the qualities of effective learning environments. In the excerpt below, I have bolded words to highlight the tiresome repetition:

> The people who live in this environment must take the role of an **intellectual**. They must first be **intelligent**. Without **intelligence** there will be no discussions, only foolery and actions. While **intelligence** will give the people the ideas and

allow them to think of ways to spread them effectively, it is nothing without **friendliness**. For ideas to be exchanged all the people involved in the discussion must be **friendly**. They will then be willing to **talk**. Not only will they **talk** but they will hear. Each person will listen to what is being **talked** about, think on it, and present what he or she believes on the subject. This will transform the conversation from the blurting of ideas into the thoughtful contemplation of what each person knows.

Of course the main problem here is that the writer is not backing up assertions with specifics and examples. That he seems to be chasing his own tail is coming unwittingly from the sound the repetitions are making.

Compare the repetition in this unworked draft to that in master orator Martin Luther King Jr.'s "I Have a Dream" speech (www.americanrhetoric.com/speeches/mlkihaveadream.htm). Here are some of Dr. King's famous repetitions:

I say to you today, my friends, so even though we face the difficulties of today and tomorrow, I still have a dream. It is a dream deeply rooted in the American dream.

I have a dream that one day this nation will rise up and live out the true meaning of its creed: "We hold these truths to be self-evident: that all men are created equal."

I have a dream that one day on the red hills of Georgia the sons of former slaves and the sons of former slave owners will be able to sit down together at the table of brotherhood.

I have a dream that one day even the state of Mississippi, a state sweltering with the heat of injustice, sweltering with the heat of oppression, will be transformed into an oasis of freedom and justice.

I have a dream that my four little children will one day live in a nation where they will not be judged by the color of their skin but by the content of their character.

I have a dream today.

Since this writing was delivered by Dr. King himself, it is hard for some of us to separate the text from our memory of his soaring voice. But this speech works equally well as a written document. The artful, intentional drama created by repeating the phrase "I have a dream" is a lyric device that keeps the reader moving down the page and experiencing all that has been denied those whose skin color is not white. Even those unmoved by the fight for equal rights for all races could not have avoided experiencing the passion and dignity of the music in Martin Luther King Jr.'s argument.

Repetition is forceful in carrying the reader into the deeper emotions of a story. In Tim O'Brien's famous "The Things They Carried," (http://web.archive.org/web/20011222025122/www.nku.edu/~peers/thethingstheycarried.htm)

the emotional weight of serving in Vietnam accumulates in readers just as it does in the bodies and souls of the soldiers O'Brien describes. In one passage, the word "as" is repeated to introduce the specific roles of each soldier:

> As a first lieutenant and platoon leader, Jimmy Cross carried a compass...
>
> As an RTO, Mitchell Sanders carried the PRC-25 radio...
>
> As a medic, Rat Kiley carried a canvas satchel filled with morphine and plasma and malaria tablets...
>
> As a big man, therefore a machine gunner, Henry Dobbin's carried the M-60...
>
> As PFCs or Spec 4s, most of them were common grunts and carried the standard M-16 gas-operated assault rifle...

In another passage, the repetition O'Brien uses involves the phrase "they carried" at the start of successive sentences. The soldiers are no longer singled out by role but have become a collective:

> They carried USO stationery and pencils and pens. They carried Sterno, safety pins, trip flares, signal flares, spools of wire, razor blades, chewing tobacco, liberated joss sticks and statuettes of the smiling Buddha, candles, bush hats, bolos, and much more.

Again, as in King's speech, the repeated words make us look up close at the writer's subject. They create a music of persistence.

In August, 1970, Judy Syfers read an essay she wrote, "Why I Want a Wife," (www.cwluherstory.org/why-i-want-a-wife.html) before a San Francisco crowd celebrating the 50th anniversary of the 19th amendment to the U.S. Constitution, which gave women the right to vote. A year later, the essay appeared in the first issue of *Ms. Magazine*. The essay travels down the page via the repetition of the phrase, "I want a wife who will..." The phrase introduces and occurs inside paragraphs on caring for children, meeting the needs of a husband, and selflessly giving up one's own life. Here are some of those phrases:

> I want a wife who will work and send me to school...
>
> I want a wife to take care of my children...
>
> I want a wife to keep track of the children's doctor and dentist appointments...
>
> I want a wife who takes care of the children when...they are sick...
>
> I want a wife who will take care of my physical needs. I want a wife who will keep my house clean....
>
> I want a wife to go along when our family takes a vacation so that someone can continue to care for me and my children when I need a rest and change of scene.

At the essay's conclusion, the syntax changes:

> If, by chance, I find another person more suitable as a wife than the wife I already have, I want the liberty to replace my present wife with another one...When I am through with school and have a job, I want my wife to quit working and remain at home so that my wife can more fully and completely take care of a wife's duties.

We read our way to the essay's last sentence feeling a sense of momentum. When that last sentence turns out to be the question, "Who wouldn't want a wife?" the answer we feel inside plays off of the list of "I want a wife who" phrases. In the same way that Dr. King gets his listeners to internalize the knowledge that those discriminated against are as real and human as those doing the discriminating, Syfers gets her listeners to understand that seeing a woman only as a role causes her mate to dehumanize her.

Another famous document that employs repetition artfully is Thomas Jefferson's "Declaration of Independence" (www.ushistory.org/Declaration/document/), where he uses this rhetorical tool of phrase repetition to build the case against the King of England:

> He has refused his Assent to Laws, the most wholesome and necessary for the public good.
>   He has forbidden his Governors to pass Laws of immediate and pressing importance, unless suspended in their operation till his Assent should be obtained; and when so suspended, he has utterly neglected to attend to them.
>   He has refused to pass other Laws for the accommodation of large districts of people, unless those people would relinquish the right of Representation in the Legislature, a right inestimable to them and formidable to tyrants only.
>   He has called together legislative bodies at places unusual, uncomfortable, and distant from the depository of their Public Records, for the sole purpose of fatiguing them into compliance with his measures.
>   He has dissolved Representative Houses repeatedly, for opposing with manly firmness his invasions on the rights of the people.

What if the student working to define an effective learning environment took a lesson from these master writers? Here's a possibility:

> Intelligence is not the mere blurting of ideas. Intelligence is the opposite of foolery and meaningless action. And intelligence is nothing without friendliness, for if ideas are to be exchanged, all of those involved in discussion must be willing to talk—not only willing to talk but to hear, and to think about what they've heard.

Not a perfect piece of writing yet by any means, but listening for music that the repeated words can make has changed the sound into that of a march toward a patient persuasion rather than the annoying sound of a needle stuck in the groove of a record.

Your Turn

Try your hand at using repetition and experiencing its force for helping you evoke both emotion and thinking.

1. Think of something you believe in or wish for and write five or more passages, each starting with the same line: "I believe in running free and fast" or "I have a wish to swim in the ocean" or "If I could talk with my mother for just one moment more."

   After you have written the passages about your topic, end by repeating the line you started with three times in a row. Think about the way this builds emotional content in your writing.

2. Think of something you can describe well by writing a "Declaration of Independence" from it. You might address the 10 pounds that you've wanted to lose for ages, the weeds in your garden that get you down, or the person who seems to have inordinate power over the way you think of yourself (your inner critic will do as a subject here).

3. Think of a role you've taken on in life that you can describe well by listing what you must wear or carry or perform in this role. Write about it using sentences that start off repeating a verb: I run, I dress myself in, I mix, for instance. Alternatively, write about the role by using the verb "want": I want to write a book that..., I want to tell the president..., I want to learn to... ."

More on Repetition

Remember Edgar Allan Poe's "The Raven" (www.heise.de/ix/raven/Literature/Lore/TheRaven.html)?

> Once upon a midnight dreary, while I pondered weak and weary,
> Over many a quaint and curious volume of forgotten lore,
> While I nodded, nearly napping, suddenly there came a tapping,
> As of some one gently rapping, rapping at my chamber door.
> "Tis some visitor," I muttered, 'tapping at my chamber door—
> Only this, and nothing more.'

In school, even those of us who shied away from poetry were drawn to this poem for its eerie momentum. In 1850, Poe wrote "The Philosophy of Composition" http://xroads.virginia.edu/~HYPER/poe/composition.html. Explaining his process in writing "The Raven," he mentions his thoughts about one of the kinds of repetition in the poem:

> …bethought me of the nature of my refrain. Since its application was to be repeatedly varied it was clear that the refrain itself must be brief, for there would have been an insurmountable difficulty in frequent variations of application in any sentence of length. In proportion to the brevity of the sentence would, of course, be the facility of the variation. This led me at once to a single word as the best refrain.
>
> The question now arose as to the character of the word. Having made up my mind to a refrain, the division of the poem into stanzas was of course a corollary, the refrain forming the close to each stanza. That such a close, to have force, must be sonorous and susceptible of protracted emphasis, admitted no doubt, and these considerations inevitably led me to the long o as the most sonorous vowel in connection with r as the most producible consonant.
>
> The sound of the refrain being thus determined, it became necessary to select a word embodying this sound, and at the same time in the fullest possible keeping with that melancholy which I had pre-determined as the tone of the poem. In such a search it would have been absolutely impossible to overlook the word "Nevermore."

Poe wrote "nothing more" at the end of his first stanza, "evermore" at the end of his second stanza and then returned to "nothing more" for five stanzas before the raven speaks his name "Nevermore;" then that word is repeated at the end of 10 more stanzas:

(*Stanza 2*)
Ah, distinctly I remember it was in the bleak December,
And each separate dying ember wrought its ghost upon the floor.
Eagerly I wished the morrow;—vainly I had sought to borrow
From my books surcease of sorrow—sorrow for the lost Lenore—
For the rare and radiant maiden whom the angels named Lenore—
Nameless here for evermore.

(*Stanza 3*)
And the silken sad uncertain rustling of each purple curtain
Thrilled me—filled me with fantastic terrors never felt before;
So that now, to still the beating of my heart, I stood repeating
'Tis some visitor entreating entrance at my chamber door—
Some late visitor entreating entrance at my chamber door;—
This it is, and nothing more,'

(*Stanza 8*)
Then this ebony bird beguiling my sad fancy into smiling,
By the grave and stern decorum of the countenance it wore,
'Though thy crest be shorn and shaven, thou,' I said, 'art sure no craven.
Ghastly grim and ancient raven wandering from the nightly shore—
Tell me what thy lordly name is on the Night's Plutonian shore!'
Quoth the raven, 'Nevermore.'

(*Stanza17*)
And the raven, never flitting, still is sitting, still is sitting
On the pallid bust of Pallas just above my chamber door;
And his eyes have all the seeming of a demon's that is dreaming,
And the lamp-light o'er him streaming throws his shadow on the floor;
And my soul from out that shadow that lies floating on the floor
Shall be lifted-nevermore!

Of course, hearing words that rhyme at the ends of sentences and inside sentences is part of the pleasure for any listener. But certainly the ear's expectation of a stanza ending with the word "more" in it contributes. The fun also comes from repeated words and phrases on the interior of sentences. These make us feel the suspense the speaker feels as well as his sadness: "rapping, rapping;" "surcease of sorrow—sorrow for the lost Lenore," "some visitor entreating entrance at my chamber door—/Some late visitor entreating entrance at my chamber door."

Walt Whitman is another poet who used repetition effectively for staying power with listeners as well as to mimic the intensity of his longings and perceptions. In "A Noiseless Patient Spider," notice the places where the poet repeats words and phrases:

A Noiseless Patient Spider   *By Walt Whitman*

A noiseless, patient spider,
I mark'd, where, on a little promontory, it stood, isolated;
Mark'd how, to explore the vacant, vast surrounding,
It launch'd forth filament, filament, filament, out of itself;
Ever unreeling them—ever tirelessly speeding them.
And you, O my Soul, where you stand,
Surrounded, surrounded, in measureless oceans of space,
Ceaselessly musing, venturing, throwing,—seeking the spheres, to connect them;
Till the bridge you will need, be form'd—till the ductile anchor hold;
Till the gossamer thread you fling, catch somewhere, O my Soul.

The art of repeating phrases creates impact beyond a poem's length. Repeated three times in a row, the word "filament" mimics the act of the spider throwing its threads. The word "mark'd" used twice as the verb in a sentence keeps the readers feet on the ground with the poet pointing out his observation of the spider. "Surrounded, surrounded" emphasizes the vastness of the universe and puts us as human readers to scale in our universe as the small spider is on the promontory. When the poet uses the phrase "O my Soul," both at the opening and closing of the second stanza, we move with him from observing something tangible in the world (the spider) to an intangible hopefulness about the ongoing life of the soul, though it be alone in an unknowable vastness.

In the short story "The Pier," Mori Ogwai repeats one sentence: "The pier is long—long—" throughout about every five hundred words (page 55 on www.archive.org/stream/paulowniasevens00erskgoog#page/n86/mode/1up). This kind of repetition creates foreshadowing, convincing the reader to bring along feelings of suspense from one part of the story to another.

Ernest Hemingway is another prose writer skilled at repeating words and phrases inside of sentences. He did this in "On the Blue Water," a short story that he published in *Esquire* in April, 1936, and then made into the novella *The Old Man and the Sea*:

> Certainly there is no hunting like the hunting of man and those who have hunted armed men long enough and liked it, never really care for anything else thereafter.

To develop your ability to employ repetition to heighten emotion, when you read, note moments you come across word repetitions you enjoy. Here are some from authors whose work you might know:

Ernest Hemingway: "And then it just occurred to him that he was going to die. It came with a rush, not as a rush of water nor of wind… ("The Snows of Kilimanjaro" http://books.google.com/books?id=QjgiXnMHHtIC&printsec=frontcover&cd=1& source=gbs_ViewAPI#v=onepage&q&f=false)

Charles Dickens: "It was the best of times. It was the worst of times." (*A Tale of Two Cities* http://books.google.com/books?id=YqfPAAAAMAAJ&printsec=front cover&cd=1&source=gbs_ViewAPI#v=onepage&q&f=false)

Emily Dickinson: "I'm nobody! Who are you?/Are you nobody too?" ("I'm Nobody! Who Are You?" www.americanpoems.com/poets/emilydickinson/10240)

T. S. Eliot: "Because I do not hope to turn again/Because I do not hope/Because I do not hope to turn..." ("Ash Wednesday" www.poemhunter.com/poem / ash-wednesday/)

Samuel Taylor Coleridge: I looked upon the rotting sea /And drew my eyes away; / I looked upon the rotting deck/And there the dead men lay." ("The Rime of the Ancient Mariner" www.online-literature.com/coleridge/646/)

Alfred Noyes: And the highwayman came riding—/Riding—riding—/The high-wayman came riding, up to the old inn door. ("The Highwayman" www.potw.org/archive/potw85.html)

Your Turn

Copying patterns authors use can inspire new pieces you might not have written if you weren't trying to emulate others.

Think of a decision you made. Picture yourself in a particular place where you think you made or might have made the decision. Now write a description of that moment using repetition. For example, I am thinking about the time years ago when I finally made the decision to get a divorce. Recalling that moment in a freewrite, I say: "I looked at the kitchen counter full of bottles, juices, milk, and dressings/and I read the labels on them one by one./I did not put them away, but looked at a kitchen counter full of sustenance displaced."

Then, I try a different pattern: "Because I wanted more and hoped to find it, because I wanted less and would give up much of what I had, because I wanted to mine the depths of me, I left the kitchen, the counter as it was and opened my door to earth and trees, the sun."

If I put this all together and practice compression that allows for some of the repetition, I might have a poem:

Meaning It

I saw my kitchen counter full of bottles,
juices, milk, and dressing, read the labels
one by one. I left the kitchen counter
full of sustenance displaced, this first
of many days, this last of many others.
I wanted more and hoped I'd find it;
I wanted less. I left the counter as it was,
opened my door to earth and trees and sun.

Now you try it: Invent lines that use repetition to describe where you were and what you were thinking when you made an important decision. Or try writing in present tense and see what decision you might be making about something you are thinking about.

Perhaps what you write will stand as a finished piece or it might become incorporated into a longer work you have in mind. But whether or not you use the particular lines you invent for the exercise, you will get the hang of using repetition; you will feel the stride it creates and how it draws writing from you.

Onomatopoeia, Alliteration, and Rhyme

Onomatopoeia

The term onomatopoeia comes from the Greek for "word-making." It means the employment of one or more words to imitate, echo, or suggest the sound of the thing or action described. Such words include bang, click, fizz, hush, buzz, moo, quack, and meow. When you pay attention to the sounds of our language, you soon realize how many of our words are onomatopoetic: bounce, boom, clap, clang, crackle, hiccup, ping pong, pitter-patter, plop, poof, snore, swoosh, slither, slop, splat, thud, tick-tock, and zap.

In *Spunk and Byte: A Writer's Guide to Punchier, More Engaging Language & Style*, author Arthur Plotnik writes on the value of using good sound words like click and gulp, whomp and wallop, garble, gobble, and squawk. Onomatopoeia represents sound on the page even when we can't find a word to do it: brrrinnggg, ka-ching, vroom, thunk, ka-zoom, and psht psht, for instance.

Here are several examples that are often chosen from literature to illustrate the use of onomatopoeia:

Edgar Allan Poe's "The Raven" (www.heise.de/ix/raven/Literature/Lore/ TheRaven.html) includes "the silken, sad, uncertain/Rustling of each purple curtain," rustling being a word that mimics the sound the curtain is making.

Lord Byron wrote in part LXXVIII of "Canto the Seventh" (www.online-literature.com/byron/don-juan/8/):

Bombs, drums, guns, bastions, batteries, bayonets, bullets,—
Hard words, which stick in the soft Muses' gullets.

Alfred Lord Tennyson wrote in "The Princess, Part vii" (http://oldpoetry.com/opoem/25334-Alfred-Lord-Tennyson-The-Princess—part-7-):

> Myriads of rivulets hurrying through the lawn,
> The moan of doves in immemorial elms,
> And murmuring of innumerable bees.

Taking lessons from poets, we can infuse both our poetry and our prose with onomatopoeia by concentrating on using verbs, adjectives, and nouns that imitate the sounds of the lives we are portraying. If you want to talk about how a brisk household employee walks, you might use onomatopoeia in a verb: "All day, her heels **clicked** their way between the kitchen and the living room." If you want to show the way a dripping faucet bothers a lonely man as he is trying to fall asleep, you can use onomatopoeia in nouns: "The **drip, drip, drip** of the tiny kitchen's sink faucet kept him awake as if it were the dawn to dusk **chirping** of a chipmunk in heat." Here is a phrase with an adjective that has onomatopoeia: "The **snappy** rhythm of her pea shelling made him feel welcome."

Your Turn

You can practice using onomatopoeia by concentrating on describing the sound of events in your experience. In the passage I wrote about garbage collection day in Los Angeles, using onomatopoeia came naturally. Here it is again:

> On garbage collection days, the disposal company my husband calls Loud and Early **slams** and **smashes** its way into our sleep. We hear garbage cans **scrape** the top of the thick rusty truck, then **clatter** across the asphalt and cement of street and curb. When we hear the garbage truck **grind** the dregs of our existence to a pulp, we **slide** our feet to the floor. A police helicopter **hurls** its hello from overhead, shaking the walls and **shattering** any memory of our dreams.

Describe a noisy situation you routinely encounter. Look for opportunities to use onomatopoetic words or inventions.

Next, choose a quiet place to describe; are you using words like whisper, shush, and hum?

And try this: Write about a person you know well. Describe the sound this person makes as he or she goes about some part of their daily routine or enters a room. Does this person clank a row of coffee cups? Crack gum? Snap rubber bands?'

Finally, play with onomatopoeia this way: ascribe sound to other senses. For instance, here I've given a sight image a sound: Sunlight **crackle**d through the broken window.

You can give sound to smell: Her perfume **sashayed** through the room before she did.

You can give sound to taste: The curry **clamored** over his uninitiated tongue like an invading army.

And you can give sound to touch: Her fingers **hushed** over the 1,000 thread-count sheets.

Sometimes words sound like something feels: sleaze, grease, sneer, glitter, wrinkle, and pulp, for instance. These, too, are vibrant words in description and combine well with onomatopoeia: The **grease sizzled** in the hot iron pan, **splattering** into the depths of her **wrinkled** apron.

Give this a try: Describe a person involved in some action (like cooking, sewing, playing ball or tennis or golf, gardening, or driving) by using words that imitate the sound of the action as well as words that sound like something feels:

He placed the golf ball on the tee, taking pleasure in the feel of its **dimpled** surface. When he hit the ball correctly, the **thwack** of his club left him exhilarated. He bent down to retrieve the tee and walked confidently toward his next shot, the wheels of his pull cart **chirping** over the grass.

Alliteration

Alliteration is the name for neighboring words with the same beginning sound. In my description of garbage collection day in Los Angeles there are a few uses of alliteration: "slams and smashes," "feet to the floor," "helicopter hurls," and "shaking and shattering." Whether the words start with soft sounds or hard sounds, having the beginning sound repeat evokes feeling as well as supplies energy to a description, making it memorable.

Here are examples of alliteration from literature:

Robert Frost's poem "Acquainted with the Night" (http://oldpoetry.com/opoem/6334-Robert-Frost-Acquainted-With-The-Night) has this line: I have **stood still** and **stopped** the **sound** of feet."

Helen Keller's prose "Three Days to See" (www.theatlantic.com/past/docs/issues/33jan/keller.htm) includes: "Hear the music of voices, the **song** of a bird, the mighty **strains** of an orchestra, as if you would be **stricken** deaf tomorrow. **Touch** each object you want to **touch** as if **tomorrow** your **tactile** sense would fail."

In the novel *A Raisin in the Sun*, Lorraine Hansberry wrote: "There is always something **left** to **love**. And if you ain't **learned** that, you ain't **learned** nothing."

Your Turn

Look at what you wrote describing a quiet or a noisy place. Notice any alliteration that entered the writing. See if you can expand on what you started.

Next, think about a sound from childhood that you heard often that you found uncomfortable: the sound of pots clanging as your mother looked for just the right one, the sound of doors slamming or doors squeaking, the sound of your father's razor blade tapping against the porcelain sink, the sound of a drill when you were at the dentist's office. Or think of sounds you found comforting: the hum of your mother's Mixmaster as she mixed ingredients for a cake, the chime of the doorbell on Saturday morning that meant your favorite uncle was arriving, the thunk of the newspaper landing at your door early in the morning, the sound of Sunday football games on TV when you gathered with cousins to watch.

With a specific image in mind, write a description of yourself hearing the sound and use alliteration as much as you can. Some of the alliteration will be to get the sound of your experience in the readers' ears. And some of the alliteration you use will tell readers about the emotions of the time:

I sat in the dentist's chair, every inch of my eight-year-old self braced against what I knew was coming because I'd been there before. My hands on the armrest made a **clench** to **calm** the **cracking** sound I knew I'd hear inside my head. This was the third baby tooth he'd taken since the roots hadn't dissolved and the **big** teeth were **blocked** and held **back** from their rightful place.

Rhyme

Most of us were brought up on limericks, nursery rhymes and greeting card verse and can easily identify the words that rhyme in the traditional way, from the "blue" and "you" in "Roses are red/Violets are blue,/Sugar is sweet,/And so are you" to the rhyming "sicken" and "thicken", "die" and "cry" in Mark Twain's lampoon in *Huckleberry Finn* (http://books.google.com/books?id=BHVaAAAAMAAJ&printsec=frontcover&cd=2&source=gbs_ViewAPI#v=onepage&q&f=false):

> And did young Stephen sicken,
> And did young Stephen die?
> And did the sad hearts thicken,
> And did the mourners cry?

Our ears are also tuned to the entertaining sound of words inside lines rhyming fully: I did cry because the fly/was ready to eat the meat.

When we chant the famous nursery rhyme "Hickory Dickory Dock," (www.dltk-teach.com/rhymes/hickory/words.htm) we hear a familiar full rhyme in the first and second words and then at the ends of line one and two, but there is also a more subtle rhyme, one we call a *slant* rhyme, in the third and fourth line endings:

> Hickory dickory dock
> The mouse ran up the clock.
> The clock struck one,
> The mouse ran down,
> Hickory, dickory, dock

"One" and "down" rhyme because of their vowel sounds, the long "o" in one and the "ow" sound in down. This kind of slant rhyme is called assonance. When the consonants that begin or end words with stressed syllables rhyme as in "clock" and "struck," the slant rhyme is called consonance. Some more examples: "Or" and "horn" create a slant rhyme that uses assonance; "blanket" and "forget" create a slant rhyme that uses consonance. It gets more complicated with other terms that further define how many parts of the words rhyme, but understanding that insides and outsides of words can rhyme will help you bring good sound to your writing and is enough of an understanding to work with effectively as a writer.

Most writers today prefer slant rhyme to full rhyme. Full rhymes are thought to easily detract from the emotional message of writing because they become chimey and sing-songy. It may be that in times past full rhyme was a means to remembering what one heard; the change in what writers and readers favor is probably due to the fact that today we usually read rather than listen to writing. It may also be that the subtle sound of slant rhyme brings more pleasure because this sounds modern and sophisticated.

Here are a few lines from Richard Hugo's poem "Letter to Snyder from Montana" (www.aprweb.org/poem/letter-snyder-montana), which appeared in *31 Letters and 13 Dreams*, now a part of Hugo's collected works, *Making Certain It Goes On*. These lines convey feeling with slant rhyme at both the line endings and in the interior of lines, and there is onomatopoeia and alliteration.

> Dear Gary: As soon as you'd gone winter snapped shut again
> on Missoula. Right now snow from the east and last night
> cold enough to arrest the melting of ice.

"Again," "night" and "ice" employ slant rhyme in line endings. "Soon" and "you'd," and "Now" and "snow" and "east" and "last" employ slant rhyme in the interiors of the lines. Of course "snapped shut" employs both onomatopoeia and alliteration.

Look at lines from another of Hugo's poems. "Letter to Wagoner from Port Townsend" is also from *31 Letters and 13 Dreams*:

> all said, this is my soul, the salmon rolling in the strait
> and salt air loaded with cream for our breathing.
> And around the bend a way, Dungeness Spit. I don't need

Can you identify the long e sound of the vowels rhyming in the last two line endings? Do you notice the way five words that start with "s" come close together, causing alliterative sound—said, soul, salmon, strait, salt?

Your Turn

To experiment with these kinds of sounds, write a paragraph as if you are:

1. A person who is slamming the door and leaving the house because of a fight with someone you live with. Write about where you are going and what you hope to do there and what will be there and why it is necessary for you to leave. Do the words sound angry? Lonely? Sad? Where in the sounds of the words are those feelings coming from? What terms would you use to describe them: assonant or consonant slant rhyming? Alliterative, onomatopoetic?

2. Now, write a paragraph that expresses the thoughts of someone who has needed a place to rest after traveling, running out of money, or having been thrown out of a situation. Write about what the person notices in the new environment. Again, ask yourself about the feelings the words convey, and check to see if you have used the sound techniques we've been talking about.

My experience is that when we are writing well from an emotional situation by using specifics and the five senses, the words almost automatically use slant rhyme, onomatopoeia, and alliteration. Our job as writers is to notice the tone of the words that sound right and then to weed out the words that don't convey the meaning we find in our words. For instance, at first, I wrote the example about the golfer this way:

> He placed the golf ball on the tee, taking pleasure in the feel of its **dimpled** surface. When he hit the ball correctly, the **thwack** of his club left him exhilarated. He bent down to retrieve the tee and walked confidently toward his next shot, the wheels of his pull cart **squeaking** over the grass.

The word "squeaking" seemed out-of-tone, more like something annoying than pleasurable. So I substituted chirping, which seems merry, like the golfer in this situation.

When you practice with sound, make bold strokes and do the best you can. When you read what you wrote and work on revising, be sensitive to tone. Most of the time, once you are working "in flow," the in-tone words will dominate, but sometimes, you have to work a little to find just the right sound word.

Vary Sentence Length and Subject-Verb Positions; Use Parallel Construction

Here is a passage from my memoir, *A New Theology: Turning to Poetry in a Time of Grief.*

> With the box of Seth's ashes by my feet on the passenger side of the car, I realized that I wanted to take pictures of the wedding site, so we stopped again to buy a disposable camera. One hour outside of Denver, snow was falling over aspens. When Seth was a student in Colorado, we had visited him here and hiked this forest. We sat on rock ledges in spring and in fall, quiet and dwarfed, overlooking

the Continental Divide, feeling overwhelmed by the majesty we were viewing. My life now was a Continental Divide. One continent with Seth on the earth with me; the other one without him here.

When I read this passage, I notice that the first three sentences start with prepositional or adverbial phrases that modify the subjects I, snow, and we. Then the next two sentences have a simple subject-verb structure: "We sat on rock ledges;" "my life now was a Continental Divide." And I end the paragraph with two sentence fragments joined with a semicolon. Each fragment has noun phrases but no verb. So, I have varied sentence length and subject-verb positions in groups. My last group of two fragments sounds right to me because it is a description of a fragmented life.

Your Turn

Write a passage about a time that you felt the reality of something that had happened—something tragic or joyful, frustrating or mysterious. If your sentences sound good to you, check out what you are doing with your sentence construction. Try to see where you have varied construction and where you have repeated it.

If your sentences sound dull, see what you can do to create a variety of sentence lengths and word positions as well as introductory phrases. Can you combine some sentences to make things interesting? Can you add modifying material by using the "-ing" form of words (participial phrases such as "feeling overwhelmed by the majesty") as I have?

See what happens when you change things from dull to more varied:

> Dull: The cat lay on my bed all day. He purred when I came to pet him. The rain poured down outside. I knew he didn't want to get his feet wet. It wasn't cold outside. It was colder inside the house.
> Varied: When the rain poured down outside, the cat lay on my bed all day, purring when I petted him. It was colder inside than outside, but he didn't want to get his feet wet.

This kind of editing can come after you have written. In doing the editing, you start to hear music where it may have been lacking before and you rekindle your interest in the passages you are writing. When you sound interesting, your readers will be more interested and apt to continue reading what you've written; but most importantly, when you realize you can make yourself sound interesting on the page employing sentence variety, you will be less upset with the sound of your first drafts and you will keep writing, knowing you can go back and make new sound on the page.

The ear likes both to recognize what is coming and to be surprised by how what comes is different than what the ear expected; the ear likes to feel it is on a ride, a sail, is in hiding or dancing in the sunlight, whichever rhythm, tone, and sound most evokes the mood of the subject. Some of this sound will come naturally as you immerse yourself in your subject; but often we have to go back to our work, and, like a conductor guiding an orchestra, help our words do their work.

Employ Locution

In *Spunk & Bite: A Writer's Guide to Punchier, More Engaging Language & Style*, Arthur Plotnik illustrates the value of using phrases and expressions to mark particular styles of speech. He reminds us, "As distinctive ways of saying something, locutions tend to be judged on their aptness, inventiveness, color, sound, rhythm—the qualities that stimulate us, that make expression fetching or thrilling."

In writing fiction or writing in persona, we must assign different characters different ways of phrasing things so everybody doesn't sound the same (and just like the author). When we write about others in nonfiction, it is important to have them sound like they characteristically sound, not like we want them to sound (or like us). This kind of attention to the voices of others pays off, making our writing memorable and entertaining to readers, helping them think of specific people in their lives who sound like those in ours, and also allowing them to enjoy the idiosyncratic nature of those we put into our writing.

To write well, we must also notice our own characteristic phraseology, the sound of our thinking. If it isn't as vivid and interesting as possible, we must look for the reasons. Do we use the same words over and over when other words would make sharper distinctions (in other words, are we being lazy with our vocabulary—not that higher diction words are better than lower diction words, but "thing" is often better replaced with a specific)? Do we not pay attention to our use of "this," "that," "also," "in order to," and "so"? Do we use lots of words to describe something when a well-chosen metaphor would be more interesting?

Here's an example of poor locution from that first draft a student wrote about value in an educational setting:

> The people who live in this environment must take the role of an intellectual. They must first be intelligent. Without intelligence there will be no discussions, only foolery and actions. This is why honor codes only work in schools of the

highest academic level. The students who go to those schools are at a high mental level that lets them go beyond what is in front of them and understand the world in a greater way. While intelligence will give the people the ideas and allow them to think of ways to spread them effectively, it is nothing without friendliness.

If this were my freewrite, I'd look back into it and ask myself about repetition. Does going from intellectual to intelligent to intelligence to high mental level and back to intelligence help me share my thinking? Does it help me think about my subject? Is there music to this that helps? In all cases, my answer is no.

What should I do next? I should invoke phraseology that shows who I am and what I mean:

> What is the role of the intellectual and what furthers that person's ability to share his ideas, be heard, and consider the ideas of others? I believe that honor codes are of importance in fostering the comfort of an intellectual in pursuing his goals.

By taking out the constant repetition of words with the same root, I have reduced six sentences to two, but I have focused my work, and I see where I must go next. I must show what honor codes are and how they support intellectuals. I must show what intellectuals can do to foster their ideas. I have become a more interesting writer just by making my assertion succinct.

Arthur Plotnik would say I must use locution to make phrases that are "bell ringers." I might add to the two sentences this way:

> When you've got an idea you want someone to love hearing it and tell you if it is not yet fully formed by asking questions and playing the devil's advocate. What better place is there to do this than in classrooms where grades and competition for them is not the overriding feature of learning? When I can say something stupid on my way to being able to win the Nobel Peace Prize or a Pulitzer, I am in the best company I can find.

Your Turn

Look at a report you have written recently or a letter or e-mail you've sent off. Underline words you have repeated. Decide whether the repetition is musical and makes the emotions of the work more vivid or if there is that "I am not thinking very deeply about this" sound to the words. First, tighten up your words; then, come up with some "bell ringers" to show your point—phrases a reader might start to find characteristic of your tone.

Use the Epistolary Form

Letter writing is an art, and writers frequently use the form as a structure for poems, essays, novels, and nonfiction work as well. Richard Hugo's volume of poetry, *31 Letters and 13 Dreams*, surprised critics with its intensity and intimacy. Writers often publish "open letters" in magazines and newspapers as a way of reaching others. President Obama did this shortly after his inauguration. His "A Letter to My Daughters" (www.parade.com/news/2009/01/barack-obama-letter-to-my-daughters.html) explains why he ran for the presidency. His explanation reveals the reasons he respects and loves his country and its democracy as well as his hopes for the future his daughters will inhabit. A recent bestseller, *The Guernsey Literary and Potato Peel Pie Society* by Mary Ann Shaffer and Annie Barrows, tells the story of survival during WWII through the letters of a writer who goes to an isolated British town to do research. Kit Bakke's creative nonfiction work *Miss Alcott's E-mail: Yours for Reform of All Kinds* is the story of how the author imagines Louisa May Alcott e-mailing her wisdom and advice on how to live the second part of one's life.

In Bakke's book, after the speaker writes to Miss Alcott the first time and proposes a correspondence, she imagines Miss Alcott writing back:

> …I admit that the singularity of this potential interchange is most intriguing. You say we are communicating across "time zones" in a way much imagined, but never reliably accomplished. I will have to take you on faith for that, as the concept of time zones in not familiar to me, although the railways are rumored to be trying to do something about time. Perhaps your letter is related? You say we are inhabiting different centuries? If so, this could be the most amusing correspondence I have had in years.

Whether you write poetry or prose, writing letters is a valuable way to exercise your creative writing muscle.

Your Turn

Think of someone you wish could write you a letter, whether that person is alive, dead, real, or a character in someone else's book, play, or television show. Write a letter to that person. Have that person write back to you. Imagine that person talking from the conditions and places in his or her life. Use those details.

If you'd like to choose an inanimate correspondent, try writing from the point of view of an instrument you no longer play or from the point of view of an article of clothing in your closet. What you learn from the mouths of the inanimate can be very surprising.

A Note on Voice—It Will Come When You Employ the Elements of Good Creative Writing

Many people who write talk about looking for their voice or finding their voice. There are people who spend years and years looking. It can become something that preoccupies them to the extent that they don't develop their writing, so concerned are they about their voice. My own advice is write, practice the elements of good writing, experiment with the genres as we will in the next section of this book, and you will notice your voice in each piece.

When the elements of good writing are all in place and the do-nots are vanquished, "voice" emerges—the distinctive sound a particular writer makes on the page or has his or her characters make. Voice results from word choice, from the choice of details and situations presented, from the figures of speech employed to evoke a speaker's, narrator's, or character's age, background, location and place in time, and from the grammatical mix of sentence syntax a writer's feelings adopt. The use of personas; specifics, images, and metaphor; scenes, dialog, and lyric techniques contribute heavily to voice, producing vivid, engaging work. When you concentrate on developing a knack for using the elements of good writing, you are instinctively finding and expressing your voice.

If you are talking about what impassions you, your voice is usually compelling. When you trust what occurs to you, you do not try to control what you say; you are in flow with your idiosyncratic, association-making mind. You sound right, at least to the heart, if not to the socialized being that you have become. Think about phrases you have heard people blurt out in anger or in surprise. When the editing part of the brain is not involved, the true voice speaks. Although in writing you will edit eventually, it will not be to edit out the sound of the true voice but what interferes with it. If you go about editing too soon, before enough material is on the page, your editing self will usually chop away at the idiosyncratic, "unsocialized," unique sounds on the page. But if you wait until you have much that is original on the page, your editor self can go about making sure the words your passionate self wants to use are clear and without muddle.

In *Telling Writing*, Ken Macrorie writes, "If you can find the feeling that belongs to a piece of writing you want to create, then the composing may be accomplished almost without your help, and it will be true in tone, and compelling."

By using your developed writing muscle in conjunction with honoring and not discounting the images your unconscious mind throws onto the page, you will come closest to finding the true feeling in your writing and believing in it.

Sometimes that voice may seem sloppy at first or difficult to shape on the page. Feelings are like that. But sharing your work with trusted first listeners, those who will offer their feelings as they read what you've written, rather than ideas for "fixing" what you have written, can help you learn to trust your voice by allowing you to experience their interest and connection to what you have written. That's how you learn to hear where the feeling is.

Be Patient With Your Writing

It is important to think about writing in stages—inventing, shaping, and editing. I learned this from poet David Wagoner. He told his classes that at first when you come to the page, you must come as an inventor, open to any possibility, any starting point, image, or crazy idea that flows out. Then, you look at what you've invented with a shaper's (writer's) tools and find the spark that you can ignite into more writing. Finally, after you have that writing, you may come as the editor who is concerned about sentence structure, punctuation, and other rules. These are important to polish in your writing, but only after there is uniqueness. If the editor persona enters the process too soon, the voice will be wiped right out of the writing—because voice is shy and editors are not, because voice isn't rule bound and editors are, among other reasons.

This is how best-selling (over thirty published novels) author Holly Lisle writes about voice on her website www.hollylisle.com:

> Your voice does not exist in the thin and cheap places of your heart or the shallow end of your soul. Voice lives in the deep waters and the dark places of your soul, and it will only venture out when you make sure you've given it space to move and room to breathe.

That means taking risks, which Lisle thinks of this way:

> Choose to write about themes that your internal editor insists are too dangerous, too controversial, too embarrassing to be put on the paper. Imagine that your mom (or your other toughest critic) is looking over your shoulder with a raised eyebrow and a prudish expression on her face. Now shock her.

To write well, you must feel uncomfortable. Why else would you be setting words down when you could just go play tennis, talk on the phone or clean the house? Lisle is passionate when she tells us:

Voice is born from a lot of words and a lot of work—but not just any words or any work will do. You have to bleed a little. You have to shiver a little. You have to love a lot—love your writing, love your failures, love your courage in going on in spite of them, love every small triumph that points toward eventual success. You already have a voice. It's beautiful, it's unique...Your job is to lead it from the darkest of the dark places and the deepest of the deep waters into the light of day.

chapter 2

More Avenues to Keep Yourself Writing

One way to build up enthusiasm for developing drafts is to gather first-reader response. But there is a trick to gathering responses that help you as a writer. Author is the root of "authority." Never forget it. People's responses are helpful in empowering you, the author, to develop your work. If they rush in to fix your work, however, they encroach on your authority, and you will feel badly rather than eager to continue writing.

Therefore, I have developed a method that provides a structure to help readers offer responses that don't trample your writing. The structure directs readers in telling you what they feel and think as they read, so you get a sense of where you have short-shrifted your writing—where you have withheld information or summarized where readers really want the details. You will learn where you seem to have veered away into new subjects without taking the reader along. You'll learn, too, where readers are delighted and where they feel the writing no longer keeps their interest.

This structure helps writers hear what their readers have to say without feeling defensive. Teach this process, which I've dubbed the Three-step Response Method, to those you want to offer you response to your work-in-progress.

Here's how it works:

1. **Velcro Words:** Readers report the images and phrases that stick with them.
2. **Feelings:** Readers monitor and report the feelings that occur as they read.
3. **Curiosity:** Readers tell the writer where they want to know more.

If you are going to be your own reader, make sure you have managed to take time away from your draft so it will seem like a fresh piece of writing to you and you can be more impartial as you look at it using this response system. If you are going to ask others to respond to your draft, make sure they understand that you want them to give you feedback in these three separate ways.

I'll demonstrate the process with a document sent to me by writers' workshop participant, Kellie Van Atta:

I'm writing on this white board with an old, orange marker that has been in my purse for three weeks. Finally putting the tip to the board, I realize that after all this time, it is just as dull as the rest of them.

Sighing silently, I resign myself to pushing forcefully in order to write, "use commas between coordinate adjectives." They strain to see the obscure markings, but it's better than nothing.

This isn't exactly the type of teacher I dreamed of being while instructing my care bears at the age of eight. That teacher has it all. Her perfect handwriting is never wasted on a dull marker. That teacher has total control of students. They certainly never play the game going on in section 3. She couldn't even fathom students trying to insert inappropriate words into their sentences; she doesn't have to stifle giggles after a student mentions that "a new middle school has recently been erected."

It isn't that the teacher I dreamed of being is stiff or austere; on the contrary, she is witty and charismatic. After her students leave smiling, she organizes her room into stacks of graded papers and rows of tidy chairs. Writing her agenda in a fresh pen with a diagonal tip, she is over-prepared for the next day. Off to the gym, she says, delighted after a peaceful day. She loves the gym, her toned arms pumping the handles of the elliptical machine. Her meticulous make-up partially smeared from sweat. That teacher would bound home to create a culinary concoction worthy of Dionysus. She is an exceptional cook by the way.

Jarred by a beeping timer, I look back at my students as they finish their vocabulary quiz. "That was SOOO hard" Jessica moans. "What does it say on the board?" Marco asks. After another 47 minutes, the students leave chatting. I take a deep breath and close my eyes, exhausted. What was the word in section 3? Sack? Urggg. I can't even consider going to the gym. Eight hours on heels—can you blame me? I hope Scott will cook something.

"Commas between coordinate adjectives." The orange marker squeaks. I guess I'm not quite the person I hoped I would be, but maybe tonight I will buy a new marker.

Here is how I responded:

Velcro Words—Writing on this white board with an old, orange marker, in my purse for three weeks, just as dull as the rest of them, pushing forcefully in order to write, commas between coordinate adjectives, instructing my care bears at the age of eight, perfect handwriting, never play the game going on in section 3, insert inappropriate words into their sentences, stifle giggles, "a new middle school has recently been erected." witty and charismatic, stacks of graded papers and rows of tidy chairs, fresh pen with a diagonal tip, over-prepared for the next day, loves the gym, her toned arms pumping the handles of the elliptical machine, makeup partially smeared from sweat, create a culinary concoction worthy of Dionysus, beeping timer, finish their vocabulary quiz, "That was SOOO hard" Jessica moans, "What does it say on the board?" 47 minutes, students leave chatting, word in section 3? Sack? can't even consider going to the gym. Eight hours on heels, hope Scott will cook something

Feelings

A: I enjoy being in the classrooms and in the life the writer is in and the one she imagines. I feel organized in terms of time and place: I know where the speaker is in her thoughts before returning to the scene in front of her. I feel her longing to be a certain kind of teacher and her weariness with the way it is. The details of the marker, pen, board, and dialog of the students help me be right there.

B: I feel jarred having the label "old" for the orange marker that has been in the speaker's purse for three weeks. I think what the speaker means is that the marker, perhaps new when she began carrying it around, is no longer moist. If it is just as old as the others, I am not sure of the significance of it being in her purse for three weeks. Actually, I do feel left out of knowing why it is there—I would like to know if it was because she was preparing early for school or she forgot it being so busy.

"I take a deep breath and close my eyes, exhausted,"—I am not sure what has exhausted the teacher. I feel left out of knowing if it is classroom management, materials management day after day, or more. I'd like to see more of what the speaker's life entails in contrast to the dream of who she'd thought she'd be, as that side of things is well drawn. I am not sure how the reference to the word "sack" in section 3 (the game players in the classroom?) works here to let us know what the speaker is thinking about herself. Or perhaps Section 3 is on the test; I am confused here.

Curiosity—Why has the speaker been carrying the marker around? Does she have only one at a time to use? By the essay's end when she says she hopes that Scott will cook, I wonder if she is imagining having or not having the energy to drop into a store, rather than the gym, to buy a new marker—that would loop nicely back to the opening. And why must the teacher buy her own marker? It seems the school would supply those! So there must be something else interesting here.

Should "care bears" be capitalized? What is the game going on in section 3? Is it among the students or is this a reference to the test? What does the speaker observe about it? What does the teacher's room look like after her students leave if there are not tidy stacks of papers and rows of chairs? Does this teacher think of what she feels like not being able to go to the gym? What does her make up look like if not smeared from sweat at the gym? What might be some of the dishes in a culinary concoction worthy of Dionysus?

As a writer, it feels good to know your readers' delights, disappointments and expectations. It is important that both the feelings that feel good to the reader and the feelings that don't feel good to the reader get reported. Hearing both categories allows you to understand that your readers are interested in your material. With all of this in mind, you have much to go on in reworking your writing, and, most importantly, you will remain enthusiastic about continuing.

The Key Again: Writers Write

That's the basic definition of a writer; when we don't know what to write, we still write, calling what we are doing "free writing." The simplest freewrites start with a keyboard and screen or pen and paper. The writer sets a timer and writes, about anything, for 10 to 20 minutes. Sometimes writers like to have a bit more direction for freewrites, and they use prompts. There are many online sites and books that share writing prompts, and I have included many of them throughout this book and in the Q & A section at book's end). Groups of writers sometimes meet regularly to do free writing together and members take turns providing prompts for the group to use. Although freewrites are raw, many groups provide the opportunity for members to share what they've written in the timed writings. This builds confidence in the idea that our writing starts are valuable for future writing, as well as allowing us to make contact with listeners.

Here are some examples of how several authors have cultivated the use of free writing to help students:

Use Events as Prompts

Nahid Rachlin, author of the memoir *Persian Girls* as well as novels and short stories, suggests these prompts to her students:

Write about finding out a shocking truth about a loved one and how you coped with it.

Fictionalize a news item.

Write about an incident that happened while traveling that awakened you to a new reality.

Use the First Lines of Stories as Prompts

Bharti Kirchner, whose most recent book is *Darjeeling and Pastries: A Novel of Desserts and Discovery*, believes in using the lead sentence of a published short story as a prompt. You could, for example, she says, use the following first sentence from her short story, "Promised Tulips," which appeared in *Seattle Noir*, Akashic Books, 2009: "I am floating between dream and wakefulness in my cozy tree-house nestled high in the canopy of a misty rainforest when he murmurs, 'You're so beautiful with your hair over your face.'"

Set that timer and write; try not to lift your fingers from the keyboard or pen from the paper. If you aren't sure where you are going or what to write, write, "I'm not sure what to say or where I am going with this" as many times as you need to. Your mind will start supplying more to write about, as it doesn't like to be bored!

Make Use of Disruptions to Keep Writing

Lori Brack, whose chapbook manuscript, *Another Case for the Dead Letter Detective*, was a finalist in the 2009 Pilot Books call for manuscripts, encourages you to "crack open what you write about and how you write it by disrupting the shape, size, and rhythms of your writing practice. Add a fresh roll of adding machine tape, available in office supply stores, to your usual writing materials." Brack says:

First, respond for three to five minutes to each of the following prompts designed to evoke memory or sensory responses:

a lost love

something that happened late at night

a thing found out of place

the way a familiar animal moves

names of streets where something important happened to you

a recurring dream or dream image

the kinds of plants you have tended

Jump from your notebook or computer to the adding machine tape. Take out a pen, pencil or marker and begin with something your warm-up writing just generated that interests you or that deserves more time and exploration. You can write the long way, so that your words flow down the long, unrolling paper, or you can write across the narrow width, following the long snake of the never-ending "page."

Write for at least 30 minutes, allowing the written coil of paper to slip through your hands and to gather and puddle onto the floor at your feet. At the end of your writing period, tear off your writing and roll it up. Go back to it on another day and cut it into shorter sentences, phrases, paragraphs, stanzas, lines, or lengths. Transcribe parts of it in your notebook or into your computer. Hang evocative sections on the wall and live with them as part of your visual environment, or hang several and rearrange them now and then. Repeat the exercise when you feel stuck in recurring forms, when the material you produce is repetitive in other ways, or when you need the physical sensuousness of the whispering paper unspooling as you write.

Make Heart Journeys

Dorothy Randall Gray, author of *Soul Between the Lines: Freeing Your Creative Spirit Through Writing*, provides her students with what she calls "heart items."

It would do my heart good to…	With all my heart
I had a change of heart	A woman/man after my own heart
I was heartbroken	I wore my heart on my sleeve
I lost my heart to…	In my heart of hearts
I didn't have the heart to…	A subject close to my heart
I knew it by heart	Have a heart
I had my heart set on it	Heartache
I had my heart set against it	Heartless
Cross my heart and hope to die	Heartfelt
From the bottom of my heart	Heart and soul
Do it to my heart's content	Hearts and flowers
Eat your heart out	Get to the heart of the matter
Heart to heart talk	Heartsick
Heart attack	Heartwarming

Gray asks students to ask themselves, "Which one of the heart items calls me, evokes emotions, or makes me remember experiences I've had, or people I've known?"

"Place that heart journey item at the top of your paper," Gray says:

> …and then write about it as fast as you can without stopping to correct, punctuate, change, think about or judge anything that appears on your page. Let the journey take you where it wants to go. Do this for at least five minutes, and continue as long as you can.
>
> Now stop and catch your breath. Take a look at what you've allowed to come through you. Look for lines, words and phrases you might like to expand on, rewrite or continue. Copy them on a new sheet of paper, but always keep this original writing exercise intact. You never know what you'll find in it next time you read what you wrote.

Flashcard Magic

Cheryl Merrill, whose creative nonfiction won special mention in the 2008 *Pushcart Prize* anthology and has appeared in the college text *Short Takes: Model Essays for Composition*, studied with Terry Tempest Williams when she knew she wanted to write a book about her visits with elephants. In Williams' class, she learned about using flashcards as "strike moments" to bring new energy into her writing. As she "fumbled" her way into draft chapters, Cheryl realized the flashcards she had selected were actually signposts: "Whenever I came to a fork in the path," she says, "I consulted the next flashcard message in the order I'd selected them in class":

Ask a Question

Become the Other

Learn from the Masters

Ask a Question

Rhyme

Dedicate

Learn from the Masters

Think Architecturally

Rearrange

Follow the Scent

After I began my second draft of *Larger than Life: Living in the Shadows of Elephants*, flashcard-style messages popped into my mind unannounced as I worked:

No Extra Words

Project the Familiar onto the Strange

Reclaim an Extinct Way of Being

Interesting Questions Find Interesting Answers

Read it Backwards

I regard the commands seriously, though with a mixture of dread —they make my job harder—and joy, since they are guides to follow, no matter their woo-woo origin. I now have 106 flashcards.

Your Turn

Make yourself a set of writing flashcards—start with five to 10. Use messages from the ones Merrill lists or take some from the exercises in Chapter 1: "Show, Show, Show," "Build Scenes," "Employ Locution," "Find a Metaphor," "Use Alliteration."

* * * * *

You've now filled computer files and/or notebooks with the results of exercises aimed at helping you get in the groove of writing well by paying attention to the use of specifics and the use of the senses. You've gotten the sound of your thinking on the page. You've begun to form writing habits (writers write!) that will serve you well you in whatever genre you write.

In the next sections of this book, I present genre-specific exercises I've developed, as well as many from other writers. After you do the exercises in this chapter and in the following chapters, look up the authors' books. When you read them, notice their advice and experience at work in the writing they publish. As writers, we need many, many mentors—some we meet in person and many we meet only in their books. I am pleased to be able to introduce you to many whose work will inspire and help you.

Part 2

Poetry

chapter 3

What Is Poetry?

William Wordsworth famously defined poetry as "the spontaneous overflow of powerful feelings," and Emily Dickinson explained the sensation of poetry this way, "If I read a book and it makes my body so cold no fire ever can warm me, I know that is poetry." Today, Mark Flanagan writes for About.com (http://contemporarylit.about.com/od/poetry/a/poetry.htm) that poetry is "the chiseled marble of language," because poets use an economy of words and consider emotive qualities, musical value, spacing, and even words' spatial relationship to the page to evoke intense emotion. "Defining poetry," he writes, "is like grasping at the wind—once you catch it, it's no longer wind."

These days, this grasping at the wind is usually done in a form named free, open, or blank verse. These forms do not require set rhyme patterns or particular line lengths or numbers of lines. The ends of the lines, though, are significant for the sound and to the meaning as are the stanza breaks (the way the lines are grouped in the poetic equivalent of paragraphs). Poets also continue to use prescriptive forms as practiced over the centuries by poets around the world: sonnet, ballad, sestina, ghazal, couplets, villanelle, acrostic, chant, cinquain, ode, pantoum, haiku, and tanka, among others. Many poets report that working in these forms provides the resistance they need (meter, rhyme, patterns of repeated lines, and numbers of total stanzas and lines) to struggle against and find new ways of mining their interior selves for wisdom and beauty. Although there is no way to grasp the wind, there are many shapes to the structures through which it blows.

Why Do People Write Poetry?

The German poet Rainer Maria Rilke writes in *Letters to a Young Poet*:

> As the bees bring in the honey, so do we fetch the sweetest out of everything and build Him. With the trivial even, with the insignificant (if it but happens out of love) we make a start, with work and with rest after it, with a silence or with a small solitary joy, with everything that we do alone, without supporters and participants…

Poets believe, as Louise Glück phrases it in *Proofs & Theories: Essays on Poetry*, that "speech and fluency seem less an act of courage than a state of grace." Poets feel that in experiencing this act of grace, they are in a "continuing conversation" with their culture—"querying it, amplifying it, rebelling against it, subverting it, anesthetizing it, enhancing it," as Harvard poetry scholar Helen Vendler explains in the second edition of her book, *Poems, Poets, Poetry: An Introduction and Anthology*.

Individual poets have idiosyncratic ways of explaining what it feels like to blend imagination with a sense of language. In *On Being a Writer*, Bill Strickland records famous poets' words on what they do. Allen Ginsberg: "You say what you want to say when you don't care who's listening….so it's a matter of just listening to yourself as you sound when you're talking about something that's intensely important to you." Nikki Giovanni: "I shoot the moment, capture feelings with my poems." May Sarton: Writing poems means "not being knotted up to a purpose, but open to any accidental and fortuitous event." Poet Susan Rich told me writing poems is a love affair that "doesn't need to be perfect, but life-sustaining." And Diane Lockward explains that writing poetry feels like "finding my way home when I hadn't even known I was lost."

On Poems Outloud.net (http://poemsoutloud.net/poets/poet/bh_fairchild/), B. H. Fairchild says, "There is also the endless work/eat/sleep routine…, which can make one search for some point to it all and then eventually to locate it in literature, where life always comes to a point." Philip Levine told an audience during a Seattle Bumbershoot arts festival that if he doesn't write, he feels ill.

Whether we write from joy, sorrow, or wonder, our poems record our responses to being intensely alive. Today, many authors are writing about the way only poetry, both reading and writing it, has helped them cope with sorrows: I do in my memoir, *A New Theology: Turning to Poetry in a Time of Grief*, as has Madge McKeithen in *Blue Peninsula*. Writers have also turned their attention to the way poetry helps when most other therapies and conversations don't: David Rico in *Being True to Life: Poetic Paths to Personal Growth* and John Fox in *Poetic Medicine: The Healing Art of Poem Making.*

Writing poetry, we mourn the passage of time, celebrate connections, yell out at injustice, cry from the pain of unrequited love, and exclaim our joy and gratitude. Over the years, I have known I would start poems because of attending a traditional tea ceremony with my daughter as she was coming of age and the tea ceremony hostess's mother was dying, and because of awe I felt at the fragility of human life after looking down the Columbia River Gorge with my young son. I've written a poem because a blue moon in August made me sit down and consider the feelings I had when my daughter left for studies in Japan. Usually, I have the feeling of needing to write and no knowledge of what I will write. But as I write poems, I begin to understand poem-making as a way of finding out what I might not otherwise have known I had to say. And the more I write poetry, the more I read poetry, as absorbing other poets' strategies for delivering perception always helps.

Poet William Mawhinney, author of *Cairns Along the Road*, reflects on reading others' poems and concentrating on their sound:

Let me dip into my commonplace notebook and share some resonant snippets and lines that've rung my bell over the years. I'm a sucker for such paths of shimmering music as these:

"The day waves yellow with all its crops."

—Virginia Woolf

"We sit together, the mountain and me/Until only the mountain remains."

—Sam Hamill

"To follow the sea-bright salmon home."

—inscription on a bell cast by Tom Jay

"Clouds dance/under the wind's wing, and leaves/delight in transience."

—Basil Bunting

"Time stops when the heart stops/as they walk off the earth into the night air."

—Jim Harrison

"Down the rivers of the windfall light"

—Dylan Thomas

"After many a summer dies the swan"

—Alfred, Lord Tennyson

"Man is not a town/Where things live,/But a worry and a weeping/of unused wings."

—Kenneth Patchen

"Down their carved names the rain-drop ploughs"

—Thomas Hardy

"I had the swirl and ache/From sprays of honeysuckle/That when they're gathered shake/Dew on the knuckle."

—Robert Frost

"Bare ruined choirs, where late the sweet birds sang."

—William Shakespeare

"But something in the sad/End-of-season light remains unsaid."

—James Merrill

"…in the silent, startled, icy, black language/of blackberry eating in late September"

—Galway Kinnell

I don't invite my left brain to take charge when I engage a poem. I cringe when I recall the poetry courses at Pitt in the 1960s that encouraged me to tear wings from these butterflies. When I flunked my master's oral exam, I was told to "hold my nose and read more of the source material." I fled graduate school after that. For me, poetry is a physical experience, not an object for arms-length analysis. Today, as I read poetry, my right brain relishes the sounds of words, their physical and sensual presence—the original "mouth-fun" in baby talk, bedtime tales, and nursery rhymes.

If a poem gets up and starts to dance, I'll speak it to myself; I'll give it voice—a poet's medium is breath, not black marks on the page. And, when it's a real winner, I'll offer it my entire body by walking along the nearby roads and reciting it out loud. My neighbors already know I'm strange!

Phrases like these from my notebook are a species of remembering. They stick like Velcro to tender places; they light up dark spots inside, helping me to confront what Mark Doty calls "the unsayability of experience."

I jot them down in my commonplace book; otherwise they'll evaporate. That's the only "writing exercise" I use: I scribble down bits and shards of language that come my way, never knowing how I'll use them, if at all. One may become the seed of a poem, but because they all plunk my magic twanger, they become my word hoard. I'm a scavenging magpie tucking shiny objects into my nest.

I never know where this scribbling will take me. Writing poetry, for me, is a guideless journey. To the best of my ability, I ignore a voice that whispers from the shadows of my brain, "What a raging piece of crap!" and just get to work. Resonances from a few shimmering words will start percolating. Then something will occur to me and something else will occur to me, then something else that I reject may push me in another direction. Slowly, accretions of images begin to form around the seed words, lustrous deposits around an irritating grain of sand that perhaps end up as a pearl. I follow the poem as it emerges, remembering the words of an old Zen cowboy: "Always ride the horse in the direction it's going."

The Three Main Subgenres of Poetry: Lyric, Narrative, and Prose

Basically, although all poems operate by heightened language, there are three categories into which most poems fit.

Lyric

The term *lyric poetry* comes from the Greek, "sung to the lyre," and preserves the idea that sound is of utmost importance in the lyric poem. In today's lyric poetry, the speaker is speaking from here and now even when thinking about a there and then; the poet is addressing an absent listener upon a specific emotional occasion. When a reader reads the poem, he or she feels at one with the speaker and understands the poet's urge to speech.

Here's an excerpt from Stanley Plumly's lyric poem "Wildflower" (www.poets.org/viewmedia.php/prmMID/15494):

It is June, wildflowers on the table.
They are fresh an hour ago, like sliced lemons,
with the whole day ahead of them.
They could be common mayflower lilies of the valley...

Struck by the flowers, the poet goes on to reflect on all the flowers he has had in jars, named and pressed.

Although most lyric poems today are written in blank or free verse, poets often return to the lyric forms I've mentioned—the sonnet, villanelle, pantoum, ghazal, and sestina among them. You can read examples of contemporary lyric poems in traditional forms at sites like Poets.org and Poemhunter.com by typing the name of the form you are interested in into the search box. Two print anthologies are particularly good sources, as well: *An Exultation of Forms: Contemporary Poets Celebrate the Diversity of Their Art*, edited by Annie Finch and Kathrine Varnes, and *The Making of a Poem: A Norton Anthology of Poetic Forms*, edited by Mark Strand and Eavan Bolan. In addition, *The Teacher's & Writer's Handbook of Poetic Forms*, edited by Ron Padgett, offers a good introduction to forms.

Narrative

The word "narrative" comes from the Greek word for story. Older narrative poems were usually lengthy and concerned a serious subject and heroic deeds performed during culturally significant events. Homer's *The Odyssey*, Virgil's *Aeneid*, and Milton's *Paradise Lost* are examples of long narrative poems. Ballads are less formal narrative poems; they tell a story, often elevating a local figure to hero status in common language: "God's Judgment on a Wicked Bishop" (www.poemhunter.com/poem/god-s-judgment-on-a-wicked-bishop/) by Robert Southey and "Casey at the Bat" (www.poemhunter.com/poem/casey-at-the-bat/) by Ernest Lawrence Thayer are two examples.

Here are two stanzas from Southey's poem:

> Rejoiced such tidings good to hear,
> The poor folk flock'd from far and near;
> The great barn was full as it could hold
> Of women and children, and young and old.
>
> Then when he saw it could hold no more,
> Bishop Hatto he made fast the door;
> And while for mercy on Christ they call,
> He set fire to the Barn and burnt them all.

What is the difference between lyric and narrative poems? Lyric poems often tell stories as part of what they do (since we are temporal beings and to us everything moves through time, everything we compose has plot or story), and narrative poems obviously must use sound and rhythm to tell their stories with force. So what is the difference between the two subgenres? I think it is the difference between intending to write a poem to tell a story and having a story creep into a poem as one searches to evoke a feeling and perception. In narrative poems, the form is used foremost to tell the story. The focus is not on the poet observing the story, but on the story itself. In a lyric poem, the focus is on the poet's observations, feelings, and thinking. Search poemhunter.com for "narrative" and then for "lyric" poems to experience the difference.

Prose

Peggy Shumaker, author of *Gnawed Bones* and *Just Breathe Normally*, writes on Brevity.com (www.creativenonfiction.org/brevity/craft/craft_prosepoems.htm) that prose poems are brief pieces of prose, meant to stand on their own and capture our attention "via compression." She admires Naomi Shihab Nye for taking "on big questions" in her book of paragraphs entitled *Mint Snowball*. Shumaker quotes Nye as saying, "I've never heard anyone say they don't like paragraphs. It would be like disliking five minute increments on the clock." Shumaker says to write the prose poem, poets give up line breaks, but to be as cutting as a stiff wind, they rely on "bits of dialogue, quick exposition, complex rhythms" and sentence variety in the highly compressed prose they use.

Ideas about prose poems seem to date back to 1842, when Aloysius Bertrand wrote *Gespard de la nuit*, a collection of fantasies written in rhythmical language. In 1869, Charles Baudelaire introduced what we call prose poetry to a larger audience with his volume *Little Poems in Prose*, in which short prose pieces employed regular rhythm; a definitely patterned structure; vivid, sometimes surreal, images; and emotional heightening. He explained the form this way:

> Which one of us, in his moments of ambition, has not dreamed of a miracle of poetic prose, musical without rhythm and without rhyme, supple enough and rugged enough to adapt itself to the lyrical impulses of the soul, the undulations of reverie, the jibes of conscience?

Today, Michael Benedict writes in his introduction to *The Prose Poem: An International Anthology* that there are "special properties" of the prose poem: "attention to the unconscious, and to its particular logic"; "an accelerated use of colloquial and everyday speech patterns"; "a visionary thrust"; a reliance on humor and wit; and an "enlightened doubtfulness, or hopeful skepticism."

This is an excerpt from a prose poem by James Tate entitled "The List of Famous Hats," which displays these traits:

> Napoleon's hat is an obvious choice I guess to list as a famous hat, but that's not the hat I have in mind. That was his hat for show. I am thinking of his private bathing cap, which in all honesty wasn't much different than the one any jerk might buy at a corner drugstore now, except for two minor eccentricities . . .

A Few More Contemporary Poetry Subgenres: Language, Performance, and Cowboy Poetry

Language Poetry

For language poets, the structure of language dictates meaning rather than the other way around. By breaking up poetic language, the poets require readers to find a new way to approach the text. In her book of essays, *The Language of Inquiry*, language poet Lyn Hejinian writes:

> Language is nothing but meanings, and meanings are nothing but a flow of contexts. Such contexts rarely coalesce into images, rarely come to terms. They are transitions, transmutations, the endless radiating of denotation into relation.

Writing about language poetry, or as the language poets write the term, *l=a=n=g=u=a=g=e p=o=e=t=r=y*, on www.worldlitonline.net/art3.pdf Suman Chakroborty quotes David Melnick's 1978 contribution "A Short Word on My Work," published in L=A=N=G=U=A=G=E: "The poems are made of what look like words and phrases but are not … What can such poems do for you? You are a spider struggling in your own web, suffocated by meaning."

Charles Bernstein maintains in an interview at http://home.jps.net/~nada/bernstein.htm that this kind of poetry contains "features of language" that can "roam in different territory than possible with tamer verse forms" so "the poems do not necessarily mean one fixed, definable, paraphrasable thing."

Here are some lines from Charles Bernstein's "These Horses Do Not Move Up and Down" that illustrate the features he identifies in language poetry:

> Teapots explode, asterisks expound.
> The silly sailor says to us the ship
> He built is broke. Heaven help the
> Nincompoop who shakes instead of bloats.
> Take two steps forward, you are half-way there . . .

Performance and Slam Poetry

During the 1980s, performance poetry became the term for describing poetry written or composed for performance rather than print distribution. According to Wikipedia (http://en.wikipedia.org/wiki/Performance_poetry) a 1980s press release used the term to describe Hedwig Gorski's audio recordings of her poetry in collaboration with the music of her band, East of Eden. Gorski, who relied on the rhetorical and philosophical expression of her poems, wanted to distinguish her text-based vocal performances from other performance art, whose work was based in music.

Performance poetry practitioners believe in person-to-person transmission through in-person and broadcast performances. They see themselves as keeping the oral tradition alive in an age where broadcast technology surpasses books in reaching mass audiences. They believe that poetry created for performance has the most in common with the original art than written poetry, because written verse evolved to make use of books, journals, and newspapers as printing and mass distribution evolved.

Chicago poet and construction worker Marc Kelley Smith started the slam poetry subgenre of the performance movement at a reading series in a Chicago jazz club. In the 1990s, San Francisco, New York, and Austin became centers for the small clubs in which slam poetry artists fostered competitions by performing poems on the spot. Their work was performed alone or in teams before small audiences who judged the performances. The Nuyorican Poets Cafe and Def Poets flourished using the performance and slam forms.

Performance poets see the form as a democratic voice for those outside of academia and the unheard, starting with Beat poetry readings of the 1940s and 1950s. Hip-hop and rap poetry are two contemporary extensions of the performance poetry movement. In these forms, too, words and the sounds of the words convey feeling and intensity not possible if not performed. To get a sense of the energy in performance poetry and audience reaction, view poet Taylor Mali at www.youtube.com/watch%3Fv=SCNIBV87wV4.

Cowboy Poetry

Cowboy poetry grew out of a tradition of composing on the spot in the evenings after cattle drives and work on ranches. Around a campfire, cowboys entertained one another with tall tales and folk songs using poetic forms to help them memorize their work. The genre's audience today is composed of performance lovers and those with an interest in preserving the themes and lifestyles of the American West, as well as creating and reciting new cowboy poetry. The frequent rhyming couplet style in cowboy poetry is like country music; most cowboy poets use rhyming verse rather than free verse, just as earlier practitioners of this form did. "The Walking Man" by Waddie Mitchell is a famous cowboy poem. Here's an excerpt:

> Sunny summer day it was when loping in to Laramie,
> I overtook the Walking Man, reined up and nodded "How!!"
> He'd been a rider once, I knew. He smiled, but scarce aware of me
> He said, "If you would like me to, I'll tell my story, now.
> They'll tell you that I'm crazy—that my wits have gone to glory,
> But you mustn't be believing every Western Yarn you hear."

* * * * *

Poets invent, copy, and alter ways to use language for getting to the heart of our minds and hearts, whether they come from the court, the peasantry, work on the ranch or are among the intelligentsia who want to rebel against academia. When I read poetry, I like to remember Edward Hirsh's words from *How to Read a Poem and Fall in Love with Poetry*: "I encounter—I am encountered by—a work of art. For me, that encounter is active, inquisitive, relentless, disturbing, exuberant, daring, beholden. Poets speak of the shock, the swoon, and the bliss of writing, but why not also speak of the shock, the swoon, and the bliss or reading?"

As you use the exercises in Chapter 4, be sure to visit online poetry sites such as poets.org, poemhunter.com, and poetry180.org to keep the sound of poetry in your ears.

I write to find out... what I didn't know I knew... until I wrote about it.

chapter 4

Practice for Writing Poetry

Writing poetry does take a certain frame of mind—one in which we realize that small things hold great emotional meaning. To write poems, we have to trust that the everyday objects we notice and remember will help us identify, examine and release our feelings.

The following exercises are meant to help you find topics for poems and see how well you can do when you write without worrying about how what you are writing will work out. Many poets exclaim that their poems are smarter than they are. The words will show you the way, and using the craft of poetry, you will discover and release meaningful observations and responses to being alive.

List Ordinary Objects to Find Poems

In a well-known poem, "Things to Do Around a Lookout," poet and naturalist Gary Snyder lists things he could do while working for the forest service as a lookout for forest fires. He spent a lot of time alone in small, isolated quarters, and his poem details life there by way of listing actions he could take and objects he could use: airing out musty forest service sleeping bags, bathing in snow melt, reading the star book and the rock book, brewing Lapsang Souchong tea, and putting salt out for the ptarmigan are among my favorites from the list.

Many poems are lists. Allen Ginsberg's literature-changing poem "Howl" (www.poetryfoundation.org/archive/poem.html?id=179381) is a list of the sad and terrifying things he had seen in the people around him. English poet Christopher Smart wrote list poems in the seventeenth century. Here is an excerpt about the poet's cat from is work "Jubilate Agno":

For first he looks upon his forepaws to see if they are clean.
For secondly he kicks up behind to clear away there.
For thirdly he works it upon stretch with the forepaws extended.
For fourthly he sharpens his paws by wood.
For fifthly he washes himself.
For sixthly he rolls upon wash.
For seventhly he fleas himself, that he may not be interrupted upon the beat.
For eighthly he rubs himself against a post.
For ninthly he looks up for his instructions.
For tenthly he goes in quest of food..

Your Turn

As an exercise, listing gives the poet practice using exact names and characteristics. The only trick is figuring out a list that interests you. Here are some lighthearted list ideas to get you started without worrying what you will write about:

7 or more things you see outside a window right now that someone else looking might not notice

7 or more jobs you think you'd like, and in detail what you would wear to each of them

7 or more things that are in your refrigerator and why they are there

7 or more gifts you have been given, when, and by whom

7 or more occasions upon which you wished you could disappear—name names, places, and actions by you or others

7 or more lies you have told, to whom, and when

7 or more compliments you have given, to whom, and when

7 or more ways you would curse someone who has angered you

7 or more ways you have been complimented and by whom

7 people you think of right now and why you are thinking of them

7 or more songs you know and what they make you think of in your life—people places, events

7 titles of more lists you could make

Here is an example from Raul Gallardo, who used this exercise to generate poems. He sent his list of songs and what he thinks of when he listens to them, and I made comments. Reading through the list and my responses will help you see where you can find poems in what you have listed:

7 or More Songs You Know and What They Make You Think of in Your Life: People, Places, and Events

"Don't Panic," Cold Play—Via Andrea in Milan is not exactly the place you want to start screaming at everybody but that is what I wanted to do when I felt I needed fresh air and I became mute. I put my headphones on hoping to disappear from the world and that is exactly what this song helped me achieve.

"Sing," Travis—Friday afternoon, it's dusk and I'm on the highway going back from work. I miss my exit and I don't care. I keep on going. I could only stop the car when the disc finished.

> Re-arrange here, create a title, perhaps "September," and you are on your way to a poem:
>
> **September**
>
> "Sing." Travis. Friday afternoon, it's dusk
> and I'm on the highway going
> back from work. I miss my exit and I
> don't care so I keep on going.
>
> Now you keep writing, letting the reader know where the song has transported you.

"Colorblind," Counting Crows—It is a classic; every time I listen, it acquires new meaning. First it was the song from the movie everybody talked about and I wasn't able to watch: *Cruel Intentions*. The only song from hearing over and over that I went to the piano and got it right the first time. A couple of years ago I ended up feeling like Sebastian.

> You have written your way to a poem—the story of what happened to make you feel like Sebastian.

"Wonderwall," Oasis—We are on a school bus of my only dance in the seventh grade[*sic*]; all night I looked for her. I barely spoke English and I will never know if her name was Fey or Fade or something similar. We only danced for one song. Somebody turned on the radio and that song appeared, nobody knew who this new guy was. The first time I ever danced so close to a girl.

I believe it's a poem!

Wonderwall Oasis

We are on a school bus to my only
dance in the seventh grade. All night
I looked for her. I barely spoke English
and I will never know if her name
was Fey or Fade or something similar.

We only danced for one song. Somebody
turned on the radio and that song appeared,
nobody knew who this new guy was.
The first time I ever danced so close to a girl.

"Dime que no," Ricardo Arjona—The proper translation could be reject my date or say no to me. It's another classic that used to be a great song and then became a true story and she did end up going out with me. When I told her what that song had meant for me, she almost cried and now it's also one of her favorites

---

I think "Don't Say No to Me" could be a good title for a poem. I think the occasion of the "she" deciding to go out with the poet is a strong one to write from—the poem could include what the "she" says when she says yes and what the poet says or thinks about the song and its meaning to him.

Challenge yourself to write a list a day. Keep your lists in a journal, a box, or on your computer. Read your lists from time to time to remind yourself that you have a unique way of experiencing the world.

When you go back and read what you listed and explained, I believe you'll see poems in there and be able to identify the emotion of several of them. Then you can select just the right images and compress the language.

Another Listing Exercise

Here is another listing idea that frees you to acknowledge your unique way of seeing things. Make a list of "sometimes" thoughts. Try to fill a page:

> Sometimes when the phone rings I think it is
> the president inviting me out to dinner.
> Sometimes when I want to eat cookies
> I try to stop myself
> Sometimes when I want to eat cookies
> I just go ahead and do it
> Sometimes when I want to eat cookies
> I offer them to someone else
> Sometimes at dusk I think of when my children
> were in grade school and this was the busy time
> of day with dinner, homework, gymnastics,
> friends staying over, trumpets and piano practicing.
> Sometimes when I kiss you I imagine a girl with blue flowers.

Choose one of the sometimes lines you have written and write a longer poem. From this item on the list, I realized that I had started a poem:

Sometimes When I Kiss You

I see blue flowers,
and sometimes a young girl
in party dress, hair
fastened with roses.

You ask if she is picking
the flowers. The flowers
are wild and I never see
what she does with her hands.

Alternatively, you could choose a topic and write a list of "Sometimes when I" lines on that topic. If you include specifics more than generalities, you will most likely write a poem that evokes the effect of that topic on you. Even if your lines change topic, as mine do in the list above, with stanza formation, you might have a whimsical look at yourself that makes the list feel complete like a poem.

Extending Metaphor: After Pablo Neruda

In "The Queen," (http://oldpoetry.com/opoem/39370-Pablo-Neruda-The-Queen), the renowned Chilean poet Pablo Neruda addresses his beloved saying "there are lovelier," "there are taller," and "there are purer" than she, but he says, no one else sees her crown and the carpet of gold at her feet when she walks by. When he sees her, the world is filled with hymns and bells. He ends his poem with three short lines: "Only you and I,/only you and I, my love,/ Listen to me."

Your Turn

Print a copy of Neruda's "The Queen" and think about the way the poet uses and extends his queen metaphor to describe his beloved and his love for her. Try this: Put the real name of your love or of someone you are close to in the center of a blank piece of paper. Think of metaphors for this person, things you might rename your love (newsstand, national park, spatula). Put those names around the person's name on the page. Think of more (pyrotechnical, bee-keeper, baker, pole-vaulter). Come up with all kinds of terms: vacation, magician, maître d', silk scarf, Cracker Jacks, artist's palette, ocean crossing, take off, car chase, gardener.

Choose one metaphor that engages your attention and jot down the functions and actions of the thing or role you have selected: A gardener, for instance, tends plants, knows exactly what their soil requirements are, appreciates their colors and textures, among other things. Continue with this exercise using Neruda's strategy as a template: List as many things as you can that no one else notices that confirm your belief that your love is what you call him or her. Extend the metaphor you are making by branching into more images.

If I call my love a gardener, I may talk about how no one else sees his eyes taking in the blue of Himalayan poppies or the way he stakes the tallest stalks so they do not bend from the weight of the day's growth. After you have written the first part as far as you can take it, begin an ending stanza with the word "and" and follow it with the sensations that happen inside you when you are near your love or thinking about your love. Remember, what happens inside you is a consequence of what you've called your love. Neruda chose to name his love the queen because she set off bells in him, as the bells of churches would be set off when a queen visited. If my love is named a gardener, perhaps inside me a night-blooming lily opens. But I can't stop at one event that goes on inside of me. I must tell my love more about what nobody sees going on inside me when he is near. I must keep my thoughts in character with the name I've given my love: Not only does the night lily open inside me when I am in the presence of my love, but moonshine lights my way home, and I think of the way time prunes the weakest branches, allowing nutrients to foster thicker, stronger growth. When I awake near my love, all the cells in my body go tropic. I move from the dark to the light.

After you have described what happens inside you, end your poem with something you can share with your love. Neruda asks his love to listen with him. What do you want to tell your love to share with you? If I have chosen to call my love a gardener, perhaps I want to implore him to go out with me in noonday sun and see the top tips of manzanita leaves pointing directly to the sun, protecting the rest of the leaves' surfaces from dangerous heat: "We know how to protect the heart of love from all that attempts to bake it dry."

Put the words "After Neruda" under your title to show the debt you owe this brilliant poet. Invoking his name and thinking as he did will open you up to writing about love and its effects on you.

Start with Prose to Find the Poem—A Lesson in Compression

Here's an example of how to start with prose and then pluck poetry out of it. Kathy Lockwood wanted to write poems but was caught up in selling her house and moving. She wrote to me:

> When we bought the house I was looking for more space for a growing family. The house provided this with its ample 2,080 square feet and four large bedrooms. Everyone had their own room and we still had a family room, living room and an office. The kitchen was small, a galley style but had freshly painted white cabinets with cute rose porcelain knobs. The counter top was a country rose colored Formica with oak trim. I thought the house was beautiful.
>
> We moved into the home in February when snow was still building in the back yard. We weren't sure what we would find come spring under the white blanket that fit tight against the chain link fence. The yard looked so perfect in white with two sheds painted in country red to match the house's exterior. The yard had several birch trees with heavy limbs weighted down by the snow. It was like our own winter wonderland where I would often go late at night to pause from a long day, breathing in the joys of nature and homeownership.

When our first spring brought us yellow daffodils and lots of green surrounding the house we were so excited to work or play in the yard. The kids quickly filled the yard with friends, building friendships that are still strong fifteen years later. I planted more flowerbeds adding delphinium and bleeding hearts.

The seasons flowed into each other quickly those first few years, and the kids grew even faster. Our family room was filled each weekend night with the neighborhood kids, pizzas and movies. My early morning coffee was spent out on the deck listening to birds sing as the sun woke up or in the winter I sat at the bay window watching the neighborhood begin its day.

Over the years changes were made to accommodate the needs of the family. We added a larger second deck out back and as the kids became teens and were more interested in driving lessons or hanging out at the mall, I became more interested in gardening. I added whisky barrels full of annuals and made four more flowerbeds in the back yard. I felt like the yard was more my sanctuary than their playground. The deck was where I could be found most days and late into the night. I have even shoveled snow off the deck for me to sit outside wrapped in my coat and armed with a blanket and a good book.

We have given the house a well-deserved new look. After years of wear and tear on the carpets they have been replaced with laminate flooring in colors called Jefferson Oak and Sonoma Cherry. The walls have been painted a rejuvenating green with white colonial baseboards. The kitchen was remodeled, adding the double French doors that open onto the side deck. The new cabinets are oak and the counter top is a dark stone like Formica in a color called River Gemstone. My sink is an under countertop design, adding to the Tuscany style and feel. I love the kitchen for its colors, inviting atmosphere and its functionality. It is a smaller space in the house but the space is used very wisely.

Going through the house room to room cleaning out years of living has been like reading a book from chapter to chapter, you can see a story unfolding before your eyes. Lives have been lived in this house, children have grown up and moved on leaving behind devoted parents that are now called empty nesters.

As I cleaned out closets, I found toys like my son's old remote control car that he and his dad played with in the street out front. My husband was ever so patient teaching him how to work the controls and retrieving the car from underneath trees and shrubs in the neighbor's yard. Now my son drives his own truck and plays with a remote control car in front of his own house with his son.

I found a story my youngest daughter wrote in second grade about a bear and a moose becoming friends, she had named the bear after her brother and the moose after her uncle. Her words were written as they sounded to her and not always spelled correctly. I broke down and cried at how beautiful her innocence was and now she is all grown up spelling her words correctly.

I found an essay my oldest daughter wrote in seventh grade on the importance of a good work ethic. I also found a poem she wrote for me for mother's day that year. It spoke about the importance of a mother's job and the last line is " a mother's heart will let you in and show you the way." I sat down and cried again as I realized how proud I am of both of us. She has grown up into an incredible woman, built a great career and a good marriage and now has a baby of her own on the way. I am very proud of me for being the parent I am, especially since I had her while I was still just a kid at seventeen.

I have tried to reduce our lives lived for fifteen years down to fit into fifteen Rubbermaid totes. It hasn't been easy but I have been aggressive and determined. I gave the kids their toys, baby books, shot records, some photos, and some house wares. I have kept photographs, a small amount of knitting, half my clothes, dishes for two and my writing materials. I could not part with all my books—it was torture to decide who stayed and who had to be donated. I felt like a coach saying to her players "you made the team, but you did not." Parting with books is like parting with a member of the family. I honestly was heart-broken; I paused in the car before taking the boxes of books in to donate them. I sat there saying good-bye to my "friends" and wishing them well. How did I get so obsessed with books?

I look forward to the new experiences we will have in a new house and location but wonder if they will ever be as rewarding and challenging as the experiences we have shared in this home raising a family. I am ready to pass on this house's beneficence to the next family.

For some reason on Friday night when we talked on the phone and you told me to write about the move, the house, the things going on right now, I got it. I knew right then that I had been keeping my writing outside my lived life and that was why I struggle so to balance the two. It is funny how a person can go for years trying to get deeper into something but can't see that they are impeding the process themselves. I now see how important it is to write the life and live the writing. The two should be one, like in a marriage. There is no room for pushing one aside so that the other can be focused on; they need to work together in order to be more fulfilling.

I have started at what was happening in my life at the time, all the craziness with empting out a house we have lived in for fifteen years, and the feelings of changes that are happening in my life. I have written a rambling essay that needs work but got my feelings and thoughts out. I hope to build poems from the essay.

I thought some poems had started right there. By going back in and using the compression of poetry on the sentences, I saw this poem's beginnings:

What I Love About the House I Am Moving From

Its ample 2080 square feet and four large bedrooms
meant one for each of us and still a family room, living
room, office. The kitchen was small, galley style, but the freshly
painted white cabinets with rose porcelain knobs above the rose
Formica with oak trim made up for that.
The yard looked perfect with two sheds
painted in country red to match the house's exterior and birches

> heavy with snow. We weren't sure what we would find
> under the white blanket tight against the chain link fence,
> but I would go at night to pause after a long day,
> and dream of delphinium and bleeding hearts.

If the name of the last flower, bleeding hearts, was changed to one with happier connotations, or the poet used the Latin name for the flower, the poem might end on that last line and carry the connotation of all that was lovely there.

And here's another poem I saw shaping up:

Today I Try to Fit Our Lives of Fifteen Years into Fifteen Rubbermaid Totes

> I gave the kids their toys, baby books, shot records, some photos
> and some housewares. I kept other photos, a small amount of knitting,
> half my clothes, dishes only for two and all my writing materials.
> I donated my books, saying goodbye to them like friends wishing them well.

I like the list of what's to be parted with and how the poet accomplishes her task and that there were 15 years boiled down to fill 15 Rubbermaid totes. I wanted to hear more detail. Maybe there's a poem called "Fifteen Years and Fifteen Totes." The poem could have a stanza for each tote—what's inside, how it was decided to keep what's in it, and a memory attached to the objects. I believe the daughter's essay would find a home in this poem.

Your Turn

Make a list of places, people, and events you want to write about. Choose one and write paragraphs about it, allowing whatever enters your mind on the topic to be expressed. After at least a few hours, if not days, pick up what you wrote and look into it for the places where specifics—sounds, rhythm, and energy—reach you. Then try your hand at compression and see if there is a poem there.

Write Thanks for True Wealth

In 1914 and 1915, Carl Sandburg was writing poems against the emotional backdrop of World War I, in which men were dying at a higher rate and on a larger scale than in any previous war because of the new war technology of machine guns, tanks, and barbed wire. Here is part of one of the poems (www.americanpoems.com/poets/carlsandburg/12757):

Our Prayer of Thanks

For the gladness here where the sun is shining at evening on the weeds at the river,
Our prayer of thanks.

For the laughter of children who tumble barefooted and bareheaded in the summer grass,
Our prayer of thanks.

For the sunset and the stars, the women and the white arms that hold us,
Our prayer of thanks.

I think Sandburg was thinking about the gentleness of a mother's arms over the brawn of a father's arms tanned from fieldwork when he wrote, "the women and the white arms that hold us." Today, we might praise a father holding his baby and we would think twice about the word "white," which excludes people of color. Still, we can learn from Sandburg's poem that we don't have to look too far for the material that helps us evoke our sense of life and extract wealth from our experience.

If you want to capture the mood of a day, a day when you received a meaningful gift or felt loved, saw the beauty in the world or amazed yourself with an insight or good deed, you can go about finding the depth of your experience by imagining yourself led in a spiritual meditation by Carl Sandburg. What are the sounds, conversations, sights, textures, smells, and tastes you experienced on the day you are capturing? What opportunities, no matter how small, have you had to learn something new? To think from a perspective that is a little different than the one from which you normally think?

After rereading Sandburg, I wrote:

The Secrets and the Signals and the System
—from "Our Prayer of Thanks" by Carl Sandburg

The temperatures are only a little above freezing
well past the first day of spring
in our usually temperate climate.

We pray for the roots of the newly planted
blueberries to stay warm in our garden's dark earth,
though we are thankful for last night's snow
brightening mountaintops we see from our window.

We pray that snowmelt will mean higher rivers for salmon
in late summer when they spawn, after our berries show
their juicy blue and we gorge on thoughts of more in years to come.

Your Turn

Take a turn writing in response to Sandburg's poem by saying what you give
thanks for. Then, select a line that particularly resonates with you and use
it as your title. You can do something similar with any poem you find that
you enjoy reading. Pay attention to repeated phrases or themes and write
what you have to say on the topic by using specifics from one of your life
situations.

Wake Up Cooing

Poetry relies on sound. Sometimes we forget that and use our academic language skills in a way that squelches the magic of one sound leading to
another. The excitement and emotion of our insight vanishes under the
heavy-handed exposition we have so much experience writing for school
and at work.

Imagine yourself cooing and shrieking like a happy infant, delighting yourself
with your voice and the sounds you can make when you aren't trying for words.
Write down a string of such sounds. Next, do a free write where you start with
these sounds and free associate to images and memories:

Na-Na-Na-Na, Mum, Mum, Mum

Delicious morning. Sunlight streaming through the windows,
yellow stripes on the carpet. I drive to Shilshoe Bay, watch
cormorants on pilings spread their wings to dry,
see a great blue heron cast its shadow over blue water
then dive for a fish. In the silver glimmer of the fish's belly
I catch my own life, so startled and slippery.

Your Turn

Give this kind of freewrite a try. By using different sounds on different mornings, you can create a variety of meditations.

Scandalous Pleasures

Sometimes, at the start of a new season, you notice what is happening in nature and human life with exquisite delight. In spring, so much is beginning. In fall, we notice the trunks of trees more in view, gardens trimmed for winter, and flowerbeds dug under, perhaps mulched with straw.

One spring, I was visiting my parents' home. I lived then in Los Angeles. Walking their dog in a Seattle area neighborhood made me remember what I missed about the climate I'd moved from. What had been bare for several months now showed tender green, colorful pinks, yellows, and purples. The sight of buds and shoots filled me with a sense of the miraculous bounty in the world and created an awe of life's resiliency and quality of renewal. I wrote:

In Early March

I walk along Island Crest Way
and see clusters of daffodils,
scandalous pleasure of a parade
on the meridian. The joggers are out
in shorts after winter rains, their dogs
beside them, tongues long like stamens.
Scandalous pleasures of March:
the daffodils' height after February's
low beauty of crocus. No need
for coats, okay with thin stockings,
all the puddles shrunk to button-size.

Your Turn

Decide on a euphoric emotion or one of contentment. Give it a name: bliss, joy, satisfaction, completion, for instance. Now it will be your writing assignment to describe a specific place using details that will evoke the emotion you have chosen. In your writing, sprinkle in the word or phrase you are using to identify your emotion, as I did when I repeated "scandalous pleasure."

Whatever you are describing, use details, repeat the word or phrase you selected; insert it whenever you need help continuing. You can take out too much repetition later.

Create a Prose Poem

Let's look at two prose poems. Peggy Shumaker ends her prose poem "Moving Water, Tucson," about a boy riding a flooded arroyo on a piece of plywood, like this:

> That kid on plywood, that kid waiting for the flood. He stood and the water lifted him. He stood, his eyes not seeing us. For a moment, we all wanted to be him, to be part of something so wet, so fast, so powerful, so much bigger than ourselves. That kid rode the flash flood inside us, the flash flood outside us. Artist unglued on a scrap of glued wood. For a few drenched seconds, he rode. The water took him, faster than you can believe. He kept his head up. Water you couldn't see through, water half dirt, water whirling hard. Heavy rain weighed down our clothes. We stepped closer to the crumbling shore, saw him downstream smash against the footbridge at the end of the block. Water held him there, rushing on.

Study Shumaker's work for its repetition and lists of images that enhance the lyric sound and movement of her prose poem. Notice the longer sentence at the end that brings the event she is describing to an end.

Under the influence of Charles Baudelaire's work, especially his poem "At One O'Clock in the Morning" (www.poemhunter.com/poem/at-one-o-clock-in-the-morning/), I wrote about being fed up with not being able to say no:

Tantruming at Last!   *(With thanks to Charles Baudelaire)*

No sound but my own voice and pent up tears, all energy in my face and lungs. I will not throw dishes or books, break computer screens or tear the curtains down. Only my rage of words, calving glaciers, boulders down a mountain gaining speed, house thrown off its stone foundation, an elephant when feeding time is overdue, the sound of nuclear fusing. I have said yes and yes and yes and yes and cannot stand myself and cannot sleep. I take one to the park to play and one to the library for a lecture and one to the doctor and the first for a meal and the second to a meeting and the other to a friend's for tea. I arrange another's doctor's appointments, financial assistance, and driving needs.

> I have said yes and yes and yes and envy who says no; this jealousy leaves welts along my tongue; my words projectile as pus pushed from subcutaneous sores.
>
> You, the one I love outside my door! Don't go away. Stand in the swollen surf, the riptides you think will sink you. Pretend frequencies are higher than you can sense and come to hug me as if you couldn't hear my roaring. Hug me, hug me, hug me; I'm small and waiting and need a gentle wind to bring soft soil that will protect me.

With the rhythm and sounds of these two poems in your ears, take a stab at writing a prose poem of your own.

Your Turn

Think of a dramatic event you've experienced or watched. Start a paragraph about it with "that," for instance: that day, that father, that dog in the road, that time I. Or start with an exclamation like "Tantruming at last!" as I did modeling my words after Baudelaire's opening line, "Alone, at last!" in "At One O'Clock in the Morning."

As you write, use repetition as Shumaker does ("he stood" and all the repetitions of "so") and as I do ("yes and yes and yes" and "hug me, hug me, hug me"), and lists of images as we both do to enhance the lyric sound and movement of your prose poem. You might want to see what happens if you keep many of your sentences on the short side until a last sentence as Shumaker does—the longer ending sentence sings the event you are describing to an end.

Exaggerate, An Exercise by Poet Susan Rich

Susan Rich shares an exercise she invented for a recent poetry-writing workshop based on the interconnections between poetry and food, for:

There is no love more sincere than the love of food.

—George Bernard Shaw

At a poetry writing workshop at Lower Columbia College in Longview, Washington, I was teaching based on the interconnections between poetry and food. I had people introduce themselves with one sentence that began with their name and then mentioned a food they either loved or loathed. Going around the very large circle provided a diversity of foods and expressions. I was amazed at how passionate and confident people were when they spoke of their own personal preferences. Jeannine loved sauerkraut; Barry loathed chocolate ice cream. We expanded on those first lines with a sense of play, going wild: making chocolate a reason to live, saying we'd rather die than eat chopped liver again to create energetic and entertaining pieces.

One person started with "I'm Karen and I love wild salmon." In her poem of exaggeration, the wild salmon became a very sexy boyfriend waiting for her with a freshly prepared dinner when she came home from work. Of course, once the poem gets going the first line that the poet started out with often becomes obsolete. Although sometimes a first line, like this one, sticks: "There should be a law against a cheese smarter than me."

Susan Rich Helps You Take Your Turn

Write a poem in which you take your like or dislike to the level of the absurd. The more fun you have writing this, the better.

Enlist Poets Who Came Before You, A Second Exercise from Susan Rich

Rich tells her students:

Why choose a dead mentor? How might this help in your development as a writer? Well, for one thing, it is practical. Your relationship can transcend place and time. Pablo Neruda will not be too busy at Isla Negra to work with you. His poetry, prose, and even his memoir will be available whenever you are. Elizabeth Bishop could be demanding in person, but her poetry, letters, and paintings are smart companions. You can transcend boundaries of ethnicity, race, gender, ideology in order to learn what you need. Most importantly, you will have a poet-guide to keep you company.

Susan Rich Helps You Take Your Turn

To begin your search for the poet you want to be your dead mentor, compose a personal ad. Rich suggests:

In 100 words or less, describe your ideal mentor. It's important to ask for what you want. This process is meant to help you identify who you want to take on as your mentor. It's a decision that merits some reflection. Here are some questions to get you thinking. Should she (or he) be serious or sexy? An avid outdoors person or a bibliophile? What matters to you most? Brilliance or bravado? Is it important that your mentor worked in several genres? Do you envision a poet from Romania or the Pacific Northwest? Do you prefer that they are a genius or a prolific letter writer?

When you have selected the poet, begin a conversation:

Choose one poem from your mentor's work. Double-space out the lines of the poem in your notebook so that you can insert your own lines in-between. See what your own lines might say to the printed ones. Ask questions, further your mentor's thought, make a joke. Another take on this exercise is to merely "borrow" a refrain or a line of the chosen poem and use it as your own starting point.

Next, make imaginative leaps:

Write a monologue from the perspective of your mentor's neighbor, beloved cat, teakettle or spurned lover. What might we learn about Emily Dickinson from her next-door neighbor? How did William Carlos Williams apologize to his wife after a fight? If you are obsessed with your mentor, especially if you feel quite in awe of their work, this exercise will make it easier to spend time together.

Now that you have been mining your experiences for poems in free verse, let's turn to trying out four of poetry's many traditional forms: haiku and tanka, on the short side; the villanelle, which is of medium length and uses repetition; and ekphrastic poetry, which is longer.

Haiku: An Exercise By Margaret D. McGee

Haiku is a brief, three-line form from Japan that typically expresses the essence of the moment. Haiku is often thought of as using five syllables in the first and third lines and seven in the middle line, although English syllables are not quite the same as the sounds they count in Japanese (the word "haiku" is two syllables but counts as three sounds in Japanese, for example). These days, people are often taught the 5-7-5 in school, and then, if they like the form, end up freeing themselves from the tight syllable restrictions. What is important is that using images and senses, a haiku brings feeling to life.

Margaret D. McGee explains where her haiku come from:

It was a gloomy afternoon, and I felt tired and low on the drive from Seattle to my home on the Olympic Peninsula. The sky, water, and highway all reflected back to me in shades of gray. Then in a flash, the clouds broke apart and sunlight washed across the tall mountains ahead. Though weather changes are hardly unusual in our region, still, my spirits lifted in surprise. With gratitude, I began to compose a haiku:

sudden sun

snow peaks brighten

for the long drive home

Today, this little poem can bring that moment of unexpected light back to me. In the midst of a difficult workday, I call it to mind and feel again my spirits lift, just as they did that afternoon at the wheel.

A "haiku moment" is a moment when your mind stops and your heart moves.

Often, a haiku puts two images together, and it is the spark between the images that evokes our feelings.

a turn in the road

two—no—three—deer emerge

from the dusk

This haiku, which I shared in my Skylight Paths book *Haiku—The Sacred Art: A Spiritual Practice in Three Lines*, brings back a moment when I was walking along a gravel lane near my home. Around a bend, a broad meadow opened up in the twilight. I stopped at the sight of two deer in the meadow. Then, a vague shape that I had thought was a mound of weeds suddenly moved, and a third deer lifted her head and turned to look at me.

For me, this poem evokes a feeling of unexpected possibilities in the world. Writing haiku offers the chance to hold and honor a moment that takes you out of yourself, and it is also a way to share feelings with others. All it takes is a moment of mindfulness—quiet attention to what is happening in the world around you.

Margaret McGee Helps You Take Your Turn

Margaret suggests going outside and finding a place where you can be comfortable, but you can, of course, also do this exercise from inside:

Relax, breathe, and look around. At the top of a page, write the current season and general time of day. (For example: "winter morning.") Now simply jot down whatever you notice. What's happening in the sky? What do you hear? Smell? What catches your eye? Write down specific things you see or experience, including images, scents, sounds, and even memories. Do your best to suspend all judgment for the time being, whether aimed outward at the world or inward at your own efforts. (This is not a test!) Instead, simply offer the world your respectful attention, then write down what you see. Keep writing until your page is full. Then look over your images and choose two to put together in a short poem. One of the images might be the season and time of day that you wrote at the top of the page. Or you might feel a spark of energy between two others. Arrange the images in three brief lines.

> winter morning…
> bare branches tap, tap
> against my kitchen window

For me, this haiku evokes both the cold outside and the warmth inside—a warmth connected to food and nourishment. The feeling is one of poignancy mixed with gratitude.

What feelings are evoked by your haiku?

If you are also interested in a traditional look into writing haiku, type "Grace-guts" into your browser to find Michael Dylan Welch's site. Another useful link for reading about Haiku is www.dmoz.org/Arts/Literature/Poetry/Forms/Haiku_and_Related_Forms/.

Tanka: Exercise with an Older Japanese Form by Poet Michael Dylan Welch

Michael Dylan Welch is the founder of the Tanka Society of America. He describes the tanka form as supplying:

> …a brief touch of poetry, though not quite as brief as haiku. It has a bit more room to explore, and often carries overtly emotional content that haiku only hints at. Over centuries, the tanka form grew out of an older form known as *waka*, which also spawned linked verse and haiku. Tanka in Japanese are often written in one vertical line, but English uses five horizontal lines, often in a short-long-short-long-long rhythm. Sometimes tanka is taught as being divided into syllabic units of 5-7-5-7-7. However, the majority of literary tanka writers do not follow this pattern in English because 31 English syllables result in a poem much longer than the Japanese pattern of 31 sounds.

Tanka begin, he continues:

> …with what you feel in your heart. You write about what caused the emotion rather than the emotion itself and are receptive to feelings, even down to noticing the bodily sensations that go with them—the tightening of the chest, the widening of the eyes, or the slackening of the jaw and report these physical reactions in a poem. The tanka poet tries to catch what caused his or her emotion, such as the name on a return address label that makes a letter unexpected, or the sound of a leaf scratching across the pavement after news of a loved-one's death. Then he or she begins to record these emotive observations in words.

Welch also teaches that readers often presume tanka are written from personal experience and are autobiographical, and offers one of his tanka poems for examination:

the doctor tells us
of the baby's heart murmur—
outside the hospital window
snow half way
down the distant mountain

He says of this poem:

It turns out that our daughter's murmur was minor and cleared up in just a day or two. At first, though, my wife and I didn't know what to feel. We didn't know if the snow, half way down the mountain in the distance outside the window, would come further down the mountain or retreat to higher elevations. Would the days ahead be colder or warmer, both metaphorically and literally? It's this sensitivity to natural symbolism that so often helps tanka to carry the weight of one's emotions. My tanka doesn't state an emotion but conveys something of the tension and feeling we had by the leap or "turn" from the first part of the poem to the second.

Reading Welch's poem, we notice a turn it takes in the third line, a turn from hearing the condition of the child to looking through a hospital window and letting the natural world communicate the stunned parents' feelings. Those writing tanka strive for such a turn, often in the third line, marking the transition from the examination of an image to the examination of personal response. This connects, Welch tells us, what the Japanese call kami-no-ku, or upper poem, to the shimo-no-ku, or lower poem.

Michael Dylan Welch Helps You Take Your Turn

Here are his instructions:

Take five sheets of paper and draw a line down the middle of each one. On the left side of each sheet, write "Sensations" (for sensory experiences). On the right side, write "Emotion/Assessment" (for how you felt or what you were thinking about at the time).

Spend the next five weekdays, starting on a Monday, paying attention to each of your five senses: sight, sound, touch, smell, taste (the exercise may get harder later in the week as you progress to senses that are typically less dominant). At the end of each day, try writing at least one tanka about your sensory focus for that day. Try to avoid directly saying what you were feeling or thinking about at the time of each sensory impression. Instead, try to imply those feelings or conclusions by writing about what might have caused those feelings. In other words, if seeing a baby spread its fingers makes you feel joyful, don't write about the concept of joy, write about those fingers spreading—trust the image itself to make others joyful too! By carefully leaving out statements of feelings, you empower the poem to imply them.

The Villanelle—Circling Around What Haunts Us

The name for this form comes from *villanella* and *villancico*, from the Italian *villano*, or peasant. The name referred to Italian and Spanish dance songs, believed to be derived from what field workers sang as they worked. Later, when French poets called their poems "villanelle," they did not at first follow schemes, rhymes, or refrains, but addressed pastoral themes. It may not have been until the late nineteenth century that the villanelle was defined as a fixed form when French poet Théodore de Banville used a more rigid scheme.

The form became popular among English speaking poets. Many of us know Dylan Thomas's "Do Not Go Gentle into That Good Night" (www.poets.org/viewmedia.php/prmMID/15377) and Elizabeth Bishop's "One Art" (www.poets.org/viewmedia.php/prmMID/15212). Although a villanelle can be about any subject and carry any emotion, both of these famous villanelles are about loss. In his book *How To Read a Poem and Fall in Love with Poetry*, Edward Hirsch describes the villanelle as a form that is particularly useful for "retrieving loss." Others writing about the villanelle talk of the way it helps a writer retrieve the feelings and images that haunt them.

It can seem confusing to read a description of this form, but reading villanelles themselves helps unravel the code. So, visit one of the websites noted above or read my poem reprinted below so you have a villanelle before you as you read this description of the pattern in this form. There are six stanzas—five are made up of three lines each and the last one is made up of four lines. Of those four lines, the last two lines are ones that have alternately ended the preceding stanzas. That is, the first line of the first stanza is repeated as the last line of the second and fourth stanzas and the third line of the first stanza becomes the last line of the third and fourth stanzas. The first and third lines in each stanza rhyme at the end. The middle lines of the first five stanzas usually rhyme with one another, too, as full or half rhymes. In the last stanza, the second line rhymes with the previous middle stanzas' middle lines and the other three lines rhyme with one another and match the rhyme of the previous stanza's first and third lines.

The villanelle I wrote several months after a tragic loss was a way of putting together spiritual information I felt I was receiving in dreams that I couldn't quite say yet. Writing the poem in this form did allow me to find a way to say what I needed to say and to find out what I believed. My first-hand experience tells me that there does seem to be magic in the repetition of the lines in the pattern prescribed. As I wrote, I kept Elizabeth Bishop's "One Art" open at my left to refer to the pattern and adjust my lines. The words to fill in the rhymes and pattern did just seem to come and from the words and their rhymes, the music.

Bishop's poem begins:

> The art of losing isn't hard to master;
> so many things seem filled with the intent
> to be lost that their loss is no disaster.

Modeled on the fact that her rhyming lines that repeat would be the first and third from this stanza (the third one being used with some flexibility in phrasing, however), I found my first stanza and then could fairly easily continue filling the form from there:

A New Theology
For Seth Bender, 1975–2000

> Who has no likeness of a body and has no body
> is my son, now five months dead
> but in my dreams, my dreams he brings the peace in gardens,
>
> and I see him in his smile and he is hardy
> in the rolled up sleeves of his new shirt, well-fed
> when he has no likeness of a body and has no body.
> I see him next to me in conversation at a party
> and I believe that he is fine because this is what he said,
> because in my dreams, my dreams I sit with him in gardens.
>
> The nights he comes, the cats moan long and sorry.
> I believe they see his spirit entering my head,
> he who has no likeness of a body and has no body.

In my life, accepting death comes slowly,
but the midwifery of sadness and of shock bleeds
afterbirth, dreams that bring the peace in gardens.

I know that he is far and he is here and he is holy.
Under sun, I feel the energy it takes to come away from God
who has no likeness of a body and has no body
who is in my dreams, the dreams that bring me gardens.

Although Elizabeth Bishop's "One Art" is frequently described as a poem that doesn't offer resolution, but instead evokes echoes of compounding loss and the several emotions it elicits, including regret and grief, my experience writing a villanelle is that the repetitions allowed me to circle around the tragedy I'd experienced until I found a kind of resolution—a discovery of a perception that could soothe me. It was something I could find that I did know was born of this loss. I believe I owe the discovery to the villanelle form.

Your Turn

Think of something that bothers you deeply—the way others treat animals, the way people change their beliefs depending on the celebrity politician of the moment, the way people believe what they hear and read without testing the truth of the thoughts, the way a friend is having to deal with illness or the way some things like school funding never seem adequate—and write two lines to describe what you feel. Make sure they rhyme. Next, lay those lines out in the pattern they must fulfill for the villanelle.

Stop to closely read villanelles. You can add "The House on the Hill" by Edwin Arlington Robinson (www.americanpoems.com/poets/robinson/12637), "Mad Girl's Love Song" by Sylvia Plath (www.americanpoems.com/poets/sylviaplath/1411), "Saturday at the Border" by Hayden Carruth (www.poemhunter.com/poem/saturday-at-the-border/), and "If I Could Tell You" by W. H. Auden (www.poemhunter.com/poem/if-i-could-tell-you/) to my poem, Dylan Thomas's "Do Not Go Gentle into That Good Night," and Elizabeth Bishop's "One Art."

Now, under the spell of other villanelles, with a favorite one beside you, return to the lines that you laid out; fill in the rest of the lines to complete the pattern. You will need to do some tweaking here and there, but you will surprise yourself and see a poem with power developing.

Ekphrastic Poetry—Writing Poems from Paintings, An Exercise from Holly Hughes

Holly Hughes writes:

The term *ekphrastic* comes from the Greek *ekphrasis—ek* "out of" and *phrasis* "speech or expression." Ekphrastic poems have a long, rich history going back to the time of Homer, who described in great detail in *The Iliad* how Hephaestus, the blacksmith god, forged the *Shield of Achilles*.

Poets continue to be inspired by paintings, although in more recent times they have focused less on the details of the art and have instead interpreted, spoken to, or even tried to inhabit their subjects. Some examples of well-known ekphrastic poems are available at Poets.org, PoetryFoundation.org, and other sites.

W. H. Auden: "The Shield of Achilles" and "Musée des Beaux Arts"
Edward Hirsch: "Edward Hopper and the House by the Railroad"
William Carlos Williams: "Landscape with the Fall of Icarus"
X. J. Kennedy: "Nude Descending a Staircase"

Find these poems and read them aloud several times.

My own ekphrastic poem is about a Chagall painting. There are many beautiful paintings in the world, all deserving of poems, but in my poetry classes I like to use the paintings of Marc Chagall, the Russian painter, because his paintings do so well what we want our poems to do: take imaginative leaps. In his world, cows jump over the moon, newlyweds dance across the sky, fiddlers take flight, imagination rules! Thanks to the Internet, you can easily view Chagall's paintings online at several websites, including www.artcylopedia.com and www.masterworksartgallery.com.

Here's a poem I wrote with my students in response to Chagall's painting titled "The Shop in Vitebsk":

The Shopkeeper, Waiting

Chagall: The Shop in Vitebsk

Orange persimmons glisten in a string bag;
on the table, two plums, a mackerel await weighing.
In the shadows, the shopkeeper watches, about
to enter the room where wood planked floors sag

under the tread of feet, about to re-enter this world
where jars filled with spices line up in rank,
this world tidy, measured out, set of scales bearing
fine precision of fish bone, small heft of plum.

Here, even beauty can be weighed, measured,
before it drifts like smoke toward the sky.

What will he do when he returns? Will he measure
out a few rubles of sassafras, of comfrey? Or
will he pull out his violin, fiddle to the cow,
who will leap beyond the blue moon?

And what of the mackerel, persimmons, plum?
Will they too rise, weightless, while below,

everyone who enters will find what they need.

For more ekphrasis poetry type the following into your Internet browser:
"The Poet Speaks of Art" www.english.emory.edu/classes/paintings&poems/titlepage.html,
"Ekphrasis: Poetry Confronting Art" www.poets.org/viewmedia.php/prmMID/5918
"Notes on Ekphrasis" by Alfred Corn www.poets.org/viewmedia.php/prmMID/19939

Holly Hughes Helps You Take Your Turn

Find one of Chagall's paintings that especially intrigues you—a painting that you'd like to study closely and then interact with in a poem.

1. Study the painting carefully, noting the colors, shapes, images, mood. Note, too, what's happening in the shadows of the painting.

2. In a freewrite, describe what you see in the painting, using at least three concrete details and at least one simile and one metaphor.

3. Choose a figure in the painting and write from his/her/its point of view (the figure doesn't need to be human). Let your imagination loose here, as Chagall does, so that your words are as free as his images.

4. Write several questions that are raised by the painting, but don't try to answer them; just explore them.

5. Reread your free write, underlining the strongest lines and images and the most interesting questions.

6. From these lines, images, and questions, create a poem. In doing so, think about this as a jazz collaboration—or a dance—with Chagall. Don't worry about making literal sense; rather, try to convey the mood or feeling the painting conveys. Your poem should use enough specific details that readers might recognize the painting. It should also convey the imaginative spirit of Chagall and ask us to look at the world in a new, fresh way.

7. Try out several poetic forms—couplets, triplets, single stanza—to see what will work best with the spirit of the poem and painting. Try for an organic form, if you can, in which the content of the painting is somehow mirrored in the poem's form.

8. Again, in keeping with the spirit of Chagall, try to avoid clichés or predictable language. Better not to follow a predictable rhyming pattern, but do pay attention to the music of the words, using alliteration, assonance, consonance, or internal rhyme when you can.

Additional assignments from Holly Hughes:

- Try using Chagall's paintings as warm-ups for your own writing, choosing an image to respond to each morning before you write to put yourself in an imaginative frame of mind (instead of invoking the muse, invoke Chagall!).
- Choose another painter that you admire and write an ekphrastic poem about that painting, or a series of paintings.
- If you have a friend who is an artist, suggest collaborating on a series of paintings/poems.

More Help Exploring and Writing in Forms

There are many books and online resources for studying poetry in form. Now that you have tried your hand at working within certain parameters, I hope you see that restrictions can help you figure out how to say something extraordinary by finding language you might not have found without the vessel of the form forcing you to do that.

If you want to try your hand at other forms such as sonnets, sestinas, pantoums, ballads, odes, cinquains, ghazels, and heroic couplets, among other forms, good books to consult are the ones I mentioned in Chapter 3 under lyric poems. Poets who write in form believe that the structure of form is not a lock but a key and that the subtlety, elegance, and hunger of the human spirit is "… neither constrained by nor separable from the cadences, rhymes, lines and structures that shelter it."—*The Making of a Poem: A Norton Anthology of Poetic Forms*, edited by Mark Strand and Eavan Bolan.

Like with all poetry, if you read and read some more, a haunting will begin, and you will work in response to the forms you are taking in. Start now; visit Poets.org (www.poets.org/page.php/prmID/197) from the American Academy of Poets.

Type in the name of the poetic form you want to learn about and instruction will be there, as well as sample poems in the form that you want to learn to use.

Another of my favorite sites for a complete list of poetry forms with links to instruction for writing in those forms is The Wordshop (www.thewordshop. tripod.com/forms.html). And yet another site that lists and defines forms (and terms) is Poetry-Online.org (www.poetry-online.org/poetry-terms.htm). The Poetry Foundation website (www.poetryfoundation.org/search. html?q=poetic+forms&x=0&y=0) also maintains a list of articles about poetry in form.

It won't be long before you are conversant with many poets and many ways to seek beauty and emotion through pattern: renga, terza rima, haibun...

A Word on Tone in Poetry from Poet Jefferson Carter

Jefferson Carter says:

My 91-year-old mother bought five copies of my new poetry book sight unseen. A week later, I received a letter from her saying she wanted to give the books back to my publisher because of the profanity in some of the poems: she wrote, "I don't agree with your using cuss words for emphasis in making a point. It seems there are enough words in the dictionary to get some that will do the trick! Especially for an English major! Your cuss words are an affront to educated, refined people...."

So, for an exercise, I'd use the poem below (or some other "dirty" poem) and ask students to replace the offensive word(s) with something more "refined" and then consider the resulting effect. The exercise should initiate lively and useful thought about appropriate diction, about tone, and about self-censorship.

Otis

The vet opens our dog's mouth
& shows us the gray mass on his palate,
the tumor that's grown so big
his breath whistles through one nostril.
Our options—$6000 for radiation
or do nothing. Goddamn anyone
who denies him a soul. My wife squats
beside him on the linoleum floor,
crooning as he whistles into her palm.

Words in our lexicon of "offensive" diction are actually words that express feeling and a poet's stance in the moment. Here the speaker's exclamation "Goddamn" conveys his frustrated anger against those who consider animals' lives less valuable than humans', those who can't feel his sorrow. The two-syllable sound of the term makes us stamp our feet, stand with frustration in the moment. If we substitute "Darn," the moment doesn't become extended in the stamping of the feet. The moment is almost belittled, becoming more like a moment you walk out the door and realize you forgot your keys than a time of being struck by deep feelings of finding and showing the connection that exists between humans and their dog.

Without the "cuss" word, the whole poem would be more like dinner party conversation. True, too many offensive words can obliterate the engaging moment of a poem. But if needed, the kinds of words we may have been taught not to use bring the emotional message home. Be careful, Carter is saying, about why you put words in or substitute other words—poems do make people uncomfortable, but for the right rather than the wrong reasons.

* * * * *

Where to go from here in writing poetry? If you are an avid reader of poems, this form of expression begins to feel natural to you and whether you start with lists, first lines, or prose, you will soon be writing in stanzas, with line endings that enhance the sound and meaning in your work. Peruse the list of resources at the end of this book and read from the resources I've listed as well as from those I've included in this chapter; visit the websites for prompts and poetry discussions, and join ongoing classes and workshops in poetry writing, online or in person.

Consider keeping a special "inspired by poetry" notebook handy. It can be as simple as a fresh spiral notebook. Fill the notebook with your responses to the exercises in this chapter and with responses to poems you discover. Your notebook of passages and poems rich with imagery will be something you can mine for months to come. Put in copies of poems you've read that you love, whether you "understand" them or not. If the sound of what you are reading compels you, you do understand the poem at some level and as the sound resonates in you, it will nudge your own poems into being.

Part 3

Creative Nonfiction

chapter **5**

What Is Creative Nonfiction?

Simply put, this form of creative writing encompasses all prose that is not "untrue." While fiction supposes artifice, nonfiction supposes truthfulness. In nonfiction, writers have a contract with the reader about being truthful—if they are imagining something, they must let the reader know that is what they are doing. If they know their memory may be inaccurate, they must admit this in some way that the reader recognizes they are only human, telling a story as best as they remember it. If they believe they are making something up as a way of coping with reality, then that explanation must become part of the writing. When the writer breaks the contract of being as truthful as possible with the reader, the product is no longer creative nonfiction but semi-fictionalized prose some call "faction," a genre to which Truman Capote and Norman Mailer contributed.

In his book, *Creative Nonfiction: Researching and Crafting Stories of Real Life*, Philip Gerard notes how odd it is that nonfiction is named, "not by what it *is*," but by "what it is *not*." He points out that it is like "defining classical music as *nonjazz* or sculpture as *nonpainting*." It seems, he says, that poetry and fiction rose to the fore of the written arts and in the minds of literary critics overshadowed the more ubiquitous form of writing that pre-existed both of them.

Perhaps the handiest way to differentiate nonfiction from fiction is to say, as Gerard does in quoting Pulitzer Prize winner Ron Powers, that

> The nonfiction act ... satisfies our hunger for the real and our need to make sense, make order, out of chaos.

That hunger grows in times of conflict and uncertainty. As contemporary people struggle with changing climate, technology, and theology, as well as finding a place in a global world, the various forms of creative nonfiction from reflections to memoir to personal submersion in diverse cultures and conflicts become more and more popular among writers and readers. As our entertainment industry becomes more and more polished, so grows our hunger for nonairbrushed versions of things. We want to know what it is like for others whom Hollywood has not recast and remodeled. We are willing to accept that any particular nonfiction writer has a specific, personalized version of events. That knowledge endears us to the writer, who yearns to understand experience, and in that yearning creates accounts that help us understand our own experiences. For decades, novels and heroes in epic poems helped us through human foibles and disasters. Today, the work that helps us might more frequently be nonfiction accounts by ethnic minorities suffering the obstacles of assimilation or the work of those who have overcome difficult illnesses, survived war, or won or not won against other challenging odds.

Why Do People Write Creative Nonfiction?

In *Tell It Slant: Writing and Shaping Creative Nonfiction* by Suzanne Paola and Brenda Miller, Miller writes that the genre of creative nonfiction allows her "to discover new aspects" of herself and the world, "to forge surprising metaphors, to create artistic order out of life's chaos." She says, "I am never bored writing in this genre, but always jazzed by the new ways I can stretch my writing muscles."

Philip Lopate uses the word "borders" when he describes creative nonfiction in his book *The Art of the Personal Essay*. He asserts that personal essayists in particular investigate "the borders of the self." Memoirist Abigail Thomas writes in *Thinking About Memoir*, "Writing memoir is a way to figure out who you used to be and how you got to be who you are…(The word *memory* comes from the same root as the word *mourn*, and that should tell you something.)"

I believe that by writing personal essay and memoir, we are creating a blueprint for an experience or experiences we already lived, but for which we couldn't yet see a design that contained meaning.

Sports writers, nature enthusiasts, travelers, and those whose interest is piqued by a mystery, unsolved crime, or a cultural happening write creative nonfiction to explore both an inner and an outer story or journey. As Adam Hochschild describes in *Telling True Stories: A Nonfiction Writers' Guide*, edited by Mark Kramer and Wendy Call, the work of the creative nonfiction travel writer is to enter a world not his own; in doing so he or she notices much more and sees things normally missed. This leads to a feeling of being more alive.

The same goes for writing about nature, sports, or mysteries. By entering into this world not our own, we learn about something outside of ourselves, and, as a consequence of looking hard outside of ourselves but through our own emotional lens, we learn more than we could have imagined about ourselves.

Creative Nonfiction Subgenres

The Personal Essay

The personal essay is characterized as having the attributes of honesty and humility. The author appears as a flawed individual trying to work something out, not a godly being with all the answers. As we read writers' intimate truths, we grow closer to the essayists who are revealing who they are, how they think, and how they feel while striving toward deeper understanding. Ultimately, while reading the best personal essays, we read as if the exploration is our own—the writer and reader are one, sharing the journey of understanding experience through reflection. It's a large and important task for such a short, humble form.

In *The Art of the Personal Essay*, Philip Lopate describes the personal essay by looking into its history and likenesses to early writing. The conversational aspect of the personal essay makes the form a relative to Plato's dialogues. Lopate believes that "personal essayists converse with the reader because they are already having dialogues and disputes with themselves." The personal essayist writes in order to explore these disputes. Lopate credits the French author Montaigne as the first writer to talk to himself convincingly on the page and allow a reader to feel he or she is eavesdropping on the writer's solitary mind. Writers such as Charles Lamb, William Hazlett, E. B. White, and later, Joan Didion, among so many others, kept the personal essay form alive. Today personal essays appear in literary journals, national magazines, newspapers, and National Public Radio commentaries, as well as themed anthologies. *The Best American Essays* is an important annual publication edited by Robert Atwan and guest editors.

How can you identify a personal essay? First and foremost, you will most often see the use of the pronoun "I." It is assumed in personal essays that what is at stake is the writers' coming to know more than they did at the opening of their essays about their feelings, thoughts, and connection to whatever has hooked their interest. There is no need to be objective, but observing others in addition to one's response to them is, of course, important. No one wants to read a completely self-referential piece of writing, and no writer can actually learn and grow and make readers believe in this learning and growing without observing the who, what, where, when, and how of what surrounds him or her. Personal essays contribute information to others about the world, even as they evoke a particular author's singular emotional journey.

When the personal essay includes narratives of being immersed in travel, nature, sports, and investigations, the attitude that distinguishes them as personal essays is this: The writers are telling the readers how they cared about things that happened to them while they were involved with those travels, that time in nature, or a particular investigation. Good examples in contemporary publications are Susan Orlean's essay on raising chickens, "The It Bird," which appeared in the September 28, 2009 *New Yorker* (www.newyorker.com/reporting/2009/09/28/090928fa_fact_orlean), and Jack Heffron and John Boertlein's essay "Death on a Quiet Street," about an unsolved murder in a middle class 1960s Cincinnati neighborhood, which was published in the April, 2008 *Cincinnati Magazine* (www.cincinnatimagazine.com/article.aspx?id=47780). There are also dedicated anthologies of essays on travel, nature, and sports writing published in Houghton Mifflin's *The Best American Series* each year.

If a personal essay is not organized as narration (the telling of an event through time), it may be organized by other rhetorical patterns: description, comparison and contrast, how-to, cause and effect, division and classification, or definition and argument. Sometimes personal essayists claim argument and persuasion are not part of their realm as they are not writing to change anyone's mind but to explore their own. However, many recognize that all writing is argument—as authors we are asking people to see it our way for at least a moment. So, personal essayists sometimes apply rhetorical patterns to the task of persuading others to reconsider beliefs or actions, which produces an urgency of occasion and an avenue for thorough exploration of topics that may be controversial or misunderstood. Russell Baker's "The Plot Against People" (www.srs-pr.com/plot.pdf) argues via classification and division that inanimate objects aspire not to work. Judy Syfers's essay "Why I Want a Wife" (www.cwluherstory.org/why-i-want-a-wife.html) uses definition to argue that the role of a wife as someone whose job it is to be always at the ready to fix and make things more comfortable is dehumanizing.

Sudden Nonfiction

Some personal essays are short vignettes, often called sudden nonfiction. Editors and writers Judith Kitchen, Mary Paumier Jones, and Dinty W. Moore have done much in fostering an understanding of how short prose pieces belong in our creative nonfiction lexicon.

In the 1990s, Judith Kitchen and Mary Paumier Jones collected work for two anthologies of short nonfiction, *In Short: A Collection of Brief Nonfiction* and *In Brief: Short Takes on the Personal*. In their introduction to *In Short*, the two assert, "...something is going on out there. Almost simultaneously, many fine contemporary writers are writing in a new form: a nonfiction form, literary rather than informational, and short—very short." The writer Bernard Cooper explains in his introduction to the book that his attraction to the short form mirrors his experience viewing Dali's "The Persistence of Memory." To his surprise, this famous masterpiece measured only 9-1/2 by 13 inches. Having been surprised by its small size, he became convinced that compression intensifies a view. Life, he said, is over quickly, and from his intense experience viewing the Dali painting, he abandoned using poetic forms and lines that he felt caused his writing to sound stilted; he wrote short nonfiction prose, which sounded better to him. When Kitchen and Jones created their anthology, Cooper's work was at home with the short nonfiction of others.

A few years later, Kitchen and Jones collected more short nonfiction work to present the "reflections and musings of writers who think about what it is to live in these times and recall what it was to live in other times." They wrote that the essays in the resulting book, *In Brief*, were intended to invite us to "speculate, but always about the world we know, have known, or could know."

Over a decade ago now, creative writing professor Dinty W. Moore established an online magazine named *Brevity* (www.creativenonfiction.org/brevity/index.htm). The magazine publishes well-known and emerging writers working in essay form using 750 words or less. Dinty W. Moore's 2006 book *The Truth of the Matter: Art and Craft in Creative Nonfiction* further established the subgenre of creative nonfiction in 750 words or less. The "something going on out there" continues to gather speed.

Lyric Essays

In 1997, the prestigious *Seneca Review* added the lyric essay category to their genre list. On the *Seneca Review* website, the late editor Deborah Tall calls this form "poetic essays" or "essayistic poems," and explains that the lyric essay gives "primacy to artfulness over the conveying of information." Doing so, it might move by association, like poetry does using images and be short, or it might meander, incorporating techniques of fiction, drama, journalism, song, and film, accruing weight by collecting fragments and "taking shape mosaically." It may rely heavily on repetition for structure as poems do.

In 2003, John D'Agata edited *The Next American Essay*, proclaiming a need to read the pieces he included not for the "nonfiction" in them and not for the facts, but for artfulness of the writers writing about human wondering. D'Agata received attention for the way he threaded his own ongoing essay throughout the anthology making it, according to Michael Silverblatt on Public Radio's "Bookworm" program, "a living biography of an art form." D'Agata became the lyric essay editor for *Seneca Review*. The swell in the creation of lyric essays has now become a surge.

In *Tell It Slant: Writing and Shaping Creative Nonfiction*, Miller and Paoula quote D'Agata as having stated the "credo" of the lyric essay: "Lyric essays seek answers, yet they seldom seem to find them." In a lyric essay, the authors decide, "the quest is the focus, not its fulfillment." The lyric essay "stresses what is unknown rather than what is known."

A more traditional personal essay certainly may seek but not find an answer and still illuminate a point. It certainly may describe the journey toward an answer evocatively by relying on images and leaps of association. It may have a meditative or reflective feel to it. So, for me, the most distinguishing feature of the lyric essay is an architecture that relies on fragments strung together or housed inside another structure. The lyric essay often uses patterns borrowed from other venues. In *Tell It Slant*, Paola and Miller dub this the "hermit crab essay." Writers have created lyric essays using the names in their address books or times in a bus schedule as jumping off points for associations that accrue. They write between the stanzas of a poem or ingredients of a recipe. Paola and Miller tell us the lyric structure protects, "the soft underbelly of the essay," material that is too vulnerable to be exposed to the world without protection. In addition to the hermit crab essay, the two authors name collage, mosaic, and braided as lyric forms authors employ to do their seeking.

It seems that every decade or so, specific patterns come into vogue to name the way creative nonfiction writers explore. Colleagues, critics, and classroom teachers notice the patterns and how they help in exploration, and then names for the patterns evolve as different people notice different nuances that intrigue them and name the writing strategy for that nuance. What is important is not the nomenclature, but the way the patterns facilitate writers' thoughts and feelings by opening pathways of investigation.

Journal Form

Olivia Dresher of Seattle's Impassio Press (www.impassio.com) is dedicated to publishing a form of lyric writing she calls fragmentary writing. Her focus is on notebooks, diaries, and journals. In her essay, "Art is a Lie that Tells the Truth" (www.fraglit.com/impassio/art-essay.htm), she writes:

> The many different kinds of journals, diaries, and notebooks…what do they have in common? What links them? Form is what links them—the fragmented form of writing straight from life, drop-by-drop. This fragmented form thrives on the absence of any pre-established rules or boundary lines. It's pregnant with possibilities.
>
> The directness and intimacy of the journal form is seductive. The form says: Create your own style, write whatever you want, you're completely free here. The form says: Say it however you want to say it. The form says: Tell the blank page what you can't tell anyone else, and tell it however you want to tell it—whether several times a day, or once a day, or once a week, or once a month, or as inconsistently as you need to. The form says: Make this your own world, write it down so it won't disappear. The form says: The moment matters, your words matter, the thoughts expressed matter—now *and* tomorrow.
>
> Even a novel in diary form follows this spirit of freedom. Fiction in the form of a diary creates the illusion that it's the real thing, and within that illusion truth is expressed, as all art is a leap of the imagination.

And so, with recognition for the intensity and clarity of the short form, the focus and the freedom it allows, writers are flocking to the personal essay subgenres of sudden nonfiction, the lyric essay, and fragmentary writing. Creative writing classrooms are bustling with prompts that allow students to create these pieces and audiences are thrilled with the intense bursts of emotion and the tight focus on moments, places, people, and times.

Memoir

For a long time, memoir meant a book-length nonfiction prose narrative that allowed a writer to share a large part of his or her life. Today, publishers and authors are using the word for first-person narrative essays as well as for book-length narratives. In *Tell It Slant: Writing and Shaping Creative Nonfiction*, Paola and Miller point out: "To be memoir, writing must derive its energy and its narrative drive from an exploration of the past. Its lens may be a lifetime or it may be a few hours." They go on to discuss E. B. White's "Afternoon of an American Boy" as memoir in that he recalls a period in his teenage years when he first got up the courage to ask a girl out to a dance. To define the difference between personal essay and memoir based on page length, Sue William Silverman writes in her book, *Fearless Confessions: A Writer's Guide to Memoir*, that personal essays are usually 1–25 pages and book-length memoirs are a minimum of 150 pages.

In memoir, the writer writes with a narrower lens than in writing autobiography, which may cover a multitude more facts and events. Within this narrowed lens, especially for book-length memoir, there are three important musts noted by William Zinsser in *Writing About Your Life: A Journey into the Past*. The need to adhere to these three elements creates the necessity for memoir writers to study the craft of fiction:

"You must construct a narrative so compelling that readers will want to keep reading."

"You can never forget the storyteller's ancient rules of maintaining tension and momentum—rules you've known in your bones since you were a child listening to bedtime stories."

"You can also never forget that you are the protagonist in your story. Not the hero; most writers are uncomfortable with that idea—they weren't trying to be a hero and they don't feel like a hero. But you are the central actor in your story, and you must give yourself a plot."

—William Zinsser

In addition to understanding character development and plot, memoir writers understand the difference between outer and inner story. In *Fearless Confessions: A Writer's Guide to Memoir*, Sue William Silverman uses this quote by Soren Kierkegaard as an epigraph: "Life must be understood backwards. [Although]… it must be lived forwards." She goes on to explain that memoir is told in two voices: the "innocent voice" of the author who is telling the facts, the surface story, and the action; and the "experienced voice" of the writer that employs "metaphor, irony and reflection to reveal the author's progression of thought and emotion." She also points out that a memoir is "a search to see past events or relationships in a new light." Therefore, the "experienced voice conveys a more complex viewpoint, one that interprets and reflects upon the surface subject."

As memoirist Abigail Thomas says in the "Preface" to *Thinking About Memoir*: "Memoir is the story of how we got here from there." Therein lies the importance of literary craft: The identification of (whether for book-length narrative, traditional personal essay, a mosaic of shorter pieces collected together, or individual sudden nonfiction) where the innocent voice's story starts and ends, as well as the choosing of images and details the experienced voice knows, provide the emotionally accurate tone.

Coda on Creative Nonfiction

In the creative nonfiction genre, to a large extent, the name of a particular subgenre is in the eye of the beholder. Silverman talks about immersion essays, while I talk about investigative essays. Miller, Paola, and Silverman talk about the meditative essay and look at whether the writing moves by action or contemplation, while I talk about rhetorical patterns and look at the structure that holds the essay together. Whatever the approach, if your creative nonfiction evokes events and experiences of your life as if you are living them as you write, you will bring readers on a journey in which they learn what you have learned by writing of your experience, and both you and your readers will gain a new or refreshed way of seeing and feeling.

chapter 6

Practice for Writing Creative Nonfiction

Personal essays, vignettes, flash nonfiction, letters, and journals culminate not only in the evocation of particular human questions and insights, but in the dissemination of information and the education of readers on particular subjects, the ones the writers are exploring to find answers to life questions.

When you sit down to write creative nonfiction, you may have a word length in mind or the idea for a whole book. You may want to write in journal entries or in one long paragraph, in letter form, or in essays that follow rhetorical patterns of thinking.

The exercises that follow will help you use the material you have from your life, research, and knowledge to write first-person pieces that move and inform others as well as focus or change your perceptions about what you have experienced.

Let's start by exploring the rhetorical forms you might use to organize explorations.

Eight Rhetorical Patterns and How to Use Them to Create Essays

Narration—In this form of organization, a writer moves through time in chronological order, telling a story by relating events as they occurred. This story may be from a memory, a current happening, or one that will happen or is longed for and can be fully imagined.

Description—Although all narrations require description or readers won't feel like they are in the story, some creative nonfiction has as its mission the desire to evoke one place, person, thing, or event through the use of details that make the reader feel in the presence of the writer's subject.

How To—Using how-to (or process analysis, as it is also called) writers tell how something is done or something is made. There are always steps to be ordered and detailed. Inside the steps, anecdotes, which are short narrations, might be employed; description is always necessary as readers need to know what results, procedures, and variations look, feel, taste, smell, and sound like. They need descriptions of how they know they have succeeded and/or what the failure to receive expected results looks like.

Comparison and Contrast—We are born comparison makers. Using our abilities in our writing means we tell what is the same and what is different between two versions of something, whether they be places we swam as children, cars we've had, our grandfathers, or schools we went to.

Cause and Effect—What happens in life can often be traced back to an event or a decision we or someone else made. Writing about the results of experiences can help us relate more of our life experiences.

Classification and Division—Sometimes we like to put our experiences and thoughts into categories and compare those categories to explore more than we might otherwise.

Definition—Writing from our own perspective about what something is, we write using all of the other rhetorical devices. We describe, compare and contrast, show how something is made or done, delineate effects and classify kinds of whatever we are describing. Very importantly, we call attention to function.

Argument and Persuasion—Sometimes we write to affect how people think about a situation and to help them change their minds and hearts. People who write from personal experience can be quite persuasive. If an author suffers from an illness that most readers don't realize afflicts people—say social anxiety—that author can argue that the illness exists by sharing stories about moving through life with the illness, describing what it looks and feels like, and talking about how the sufferers are impacted by those who don't understand. The author can talk about how the condition is the same and different than other mental and emotional afflictions. To use personal experience to write an argument, the writer needs to know the point under consideration and how to make it real to the reader and pull the reader into the information.

Your Turn

You can learn to use these forms to begin, shape, and extend your creative nonfiction pieces. Ultimately, some of your writing will use one form for the overall organization and some will combine the forms to help you write your experience. You might be interested in my book *Writing and Publishing Personal Essays* for more detailed illustrations of how to develop essays.

Here are ways into each of the eight kinds of essays:

Narration—Tell the story of a time you were not allowed to eat or buy something you wanted. Where were you located? Who was there with you? What did they say? Why did you want to eat or buy this thing? What did you do or not do? What did you think about next? How did things turn out?

Another way to approach narration practice is to think about commonplace things—light bulbs, fences, or chewing gum, for instance—and tell a story that comes to mind from your experience involving one of the objects. Maybe it is a story of sitting in the dark with someone because of a power outage and learning something about them you never would have guessed, or perhaps it is a story about misunderstanding a sign and hiking on the wrong side of fence and coming eye-to-eye with a bull.

Description—Write about an environment as if you were writing an extended riddle and want your readers to guess what you are writing about (a swimming pool, a beach, a locker room, your favorite friend's house, a particular classroom or meeting room, or a garden, for instance). Describe texture, sound, taste, smell, and some of what it looks like without naming the environment. You can tell an anecdote about yourself being there, if you'd like. When you are done writing your description, title the piece with the name of the place you've been describing. The end result should illustrate your feelings about the place you have chosen.

How-to—Take on something you have never described how to do before and think of it as a title: "How to Lose a Good Friend," "How to Mourn a Break-Up," "How to Make Sure Your Loved One Doesn't Discover the Special

Present You Bought," for instance. Figure out the steps in accomplishing the goal and write your way from step one to the final step, being sure to name specific equipment needed (a Facebook page for gossiping, a box of chocolate, a gallon or two of ice cream, a cluttered closet). You may begin the piece with an anecdote about why you are the one to tell us how to do what you have chosen to write about. End with a passage about how you (or your readers) will realize the goal has been met.

Comparison and Contrast—Is your life very different than the life you or someone close to you thought your life would be by now? Have you had to move from a town thinking you'd hate your new location only to find out that you love it? Have you moved thinking you would love your new situation only to find out you are homesick for the place you came from? Have you thought you were getting fired only to find out you were being promoted or vice-versa? Think about a time that something went terribly right or terribly wrong. Write your initial vision using details and images that show, show, show how you thought things would be. Then write what actually happened, using specific details and images. You will find that you have a new perception with which you may end your piece.

Cause and Effect—Every change starts with an action or a thought. Think of a time that you did something differently than you had anticipated—walked instead of drove or drove a new route; took a job you had never imagined you would have; said yes to a date with someone you had thought you weren't interested in. Describe the action you took and tell the story of what resulted.

Classification and Division—We all experience kinds of people, events, places and situations we can write about by separating them into types. Choose a topic and figure out at least three categories into which the topic can be divided. Here are some examples: Do you think of the clothing purchases you make as having categories: things I need, things others think I need, things no one, not even me, thinks I need? You can write about kinds of entertainment in an original way: what the media thinks you want to do in your spare time, what your friends think you want to do, what your family thinks you want to do, and what you actually want to do. Think of types of phone calls received in a day and order them from those that are welcome to those that are unwelcome and those that are dreaded. Do you have types of ex-friends? Can you order them from merely annoying to downright destructive? How about types of losses, in order, from inconsequential ones to those that left you bereft?

Definition—There is so much we know deeply from our firsthand life experience that others know about only through cursory definitions: what it means to be a single parent, a caregiver, a bus driver, a self-supporting student, a diabetic, or a snake handler, for instance. Take on a role you play or have been assigned and define it for others by writing anecdotes showing yourself engaged in the role, delineating the effects of having that particular role, giving instructions on how to perform that role, and/or comparing being in that role to being in another one. You can write about what is not included in that role that others assume is, or what abilities and freedoms you lose or gain as a consequence of being in the role.

Argument and Persuasion—Here's your chance to employ any combination of the preceding rhetorical forms to write to change others' minds and/or move them to action. What you choose to write about should be something from which you have benefited or something of which you have been a victim. You can be funny or serious in your approach. Do you want to excite people about composting? Make sure they know the impact of not taking care of their teeth? Do you want to make sure they stop texting while driving? Make sure you have at least three supports to present as back up for your way of thinking and knowledge of what the opposing point of view would be and how you can overcome objections. Then order your supports and retort to the opposition in a way that builds your case. Use anecdotes from your life and the lives of those you know or have read about. Be sure to show the positive consequences of changing the behavior or thought you want to change.

Writing an Oral History, An Exercise from Kit Bakke

After writing her memoir, *Miss Alcott's E-mail: Yours for Reforms of All Kinds*, in the form of e-mails between Louisa May Alcott and herself, and as papers on transcendentalism, Bakke began writing oral histories and helping others to do so. The oral history can be a form of investigative creative nonfiction. Bakke says:

Writing an oral history is a good way to dip your pen into creating character and story out of the ingredients of the everyday life around you. An oral history is not about facts as much as it is about an individual's memory. For facts, you can go to newspaper archives and history books. Oral histories preserve the memories and stories that add color and humanity to the bare bones of the documented past. Particularly good examples of collections of oral histories are John Hersey's *Hiroshima* or Walter Lord's *A Night to Remember*. These memories were about spectacular events (the atomic bombing of Hiroshima and the sinking of the Titanic), but everyone you know has a story to tell—each person's reminiscence adds to the richness of human experience.

Many people start by collecting oral histories from grandparents or great-grandparents—family origin stories interest almost everyone. The web has many resources for the oral historian—organizations, conferences, journals, classes, books.

Kit Bakke Helps You Take Your Turn

"A good way to start is to do an interviewing exercise with yourself," Bakke instructs:

> Sort your own life into sections like childhood events, biggest struggle, biggest success, greatest satisfaction, the public event I remember most, the holiday tradition I like best, how I was introduced to a new technology, what it was like to move, etc. Then frame a few questions to ask yourself: "Describe your earliest childhood memory" or "Tell the story of your biggest success in high school" or "What video game do you first remember playing, and what was it like?" or "Describe your childhood heroes" or "How were common illnesses treated in your family when you were young?" Answer them in writing and then think of how you'd build up the story of your family by asking similar questions to your parents, siblings and other relatives.

Writing Historical Events in Memoir, An Exercise by Linda C. Wisniewski

Wisniewski, author of *Off Kilter: A Woman's Journey to Peace with Scoliosis, Her Mother and Her Polish Heritage*, teaches her students about writing history in their memoirs:

> Remember the Ken Burns Civil War series on public television? Its most beautiful aspect was actors reading aloud the personal letters of soldiers to their wives, mothers and loved ones back home. When the terrorist attacks in the U.S. occurred on September 11, 2001, many young people asked, some for the first time, what it was like to live through an event sixty years prior: the Japanese surprise air attack on Pearl Harbor, Hawaii, on December 7, 1941.
>
> "Were people scared back then?" "How did they cope with impending war?" How helpful it would have been to know how our grandparents felt about a similar event.
>
> Many of us want to write about the historical events that took place during our lives. A common mistake, however, is to forget to put ourselves into the story! Your family and friends, even readers you've never met, are more interested in your personal take on national and world events than they are in another report on the event itself. They can read that in a history book.

Linda C. Wisniewski Helps You Take Your Turn

Her idea is this:

> To get started, make a list of the historical events that have taken place during your lifetime. They should be things we all know about, events that were reported in the newspaper and on television.
>
> Next, pick one and write about it in a letter to someone you know. Be sure to tell the person things like how old you were at the time of the event, where you lived, and what you were doing when you heard the news. How did you feel about that day? Set a timer for 20 minutes.
>
> When you are finished, add a postscript: How do you feel about the event today?

Just Add Water: An Experimental Mini-Essay in a Can by Dinty W. Moore

Author of the memoir *Between Panic and Desire* and editor of BrevityMag.com, Dinty W. Moore, helps students work in creative nonfiction with this exercise:

> Many writers habitually compose memoir-based nonfiction as if someone had once ruled "all childhood stories must be told in chronological order." Though there is obvious utility to relating events in the order in which they occurred, this tidy approach can also be very limiting. Often, it is the juxtaposition of events that gives one's childhood memories meaning, and sometimes the odd juxtaposition becomes a gathering place for discovery and fresh insight. Logic, in other words, is not the only way into the truth.
>
> The following exercise *forces* incongruity. It also teaches the importance of detail—nouns and verbs, specific moments and particular things. Finally, the exercise encourages the writer to trust "chance" to a certain extent. Seasoned writers often marvel over some element or another that just seemed to show up, unbidden, in their writing, yet ended up being alive, surprising, and richer than where the author was headed. This, of course, is the unconscious reaching up and through the rational mind, but at times it seems random and capricious. If some oddity of detail or language appears in your writing, and it works, then keep it there, and be thankful. You don't have to know why!

Dinty W. Moore Helps You Take Your Turn

He says:

> The first draft that results from the eight steps listed below may result in a finished experimental mini-essay. I have assigned this to students who subsequently published the (revised and polished) version. But at the very least, it almost always generates rich and fruitful raw material.

Important Note: As hard as I know this will be to do, this exercise works best if you *do not* read ahead. Don't read step two until you've assembled your index cards and pencil. Don't read step three until you've completed step two. Trust me, it works.

Large index cards are best for this exercise, but they may not always be available, so separate sheets of paper will work as well. This can be done alone, but works even better with writing partners or small groups. You may want to set a timer—give yourself about five minutes for each step.

1. Assemble four over-sized index cards (or four separate sheets of paper).

2. On the first card: Describe a smell from your past. Don't worry whether or not it is a significant or important smell; all that matters is that it remains in your "memory bank" 10 or 20 or 30 years later. Describe the smell, the quality of the odor. Is it sour or sweet, smoky or clean, sharp or dull? Does it remind you of anything? Keep this to around four or five sentences.

3. On the second card: Describe part of someone you love, but just a *part*. Stick to one physical aspect—your mother's hair, your Aunt Lula's elbows, your little brother's teeth. Be specific. Instead of "dad had rough hands," describe the texture of the palms, the shape of the fingers, the bruises or cuts, the caked oil in the seams. No more than six sentences.

4. On the third card: Pick a snippet of conversation from your past, something you heard all of the time when you were younger. It can be significant—a parent's correction or sharp criticism—or seemingly insignificant—a dumb joke your older brother made every time you sat down to eat chili. It can be anything at all. The only requirement is that you heard it and that it remains in your memory bank, for whatever reason. Do NOT illuminate, describe, or elucidate. Just give us the quote: "Drink your milk. You want to have strong bones, don't you?" "I don't like milk." "Don't come crying to me when you're old and rickety."

5. On the fourth card: Construct a disjointed list of 30 words, primarily nouns, or nouns with some slight modification. Each of these words or phrases describes a remembered something in your past. For instance, my list looks like this: "Ringo. Sled. Uncle Clem's wooden leg. Cooked cabbage. Howdy Doody. Bugs. Sycamore tree." In this instance, it is *not* important to give enough information for the reader to fully understand. Just make your list. No phrase more than four words long. Thirty words. (It often works best to write 45 words, and then cross some out.)

6. When you have completed the five steps above, take the four cards and shuffle them in random order.

7. At the top of each card, write a number 1 through 4.

8. To the first card, add this title: "Why I Am Who I Am."

You have now written an experimental essay, in collage form. Read it out loud, including the title, and the numbers at the top of each card. Marvel at the unexpected connections and odd logic.

I Just Don't Understand You, Another Exercise from Dinty W. Moore

Dinty W. Moore continues:

Too often, we write about other people because we think we know something about that person, or because we feel that we can weigh in with intelligent correctness on their actions or the choices they have made. Too often as well, we end up sounding like mister- or ms.-know-it-all. Whether we are writing about a celebrity or politician, someone who lives just down the street, or a relative—perhaps a seldom-visited grandfather—the assumption that we actually know someone's motives and understand what factors into their behavior is a dicey one at best. Life is complicated, and people are hard to fathom.

So think a moment about the people you *do not* comprehend, and would never claim to fully understand, even if you thought long and hard about it. My list would include two friends who struggled to keep together a marriage but simply could not. Neither one of them was bad or at fault. They just couldn't find the working formula, and I have no better take on what they should have done instead. Still, it seems a shame.

I also can't understand a friend who repeatedly shoots herself in the foot just when her career is taking off. Clearly, she wants to succeed, just as we all do, but something deep inside is driving her to fail. Though I have observed this behavior for years, it still makes no sense to me at all.

A less serious but equally baffling example are the folks in my neighborhood (and in most neighborhoods, I imagine) who treat their front lawns and driveways as if they were hospital operating rooms, hosing away every leaf and acorn first thing in the morning, painstakingly digging out each dandelion and virtually every green shoot that does not look like perfect Kentucky grass. Now I like my yard to look nice, but I can't see putting eight hours a week into it, and a few leaves and twigs and weeds are, to my mind, inevitable. It's autumn as I'm writing this, and not only is my lawn covered in red oak leaves, but I just noticed a stray leaf in the living room, by the front door. Mother Nature is nothing if not persistent.

Dinty W. Moore Helps You Take Your Turn

Make your own list of the people who make no sense to you. You aren't firmly against their choices, and you don't have all the answers—they just baffle you. Put some real people on that list, some types of people (the lawn purists), and even famous folks if you'd like.

Now write about what you *don't* understand, and how unsure you are about what is going on inside the mind and heart of this person. Don't attack or suggest that you know better; just explore.

Worth 1,000 Words, An Exercise by Judith Kitchen

Judith Kitchen, author of the essay collection *Distance and Direction*, created this exercise for her students, beginning with an epigraph:

A photograph is both a pseudo-presence and a token of absence. . .
—Susan Sontag, *On Photography*

Traditionally, photographs have been used in nonfiction as confirmation. Placed in the middle of the biography, they confirm events, give face to people we've met in print. Scattered throughout the memoir, they attest to the truth of what we're being told. This exercise is intended to move beyond the realm of confirmation, making the photograph a part of the text itself.

They say a photograph is worth 1,000 words. Well, this exercise forces you to cut out those 1,000 words and find another 1,000 words that cannot be replaced by the image itself. Your job, then, is contemplation. Speculation. Meditation. You must surround this photograph with the thoughts and feelings that well up in you as you examine it for what it might reveal—about yourself, your memories, your assumptions, what you know you simply cannot know. You must probe its contents, and then move beyond its boundaries, thinking about what it doesn't say, what isn't in the frame.

Judith Kitchen Helps You Take Your Turn

She instructs:

The exercise is simple. Begin with a photograph—one that has some personal meaning: maybe a photo of your mother before she was married; your grandfather standing next to his father, a man you never knew; a place where you used to go on vacation; an album you found at a garage sale, a stranger's life sold for a dollar; your childhood pet; yourself at the age of seven, your lost tooth grinning up at you; an odd snapshot from the box on the shelf, someone you vaguely remember, but who?

Now come at the photograph from many angles. Look at it as a physical object. What is there? Look at its subject. Who inhabits its spaces? Examine the emotions it evokes. Ask it questions. What is your relationship to this scene? Who is taking the photograph? And don't forget to observe what is not there—sometimes absence is what it is all about.

Keep in mind that you may know the people in it, or the story behind it, but that your reader does not come to the photograph with any prior knowledge. Your job is to make it matter to readers as much as it matters to you—and in the way that it matters to you. You can write *about* the photograph, but not mere description, since you must keep in mind the 1,000 words the photograph could make redundant. If you want to tell its story, you will need to find words that do it justice. Bring to your reader what looking will not provide—the smells, the sounds, the texture of the day. You can write *from* the photograph, using it as a starting point, expanding on it until it comes alive for the reader, as it has for you. You can write *to* the photograph, speaking directly to the person there (even to your earlier self), or you can write it into being, telling its story right up to the moment of the camera's click. You can write *around* the photograph, or comment *on* it, moving in and out of its physical presence, making it a central part of your written text—necessary to it, and yet somehow removed from it as well.

Put in enough descriptive words that, even without the photo, the reader would "see" its sepia tint, the color of rusty water; or the odd angle of the shadow on the old man's face; or the serrated edge of the white frame that cuts across your uncle Henry's silhouette, stranding him half-in, half-out of the scene—as he seems to be in your memories, only half present, kind of ghostly. But move beyond description into the "tone" of the moment. Capture how it felt to slide down that slide, how high it seemed as you climbed those steps that, now that you look at it, was really not very high at all. The exhilarating, free-from-adults playground world. Wonder about your mother as a young woman, before you were born: what were her dreams? Where did they go? Why did she cut her river of hair? Give that stranger a life he may never have lived, but one that connects him to you in the odd, imaginative space that exists between you now that you own a piece of his life. Think about what is gone, how things have changed, what the photo holds for all time. Think about the nature of time.

What this exercise does it unlock your meditative voice and give it a focus. It allows you to step in and out of the "present" of your piece, saying "perhaps," and "I wonder if," and "Now it seems as though." By directing your own attention to the object itself—the photograph—you become a narrating sensibility; in other words, you find a "voice." The reader comes to know you by the way you have been thinking, and that is the very essence of nonfiction essays and memoir.

Find just the right title—something to give what you've written a context, a position or a stance from which you are looking. The final thing you should do is decide whether or not your words actually need the photograph to complete the text; it may just be that you no longer need it at all—that you've written the 1000 words that are worth one photograph.

Let the Holons Do the Work

Ken Wilber states in his book, *A Brief History of Everything*, that our universe is an "emergent Kosmos," which counts on creativity, the movement of chaos into form. The term *Kosmos*, introduced by the Pythagoreans, means "the patterned nature or process of all domains of existence, from matter to mind to God."

In his discussion, Wilber introduces 20 tenets of the Kosmos, the first being that, "Even the 'Whole' of the Kosmos is simply a part of the next moment's whole, indefinitely. At no point do we have the whole, there are only whole/parts forever."

Wilber adopts writer Arthur Koestler's term "holons" for these "whole/parts." Each holon strives to maintain its "wholeness" and its "partness." Each has in it the ability to maintain its autonomy and its ability to fit into a whole. Wilber believes that "creativity not chance builds a universe." He prefers "Emptiness" as a term for Spirit because it means unbounded or unqualifiable. The blank page, the blank document template on my computer screen, my mind when I have no idea of what I'll write—the perfect starting places, along with the trust that one part, one holon at a time, my writing will accrue in meaning, in depth, in making something new from what has gone before, for in Wilber's words, each moment is "part of the next moment's whole, indefinitely."

Your Turn

When you write in parts, emulating the emergent universe, of which you are a part, you can relax a little knowing you work in a larger flow.

Here are 11 prompts for taking ordinary daily images and building lyric essays. Using these prompts, you will learn to trust in your abilities to reflect and to allow details to resonate with one another until seemingly unconnected images and anecdotes unite to evoke larger meaning from your experiences, knitting them together into whole cloth.

1. Title a piece with your name or the name of your street, partner, or child. Take the letters and write a short meditation on each of the letters.

2. Take the letters ABC and write a short meditation on any subject by starting each paragraph of three paragraphs with a word that starts with each letter: an A word for the first, a B word for the second, and a C word for the third. Call this meditation the ABCs of whatever subject you are writing about.

3. Take the letters XYZ and write a short meditation on any subject, starting each paragraph of three paragraphs with a word that starts with each letter: an X word for paragraph one, a Y word for paragraph two, and a Z word for paragraph three. Call this meditation the XYZ of whatever topic you are writing about. It will probably evoke the difficulty of the topic you have chosen.

4. Put Scrabble™ tiles or children's letter magnets in a pile and pick one or pick a letter from something printed. Pick three letters from the pile or point to three letters randomly in the printed material before you; write three short vignettes, each time associating from the letter you picked to reasons why it's important to you at this moment of this day, how it seems to go with the day. You might benefit from doing this exercise at three different times in one day or over three different days or weeks.

5. Take a product out of your cupboard. Write down its name. Now use those letters and write a meditation: for example, if I chose oatmeal: O-A-T-M-E-A-L, I'd write a seven-paragraph piece, beginning each paragraph with a word that starts, in order, with a letter of the word oatmeal.

6. If you could have a special parking space earmarked just for you at work, on a street you often visit, and in your childhood town, what would the words reserving each space for you say? Why?

7. Think of a problem in your life you cannot resolve or about a situation that you are not able to change. With this problem in the back of your mind, describe the view outside your window. First, describe what is stationary in the view; then describe what is moving. Subtitle part one "Stationary" and part two "Movement." Title the whole piece after the problem you have in the back of your mind, "Now that My Children Must Adapt to Joint Custody" or "How Will I Find the Time to be a Caregiver?"

8. Imagine where you live is a place you have come to visit. Select someone living or dead to whom you might write postcards from this place. Write a series of postcards to this person similar to the kinds you would write if you were traveling as a tourist—include observations, vignettes, quotes, and text from materials you find or see in the town, snippets of history, and anecdotes about your "travels."

9. Imagine that you change your outgoing message each day on your voice-mail. Make up messages for each day of the week.

10. Think of things you haven't shared with someone who is close to you. Write about them under a title like: "Never Mentioned" or "I Wished I'd Thought to Tell You."

11. Select five or so objects from your environment, varying them from small to large, inside to outside, from new to old. After you've written in parts about each of these items, use a title like "Panorama" or "An Overview of Sorts."

Putter Inners and Taker Outers, an Exercise from Jack Heffron

In *The Writers' Idea Book*, Jack Heffron quotes exchanges in letters between F. Scott Fitzgerald and Thomas Wolfe as they debated approaches to narrative. "Responding to Fitzgerald's claim that highly selective writers were the real geniuses," Heffron recounts that Wolfe wrote:

You say that the great writer like Flaubert has consciously left out the stuff that Bill or Joe will come along presently and put in. Well, don't forget, Scott, that a great writer is not only a leaver-outer but also a putter-inner, and that Shakespeare and Cervantes and Dostoevsky were great putter-inners—greater putter-inners, in fact, than taker-outers....

"Putter-inners?" Heffron reacts. "Not exactly the type of phrase you'll want to tape to your computer or to drop oh-so-casually into conversations at the next literary fete. Wolfe liked to conceal his erudition behind a big-country-boy persona. He's well aware of what he's talking about. It's interesting to note that Wolfe was very much a putter-inner, while Fitzgerald was a taker-outer, and so their views reflect their own approaches to writing."

Jack Heffron Helps You Take Your Turn

Here's a prompt Heffron suggests:

1. Read a piece you've written and cut five details from it, ones you feel aren't essential to the piece.
2. Then add five details to it. How has it changed?
3. To extend the exercise, choose two details that are mentioned only once or twice and find ways to mention them at least two more times.
4. How has their meaning changed within the piece?

I think you can create a lyric essay from this exercise, one built in parts where the insight and emotion gain momentum across the white space that separates the parts:

Write a paragraph describing a place where you lived or hung out in a time that you wanted something—to be recognized, to be able to purchase something, to win a contest or athletic event, to be loved. Number that paragraph number one and then go on to write another paragraph that you'll number two. In this paragraph, follow Heffron's exercise by repeating paragraph one and adding five details. Reflect for several sentences on those details. Then write a list, which you'll number three, that repeats the details you previously mentioned. Write a next paragraph in which you take out all the added details and add back in only some of what had originally been in the first paragraph.

What do you feel as you exit this essay? Whatever that feeling is should help you find a title to the four paragraph piece, a piece which releases some feeling in you about the time you wanted someone or something so badly.

Learning Words by Heart

A few years ago, I invented a way of coming to writing during times when I felt overwhelmed by my need to write, yet stuck in my inability to get anything I liked on the page. The exercise I invented ultimately helped me to create vignettes and essays from life experience when I had no idea about how to find my way into my own feelings and thoughts. This exercise relies on organizing experience through the lens of randomly chosen vocabulary words. To start, I open a dictionary with my eyes closed and let my finger point to a word. I hope I'll be pointing at one for which I don't yet know the definition. Sometimes I have to repeat this action a few times, but I stop at whatever word I find for which I don't yet know the meaning. I read the definition provided. When I write that day, I work on finding a path toward applying the word I've learned to my own experience.

Starets

I have come to Northern California to accompany my husband who is working here. Because I refuse to drive in the intense and speedy Bay Area traffic, I spend a lot of time walking and waiting for BART. Today, I transfer at the MacArthur station. I walk downstairs and cross to the other side of the station and walk up another set of stairs to the opposite platform, the crepe soles of my shoes quiet on concrete. On the platform, no one is talking. We are encapsulated, cradled really, by the noisy traffic of northern California, just yards away on all sides, trucks, cars, buses and vans rushing from one highway to the next.

I stand there listening. I have been cradled by traffic my whole life. I followed along behind my hyperactive mother. I kept compulsive order like my father who often cleared our plates while food still rode our forks. At school, I was urged to "get involved," "make friends," and "be cooperative and conscientious." This was the traffic that loved me, held me, kept me, grew me, sang to me.

On some platform deep inside, I realized I was the picture faintly seen for all the static on the television, the song discernible between the words of telephone conversations when wires crossed.

This morning, in my study by a window filled with bright sky, pine branches and the boughs of willows, I opened the American Heritage Dictionary and with eyes closed, let my finger search for a word. It landed on "starets," which means "A respected spiritual advisor, often a monk or religious hermit in the Eastern Orthodox Church."

Each time I write, I know that writing is my starets and will help me find out how I can stand my ground amidst so much traffic, improve the reception, and hear my song on its own dedicated wire.

The next word I chose when I used this assignment for myself was "sederunt," which means "a long sit," and spawned a way for me to digest a recent experience:

Sederunt

It was a manicure and pedicure that I had made the appointment for, a treat at a salon I'd never been to. I was early and the little building in the little town was locked. At the appointed time, though, a cosmologist arrived and we walked inside. She was the only one working that day, she explained, and she had had to leave to pick her son up at kindergarten and take him to the sitter's. As she began filing my fingernails, the phone rang. She was also going to have to answer it, she told me, to take appointments for her absent co-workers.

The first time she got up, I felt irritated. I had come to relax and having her stop and start my nails with the ringing of the phone jarred me. I began to worry about how many times this would happen while I was there. As she spoke on the phone, I averted my vexed gaze. She took down appointment information, and I beheld Mt. Baker and Mt. Rainier filling the sky. They stood before me in white robes on the stage of Admiralty Bay's blue waters. The mountains looked like ancient Greek scholars imparting important lessons to disciples, like me, somewhere hidden at their feet.

When Dale returned from the phone and the appointment book, she started to tell me a story, full of difficulty, disappointment, hurt and bad luck. Between numerous calls, she related how once he was in recovery, her alcoholic father left his job as an engineer and started leading mountain climbs for other recovering alcoholics to share an experience that provides a high (pun intended by him, I would think) without the use of chemicals. He'd died two years before on a climb in Alaska trying to rescue a climber who'd fallen into a crevasse.

Dale's mother, who had deserted Dale's dad, brother, and Dale when Dale was very young, had 20 years later started making love with Dale's new husband, unbeknownst, of course, to Dale. Feeling unhappy in her marriage, though without knowing why, Dale told her mother she was going to leave it, and her mother pleaded with her to stay. This seemed very odd to Dale who thought her mother the very model of leaving behind what one didn't like. It was many years later, when her mother was living with Dale's ex-husband, that she told Dale one drunken evening that she'd pleaded with her to stay in her marriage because she didn't think she could keep this man without her daughter!

Now Dale was supporting her three small children with three jobs—cosmetologist, bartender, and caterer.

After finishing my fingernails, Dale straddled a very low bench to do the pedicure. She moved the phone close to me and placed the appointment book on a chair beside her. When the phone rang, she said, I could pick up the receiver and hand it to her and without getting up from her bench, she could write down the information she needed.

And so we passed the afternoon, alone together in the salon. After the last phone call of the day, Dale filled me in on her brother and how he had survived their difficult childhood. He had recently given up his job to write a science fiction novel. What would he drag from the world he experienced into the one he was inventing? I wondered. How we do somehow come to terms with events and fill the space between others and ourselves.

Daylight was almost gone when I left. My nails had a new life painted onto them, a life that came full of details about Dale's life. My sederunt with Dale in a town with more space between buildings than in my usual urban habitat taught me that people are usually doing the best they can against odds we don't even know about. When I left the salon, I imagined those two aged scholars in their white robes, the mountains that had seemed to view the whole afternoon scene, closing their books, thinking about a future lesson they'd plan for me.

Your Turn

Try this exercise to find material and new perceptions. Open your dictionary. Close your eyes. Point your finger somewhere on the page. Open your eyes and look at where your finger points on the page. If you are pointing at a word you don't know the meaning of, write this meaning down. If you need to repeat the exercise to find a word you don't know, do it now.

Next, think of anecdotes that illustrate the way the notion inherent in your word's definition operates in your life. When one of these anecdotes inspires you, start to write. Introduce the word and its meaning when it feels appropriate.

Letter to a Perfectionist—Exercise on Correspondence
As Creative Nonfiction by Meg Files

Author of *Write from Life* as well as novels, creative nonfiction, and poetry, Meg Files has helped hundreds of students write and publish their writing, and she always takes their concerns seriously. When one student's problem with writing lingered with her, Meg wrote a letter in which she imagines herself offering this student standard, useful words of writing wisdom. Once she writes those words, however, she knows that they do not quite address the real issue of the student's block. With the help of a poem she admires, Meg explores the reason she resonates with this student's particular writing problem.

While you read and receive encouragement from Meg's meditation, pay attention to the way she combines the occasion of addressing a particular person and admiration of a great poet's writing to explore a problem and come to insight. As you read Meg's letter, look for the turning point where she goes from describing the reason she is writing to figuring out an answer for herself, as well as for the person she is addressing:

Letter to a Young Perfectionist

Dear Chet,

"If it is in you to write, you will continue to write." I quote this from a *New York Times Book Review* article about rejection. I mean it to lend the courage to persist in the face of the world's (or your family's) failure to appreciate your poems and stories, in the face of the self-doubt that shivers through most writers now and then, or daily.

But then you are intense and gifted, stopped not by anyone's rejection or doubt but by Life: Life as it is visited by the perfectionist. Your studies, your responsibilities, your work consume your time, though your time wants to be eaten by writing. And if Life won't stand still long enough to allow for the perfection of the work before deadline, then in despair you are ready to give up.

I'd give a different student some ready answers: That's okay, show a draft, we have to do the crummy work to get to the good stuff, turn off the judgmental editor in your head, you're writing something and that's what matters, you're building skills, so every story isn't perfect, so what, if you write only twenty minutes a day those pages will pile up, give yourself a break, cut yourself some slack, you're only human.

But your frustration so echoes my own that I can't offer up the easy answers.

If we aren't continuing to write, then does that mean it isn't in us to write? The *New York Times* fails to address the question.

My life is crowded with work, most of it work I love. I won't take space to list it all, for I'm the one who loves it and the recitation would sound like bragging or whining. All perfectionists have their lists. Into my crowded life, I cram extra projects, projects I want to do. (And I'm the only one who can do it all just the perfect way I want it done. Go ahead and make fun, it's still the truth.) The rest of the good life—a hike with the dog, dinner made from a friend's garden produce, a hand-holding movie, books and books and books—is guilty indulgence that we perfectionists can't give ourselves up to wholeheartedly. And writing?

If it is in us to write (and, truly, we know that it is), then why aren't we continuing to write?

When I look to poetry for answers, I linger over my favorite Andrew Marvell poem, "To His Coy Mistress." In it, the suitor argues to his beloved that if they had all the time in the world, he'd lavish his full, slow attention on her because she deserves this. Two years for each breast. But. There's always a "but." "But at my back I alwaies hear/Times wingéd chariot hurrying near." Think of it: It is our beloved writing we wish to lavish long attention on, but always, always frantic duty crowds us.

And what is ahead according to Marvell? "And yonder all before us lye/Desarts of vast eternity."

I hear no promise that beyond the grave I'll have a celestial computer that will never crash or fail to save my heavenly creations. The truth? ". . . into ashes all my lust." It's a grim picture: time's a-wasting, and then we die.

Even so, I don't think the issue for perfectionist writers is really time. The perfectionist can't turn in a half-assed biology report, can't delegate: everything must be just so. We live with such intensity (I almost wrote "ferocity") that the intensity that should be hoarded for writing is depleted. We allow this activity to substitute for engaging in the true intensity of our writing. Perhaps we are afraid. Perhaps we hide in perfectionism, its safety. And we go about choosing our lives, day by day, year by hurrying year.

The answer to denying ourselves the time to write is not to provide ourselves excuses to do slipshod work but to be honest. Each of us must examine our lives and ourselves (and preferably in writing!) to find our fears and make the choices that will lead us to the courage to change our ways.

We may decide to stop and smell the roses. It's trite, it's clichéd, it's simplistic. Nevertheless, what doesn't have to be done perfectly, what truly could ease us, is what we put aside to accomplish everything else. But we can choose not to. Sometimes the rose will smell like the desert after rain, sometimes like a lover's hair. Sometimes, many times, it will smell like paper. The choice to be attentive to the person or page before us places us right in the present.

Attentiveness won't stop time, but it lets us live it more deeply. Marvel writes: "though we cannot make our sun/Stand still, yet we will make him run." With these lines, we are back to intensity: now not the frantic, frustrated variety, but a quiet, aware wakefulness. And I believe that this is the perfection we perfectionists must strive for, a perfection that writing allows in its full-bodied, fully-lived return to the moments of our lives.

This along with our awareness of what Marvell calls time's slow-jawed power may in the end be the very thing that will force us to hole up and write.

Most truly yours,

Meg Files

Your Turn

Addressing a specific person who has ignited a need in you to examine an issue or reveal a passion can help you write creative nonfiction in the traditional form of an open letter.

When have your emotions and thinking been hooked by someone else's difficulty or questions? Write down a list from the past or the present. Then try addressing a letter, one you don't necessarily have to intend on sending, to this person. In it, tell the person what most people might say are reasons for the difficulty they experienced or are experiencing. Tell them why this wisdom doesn't work for you and the ways you share the difficulty.

Sharing quotes from a piece of writing you admire or an anecdote about something that has stayed with you for years will help you in your search for the truly wise words from which you and your readers will benefit. When you write for someone in particular out of a desire to illuminate and explore a specific issue, you will find much to say and to sculpt into a strong personal essay.

Journal Writing as Finished Creative Nonfiction—Three Days and Three Nights

In his book *The Heart Aroused: Poetry and the Preservation of the Soul in Corporate America*, poet David Whyte talks about the mythic significance of the phrase "three days and three nights" in biblical stories. He says it means the time it takes for an initiation and may have derived from the fact that each month the moon is gone for three days. He writes, "In the course of a human life we get to know these dark phases of existence quite well. Bereavement and rejection, loss of friends, family and familiar way-signs."

You can write about much in your life by keeping a journal with dated entries. It is best if there is something in the background that you are working on emotionally—some decision that has to be made, for instance, or something that you regret that you are exploring on the page, or even the need to come to understanding about something in your life. The entries can vary—some can be short, some long; some can be poems, some quotes, some letters, some passages that are developed using the variety of rhetorical forms. This writing in fragments, but ordered by the chronology of the dates of the entries, will add up to a whole; you will have written your way into an initiation that is necessary for self-growth.

Your Turn

Here's one way to begin such a journal-style piece of creative nonfiction writing:

First, articulate something problematic for you: "Do I (or did I when she was alive) spend enough time with my mother (or father, grandparents, friend)?" "Can I do or could I have done anything about someone else's loneliness or distress or inability to accomplish a goal?" "How could I have told someone something he or she didn't want to hear?"

Think of a place you can describe well, either by going there or imagining going there. The place you choose might be quirky, like a busy corner in your town or in front of a school you attended, or at the kitchen sink or by a particular plant in your garden.

After deciding on the place, make a date with yourself to write from this place three times, at different times in the same day, or on different days over a week or even a month, each time keeping your question or problematic situation in your mind and heart. Use the place you have decided upon as a title for the journal entries: "At the Corner of Venice and Motor," "I Swing Through the Green Light and Think of You," "At This Dining-Room Table."

Each time you write, title the particular entry by date and the part of the day in which you are writing or with a descriptive phrase: "Afternoon, July 30" or "The Day That Makes It Leap Year." As you prepare to write, keep your question in mind, though you won't be writing directly in answer to it. As you begin each of your entries, describe what you see just then in the environment you inhabit or imagine you inhabit. Close attention to the environment will provide you with something to consider and meditate on. You will easily associate to details in the problematic situation you are holding in the background. After you have written for three sessions, your writing will most likely have helped you travel toward resolution, acceptance, or resolve.

Getting Started on a Book-Length Memoir

If you want to write a book-length memoir, it is important to know why it will take 250 to 300 pages to tell your story. Where does the story start and where does it end? What does the reader learn along the way and by book's end? Is yours a story of getting through major life difficulties? Is it a story of coming of age? Is it a story of danger and the effects of that danger? Knowing what you are aiming to address on an inner level helps in keeping focus and engaging readers.

Memoirist Steven Winn, author of *Come Back, Como*, wrote a series for the *San Francisco Chronicle* about his family's adopted dog, Como. When readers' responses to these pieces about the author's haplessness in being able to befriend a dog beloved by his daughter and wife attracted the interest of an agent, Winn wrote a memoir. He had to decide what his book-length story would be about. He subtitled his book *Winning the Heart of a Reluctant Dog* and wrote his way toward understanding how his care and concern for the dog, despite the dog's disapproval of him, allowed him deeper understanding of his family members.

The hardest part of conceiving the story as a book-length memoir, Winn said when I interviewed him, was:

> …freeing myself from the structure and narrative terms of self-contained newspaper pieces to think in longer, interlocking arcs. Shortly after I began writing the book, I put the *Chronicle* stories aside and never consulted them again.
>
> My thinking and technique were slower to come around. One thing I had to learn, for example, was not to give away information too quickly. In a newspaper piece, you want readers to feel satisfied and fulfilled. In a book, you want readers to come to the end of a chapter and *need* to keep turning the pages. I had to re-conceive the story of our adventures with a difficult dog, to explore its meanings and implications in our family life and how they would play out in the narrative.
>
> What you withhold can matter just as much as what you reveal. My book begins (after several different openings I tried) in the middle of a chase scene, with me in pursuit of the escape artist Como. After several attempts to lure and out-wit him on the street I was about to grab him. "I had him," I wrote of Como. "He was hypnotized. He didn't move, still didn't move. It was over. We were going home, with both my arms wrapped around him.
>
> "That's how it would have happened, I'm convinced, if at that very, perversely well-timed moment a gardener's truck hadn't clattered across Eleventh on Ortega. It was the first sign of other life we'd encountered all morning. The noise of it startled us both—the snarly engine, banging suspension, and rakes and hoes rattling in back. I flinched. Como sprang free. I sprang after him and ran."
>
> That scene takes place on Page 4 of *Come Back, Como*. The canine main character doesn't reappear until Page 55, and at that it takes a few more pages and another change of chapter to realize that this is the dog I was chasing back in the Prologue. What comes in between—an account of our daughter's childhood love of dogs, stories about the family dogs my wife and I had had growing up, and more—backlights the events with Como and adds weight and momentum to what unfolds in the chapters ahead. That could not have happened with a straight chronological approach. If you're paying close enough attention to your material, every story, every book will dictate the way it should be written.

Melissa Hart, author of *Gringa: A Contradictory Girlhood*, had published individual personal essays but then changed her mind about collecting them and publishing them as a memoir. Instead, she focused on creating a coming of age memoir. In an interview with me, which I posted on Writing It Real.com, she remarked:

> I began *Gringa* as a series of related long memoiristic essays. I pitched them as a book to my agent, but she didn't feel that they worked as such. She suggested that I focus on writing a coming-of-age memoir exploring the theme of culture, which informed so many of the essays. *Gringa* was born of my meditations on a Spanish/English flashcard I recalled from my mother's and my first Spanish class when I was nine. My agent was very wise in pulling out a theme and asking me to rewrite the manuscript as memoir.

Your Turn

Ask yourself what readers will learn about as they learn about your life: How cultural identity is formed? How trials and tribulations make one grow as a parent, husband, and person? About the geography of a part of the world? The pleasures and hardships of cultural diversity? The attributes necessary to face life after great loss? Next, ask yourself what *you* will be learning about and what you need to discover from writing a book: How to quell the uneasiness about your relationship with a family member? How to forgive yourself for some action, or how to face life without a particular person in your life? Create what could be a subtitle for your book. It should resonate with what you want to explore in your life experience by writing the book and information you want to share with readers: "A Hippy's Life Along the California Coast," "On Being the Only Jewish Family in a Small Town," "How I Dealt with Childhood Diabetes." Next, see if you can write a chapter outline—how many chapters do you envision in the book? What might the titles of the chapters be? Then see if you can write a preface to this book. Do you think you have identified your mission in writing this book? Do you see how you will approach your material?

More Ideas on Getting Started Writing Memoir

Rebecca McClanahan used interconnected personal essays to form her memoir *The Riddle Song and Other Rememberings*. In her instructional book *Write Your Heart Out: Exploring & Expressing What Matters to You*, she describes her process for writing her memoir's title essay, "The Riddle Song: A Twelve-Part Lullaby."

The process could certainly work for shaping the content and order of essays for an entire collection as well:

> ...I found I'd accumulated several short, unfinished pieces that seemed to be part of a larger whole. But I couldn't imagine what that whole might be. Rereading the pieces, I noticed certain images recurring: chickens, eggs, cherries, babies. I remembered a song I used to sing to my youngest sister; it contained these same images. The song had three stanzas, and each stanza had four lines. I wrote the first line of a sheet of paper: "I gave my love a cherry that had no stone." Then I searched through the unfinished pieces and found one that seemed to echo this theme. I wrote the next line on another sheet of paper, and continued the process until I began to see that the song's lyrics could provide the form I needed to tie the pieces together.

McClanahan offers another idea for how to look for uniting themes in your work:

> "If I could write about only one subject (or person, place, event, obsession) what would it be?" By limiting your choice, you'll be forced to bypass peripheral or insignificant issues. It's often said that each writer has only one story to tell, and that she continues to tell this story again and again, in various ways. Ask yourself what story claims your first attention rights. Mark Doty, in his poem "My Tattoo," poses the question in another way:
>
>> . . . . what noun
>> would you want
>> spoken on your skin
>> your whole life through?
>
> . . . Once you've chosen the subject you feel most passionate about, write about it for as long and deeply as you can without worrying about how others might respond. Remember, this is private writing; you don't need to be concerned with making your subject appealing to others. Your aim is to discover a subject so intriguing that you could come at it again and again, from any number of angles, and never exhaust its mysteries.

Your Turn

To find a perspective that will help you in writing either a both book-length narrative memoir or a collection of linked essays, think about a noun (an adjective will work, too) that could be your "guiding" tattoo. Use this word in a working title by adding a subtitle. Almost anything that pops into your head will work at this point: "Conscientious: A Daughter's Quest for Boundaries" or "Gardener: The Role That Brings Bounty."

If you choose to write interconnected essays, what could link these essays? If you choose to write a narrative story, what could organize your story? Try finding metaphor that seems accurate to your experience. As a conscientious daughter, I was permeable as wire mesh screening, I think, making my analogy. My metaphor includes not only wire mesh, something that fits into a window or door, but perhaps the dust and grime that accumulates in the corners between mesh and frame. These are all images that help me see what I will explore and how I might name sections of my book: wire mesh, frames, the grime in corners. When I think about being a gardener who creates bounty, the metaphor that occurs to me is the four elements: fire, air, earth, and water, to which I would add myself, the gardener, as a fifth element. I might write a narrative about how I became a gardener; it would move through the elements: the heat of grave loss, the spiritual quest for something thin as air, the grounding that planting provides to metabolize loss into spirit, the need for tears, who I am today.

The metaphor you choose will help you find the emotional occasion of your writing and help you decide on a unifying organization for your memoir in essays or, if it is a story, where the story will start and where it will end.

To Create Memoir from Fragments

In *Thinking About Memoir*, Abigail Thomas writes:

> You can put together fragments that contain moments of crisis or confusion or hilarity, or moments that stick in the mind for no apparent reason, and while they may not follow chronology in terms of time, they may make an emotional progression…

Of her memoir *Safekeeping*, turned down by her agent who wanted her to write a novel about her experiences, Thomas writes:

> My life didn't feel like a novel. It felt like a million moments. I didn't want to make anything fit together, I didn't want to make anything up. I didn't want it to make sense the way I understand a novel to make a kind of sense. I didn't want anywhere to hide. I didn't want to be able to duck. I wanted the shock of truth. I wanted moments that felt like body blows…

Your Turn

The poet William Stafford wrote a poem called, "Things I Learned This Week." He included things he observed by paying attention to what others generally don't take the time to see, such as on which side ants pass each other. He learned things from the newspaper such as topics famous people speak on. He learned from doing: how to unstick a door, for instance. And he learned about himself by noticing personal preferences.

You can also learn from dreams, from conversations with others, and from writings significant to you. Create a book title like "Things I've Learned So Far." List those things and where you learned them—make sure you have a variety of sources. You can learn by doing, going to lectures, reading, engaging with wise or incapable people. Perhaps you can make chapters titled by what you learned and arrange them chronologically, first lesson to final lesson. Then fill in the chapters with stories of how you learned what you learned. It can help to imagine your book as a long letter to someone you want to know about you and what you've gleaned.

Another way to organize a memoir is by listing the lessons of your life from small to large or by location or job or other activities. Name the lessons and write about how you learned each before ordering what you are writing in a logical way: east to west, kindergarten through college, or starter job to managerial position, for instance.

* * * * *

With these exercises under your belt, you have already created work that you can shape for publication in one of the most versatile and well-read genres of creative writing. Don't forget that exercises in the opening chapter on building your creative writing muscle, as well as exercises in both the poetry and fiction sections will be very useful. Creative nonfiction writers benefit from using lyrical sound and creating suspense, characters, and scenes. Experimenting with writing in parts without knowing ahead of time how what you create from exercises will knit into a whole will help you develop trust in your ability to make and discover meaning. Consulting Part Four on writing fiction will help you learn the art of managing time in writing, creating plot, subplot and conflict as well as creating scenes, strong characters (you and those you knew are characters in your creative nonfiction), and viable dialogue.

Part 4

Fiction

chapter 7

What Is Fiction?

I write to find out...

what I didn't know I knew...

until I wrote about it.

THESAURUS

The simplest definition of fiction is this: It is literary work based on the imagination and not necessarily on fact. Although many, if not most, writers base their works of fiction on a true-life event or on true-life characters, they write original scenes and dialog and invent or change aspects of the plot, setting, and character interactions. When fiction writers base their characters on people they've met, most often, those characters are composites of several people they know or have researched. When they base their characters on historical figures, they bring them to life with imagined as well as factual words and participation in events. We could say then that fiction (which means "created" or "to form" in its Latin root) can be made up or only partially made up—fiction or semifiction. Many fiction writers enjoy fictionalizing true events because it allows them to explore those events and the people involved without worrying about lawsuits and being blamed. Sometimes, a work of fiction becomes semi-factual because of future occurrences. Writers are often "see-ers," imagining events and characters that fit societal trends.

Although one purpose for writing fiction may be to inform, for fiction to succeed at that, it must contain a good story, one with characters in whom we are invested and situations where something important is at stake, whether the author is Raymond Carver in short stories, Barbara Kingsolver in novels, or Bruce Holland Rogers in sudden or flash fiction.

Why Do Writers Write Fiction?

Some writers explain they write to answer questions like, "How can a man be both right and wrong at the same time?" or "What is the consequence of a town loving its high school football team and games more than anything else about itself?" or "What is it like for a girl entering adolescence to be raised by her father after her mother has died?"

A succinct way of explaining the draw of writing fiction comes from Pulitzer Prize–winning media critic Ron Powers. He says it is "a way of creating a mythic truth from your own personal mythos. And the contract with the reader is that the reader is sharing your myth, and that's powerful because we are a storytelling species. We like stories."

Many fiction writers assert that characters present themselves to be written and tell the author their stories. Ursula Hegi explores this common feeling about fiction writers in her novel *Intrusions*, in which characters impose their views on the main character, who is a novelist, distracting her from life with her family.

When we write personal essays and memoir about our experience, we evoke real events and circumstances to come to insight about our lives and those of others who are close to us. When authors take on fiction projects, they imagine their way into others' lives, changing the circumstances and crafting storylines and outcomes. Fiction writers have the freedom to change all of the elements of a story to suit their storytelling needs. They can raise and explore questions that they didn't live out in their own lives.

By following invented characters as they confront and overcome obstacles, the fiction writer observes behavior and finds out what could have been true in "real" life. Many fiction writers report that by fictionalizing intense situations, they can cope in a way that truth makes prohibitive. Where a writer may not have been admitted to law school and thus not have earned the ability to sway a courtroom and the public in civil rights issues, by inventing a character who is a lawyer and can do that, the writer delivers the thinking she yearns to contribute. If growing up abused limited a writer's ability to be intimate with others, invented characters can learn how to do this. But as in all writing, even as writers know what they'd like to see happen, the characters' lives and situations begin to dictate new events and thoughts.

In his book *Ron Carlson Writes a Story*, fiction writer Ron Carlson says:

I write from personal experience whether I've had them or not. At first, this sounds like a joke and people laugh, but I'm not joking. Regardless of where I got the experience (or the story "idea"), I treat it personally; if it's not personal, I don't want to be involved. If it is solely intellectual, some concept or puzzle I'm tempted by (What if there were a baseball player who had killed fans with foul balls? What if Bigfoot stole my wife?), I will explore it until I find the personal element and something sparks. Having a feeling for my material means sending myself on each journey, whether I've actually been there or not...

Novelist and teacher Carol Bly believes, "Making up stories increases one's love of the universe generally: everyone knows that." For all and any of these reasons for writing fiction, the genre is so popular now among amateur writers that National Novel Writing Month (www.nanowrimo.org/) each November attracts millions who work to write 50,000 words in 30 days.

Literary versus Genre Fiction—What Do the Labels Mean?

Literary fiction is usually considered writing in which the author's concern is to be "writerly." Genre fiction is usually considered writing in which the plot and narration appeal to readers less interested in the literary merit of the writing. Authors of genre fiction, which includes mysteries, action thrillers, science fiction, and romance novels among its subgenres, are said to focus on plot and suspense for supplying reader pleasure. In literary fiction, even when utilizing plot devices like love stories or murder mysteries, authors say they work with the style of their language and the depth of their characters to investigate complex human themes, whether these themes appeal to a majority audience or not.

But there is irritation about what is exulted as literary and what is excluded. B. R. Myers wrote "A Reader's Manifesto" for the July/August, 2001 *Atlantic Monthly* magazine. It is subtitled "An attack on the growing pretentiousness of American literary prose":

> Today any accessible, fast-moving story written in unaffected prose is deemed to be "genre fiction"—at best an excellent "read" or a "page turner," but never literature with a capital L. An author with a track record of blockbusters may find the publication of a new work treated like a pop-culture event, but most "genre" novels are lucky to get an inch in the back pages of *The New York Times Book Review*.
>
> Everything written in self-conscious, writerly prose, on the other hand, is now considered to be "literary fiction"—not necessarily *good* literary fiction, mind you, but always worthier of respectful attention than even the best-written thriller or romance... What is not tolerated is a strong element of action—unless, of course, the idiom is obtrusive enough to keep suspense to a minimum.

Despite the distinctions critics, publishers, and award givers make, most of us strive to write well and find our audience after we have written. To do this, though, we must be aware of the fiction subgenres.

Fiction Subgenres

One way to break fiction into categories (whether that fiction be literary fiction or genre fiction) is by length. Wikipedia's entry for fiction (http://en.wikipedia.org/wiki/Fiction) includes these popularized page-length guidelines in ascending order:

- **Flash fiction**—a work of fewer than 2,000 words (but often 1,000 or even less by some definitions)
- **Short story**—a work of at least 2,000 words but under 7,500 words
- **Novelette**—a work of at least 7,500 words but under 17,500 words
- **Novella**—a work of at least 17,500 words but under 50,000 words
- **Novel**—a work of 50,000 words or more

Whatever the length, though, to be considered a satisfying piece of fiction, in addition to having convincing characters, settings, and plot, the author must create a tone or voice for the work through word choice, narrator personality, background, and point of view, as well as through choice of images and details.

From these elements, a theme develops; it is the point the story makes from the outcome of the actions, reactions, and interactions of the characters, as well as the narrator's thoughts and impressions. A writer doesn't often start with a theme in mind. Instead, the theme develops as the characters reveal themselves to the writer. For William Faulkner, according to his statement in a *Paris Review* interview (www.theparisreview.org/viewinterview.php/prmMID/4954), the novel *The Sound and the Fury* arose not from a grand idea but from the kernel image of a little girl in white clothing muddied by the splattering of horse hooves as her grandfather's buggy arrives home.

All fiction deals with the notion of "what if?" In fictional worlds, authors can make suppositions about what would have happened under altered circumstances, circumstances the author in fact alters. Carol Bly puts it this way in *The Passionate Accurate Story*:

I think that the moment we are processing or typing along and we change how it was to how it *might be*, the natural ethical tastes of our species jump in and begin "loading" the situation. Suddenly, something very electric in our minds, but which goes about under the boring title of "values," has entered. It joins the first-draft writer and starts steering the story...

The Novel

From Jane Austen's *Pride and Prejudice* to Nora Ephron's *Heartburn*, from Lewis Carroll's *Alice's Adventures in Wonderland* to *Like Water for Chocolate* by Laura Esquivel, from Sir Arthur Conan Doyle's *Sherlock Holmes* series to the recent mysteries of Janet Evanovich, and from Richard Wright's *Native Son* to Alice Walker's *The Color Purple*, we know that novels create ordinary as well as spectacular worlds, empathetic characters as well as antagonistic ones, and evoke both the baser and higher of our human characteristics. We look to novels when we want days of immersing ourselves in a fictional prose narrative with a plot that unfolds through the actions, speech, and thoughts of characters in whom we are interested.

Although novels date from early times (*The Tale of the Genji* was written around 1007 and *The Adventures of Beowolf* around 1100), it was only in the 19th and 20th centuries that the form gained eminence. From Amazon.com lists to librarian and book expert Nancy Pearl's *Book Lust*, *More Book Lust*, and *Book Crush*, we can find novels, as Pearl points out, to read for "every mood and season."

The Novella

Like the word *novel*, the word *novella* is from Italian, in which it means a tale or piece of news worth repeating about town and country life. Over the years, authors broadened the idea of town and country life to include whole regions of the world. Although the novella is a flexible form, most authors of novellas present one suspenseful event, situation, or conflict that leads to a surprising turning point. With a length shorter than a novel, the novella's conflicts are usually fewer, but they have more time to develop than in a short story. They are often concerned with personal and psychological development.

In introducing an anthology of novellas entitled *Sailing to Byzantium*, Robert Silverberg writes:

> [The novella] is one of the richest and most rewarding of literary forms...it allows for more extended development of theme and character than does the short story, without making the elaborate structural demands of the full-length book. Thus it provides an intense, detailed exploration of its subject, providing to some degree both the concentrated focus of the short story and the broad scope of the novel.

Although European authors use this form more often than North American writers, American authors do use the form, and we have studied many of these novellas in school: John Steinbeck's *Of Mice and Men* and *The Pearl*, Herman Melville's *Billy Budd*, George Orwell's *Animal Farm*, Truman Capote's *Breakfast at Tiffany's*, Ernest Hemingway's *The Old Man and the Sea*, Joseph Conrad's *Heart of Darkness* and Philip Roth's *Goodbye, Columbus* among them.

Other novellas we know well by British and European authors are: Charles Dickens' *A Christmas Carol*, Franz Kafka's *The Metamorphosis* and *In the Penal Colony*, and Robert Louis Stevenson's *The Strange Case of Dr. Jekyll and Mr. Hyde*.

Novelette

Shorter than a novella and longer than a short story, this form has been considered trivial or sentimental, but science fiction writers in particular are making use of it and believe it differs from a novella in word count only. Typing "science fiction novelette" into your search engine's browser will yield many titles. The Science Fiction Writers of America organization includes this form in its categories for annual awards.

Short Stories

As the novel arose, the short story, which had originated from oral story telling and the use of anecdotes to make a point, became more like a miniature version of the novel. Nathaniel Hawthorne, Herman Melville, and Edgar Allan Poe are among the form's practitioners who published in the magazines of the 1800s. Today, many national magazines continue to include short fiction stories in each of their issues or publish a yearly fiction supplement, but most short stories appear in literary magazines, and then eventually in collections by particular authors or themed anthologies.

Short stories may give the impression that the reader is coming in on the middle of things, because of abrupt beginnings and endings that leave readers to imagine what has happened before and what will happen later. Even so, readers leave a good short story satisfied. They feel that by reading it, something has occurred in their own consideration of human values and traits, even if the character hasn't yet demonstrated the results of new perceptions.

In fact, many if not most short stories take on the negative aspects of human existence and character, exposing frailties. As sobering as these stories are, they can also make us laugh. Ron Carlson's famous story "Bigfoot Stole My Wife" is narrated by a husband who we believe can't see that his wife couldn't stand their life style anymore; as we laugh, we are forced to consider ways in which we don't take responsibility and misconstrue the truth. Grace Paley is known for short fiction with a wry political spin. Her story "Wants" weaves a spell in the voice of a woman who raised children during the Vietnam War era; though the character doesn't quite get it, with her whimsical way of recounting her past, she illustrates the way that the birth of feminism caused partners' goals to become disparate, prompting divorces.

Flash Fiction

Many of us read *Aesop's Fables* as children and enjoyed the short, pithy moral lessons. Although many modern writers have produced what used to be called short short stories, the Internet has increased demand for this concise form, now usually called flash or sudden fiction. Ezines such as *SmokeLong Quarterly*, *Flash Fiction Online*, and *Vestal Review* publish the genre.

Sometimes flash fiction journals specialize in very short stories with exact word counts: Nanofictions are complete stories, with at least one character and a discernible plot, exactly 55 words long. A drabble is a story of exactly 100 words, excluding titles, and a 69er is a story of exactly 69 words, again excluding the title. The 69er was a regular feature of the Canadian literary magazine *NFG*, which featured a section of such stories in each issue. Short story writer Bruce Holland Rogers has written "369" stories, which consist of an overall title, then three thematically related 69ers, each with its own title.

Though short, flash fiction stories have a main character (usually called a protagonist), conflict, obstacles or complications, and resolution, even if some of these elements are only hinted at or implied. Flash fiction enthusiasts often quote Ernest Hemingway's six-word story: "For sale: baby shoes, never worn."

A Note About Young Adult Fiction

In the 1800s, Sarah Trimmer founded the periodical *The Guardian of Education* and in it introduced the categories "Books for Children" (those under 14) and "Books for Young Persons" (those between 14 and 21). Her lists established the idea for what we now call children's books and young adult books. In the nineteenth century, book publishers didn't cater to young readers, but, as Trimmer informed the public, many published novels appealed to young readers: *The Swiss Family Robinson*, *Great Expectations*, *Little Women*, *The Adventures of Tom Sawyer*, and *Heidi* were among those she cited.

Later, in the 1900s, novels such as *Rebecca of Sunnybrook Farm*, *Anne of Green Gables*, *The Yearling*, and *My Friend Flicka* were of interest to younger readers. In the 1950s younger readers enjoyed *The Catcher in the Rye* and *Lord of the Flies*. Because of publishers' marketing approaches, much fiction classified as young adult no longer comes to the attention of most adults unless the book, like *Twilight* by Stephenie Meyer, is made into a movie, or the series, like J. K. Rowling's Harry Potter books, is a blockbuster. However, there are books that have quietly become "cross-over" books, starting life as young adult novels before being picked up by mainstream publishing. Kyoko Mori's titles *One Bird* and *The Dream of Water* are examples.

Graphic Novels

Although many writers in the book-length comics field object to the term graphic novel and consider it a marketing term only, it seems to be sticking for describing a lengthy comics project to be understood as a single work. Many science fiction tales are told in graphic-novel form. Many books called graphic novels are actually nonfiction works. Will Eisner's *A Contract with God, and Other Tenement Stories* was one of the first such works to be labeled a graphic novel. Others of note are *The Complete Persepolis* by Marjane Satrapi (some of which was made into a film featuring the book's graphics) and *The Complete Maus: A Survivor's Tale* by Art Spiegelman. A new graphic book gaining attention is *The Book of Genesis Illustrated by R. Crumb*. That the form is used by authors taking on social oppression and telling stories from life as well as those writing fictional accounts addresses the form's ability to speak strongly in images as films do, but with intimacy, as only books can.

If you are interested in exploring the making of a graphic novel, read Nat Gertler and Steve Lieber's *The Complete Idiot's Guide to Creating a Graphic Novel* to learn the genre's background, understand current issues in the genre, and find instruction.

A Note About Experimental Fiction

J. Robert Lennon writes online in *Ward Six*:

> …how do you judge, say, a novel made up entirely of anecdotes about literary figures, delivered in a quasi-psychopathic deadpan? Or a short story in which all the words relating to sex are amusingly misspelled?…[The authors] are people whom you feel, obtuse as their writing may be, are trying desperately to express something that is deeply important to them, in the only way they know how. … it's the personality… the feeling that a writer is cackling as he types, thinking,

"This is never going to be published, NEVER!" It's the sensation, thrilling and vertiginous, that a writer is doing something simultaneously pointless, vital, and frightening.

Donald Barthelme, John Barth, Jorge Luis Borges, Robert Coover, and Thomas Pynchon, among others, all play with changing traditional form, structure, language, style, voice, and other elements of fiction to make readers put events together in new ways. Each of these writers has their own idiosyncratic way of structuring their work.

chapter **8**

Practice for Writing Fiction

Practicing with fiction writing exercises, whether you start with something from your life or an entirely made up situation, will give you practice in fully visualizing scenes and looking for the ways in which action defines character, skills you want to apply in nonfiction writing as well. What you learn about jumping right into a story will also be useful in facilitating all of your writing; avoiding unnecessary exposition and believing in your subject strengthens your effort. As you begin working your way through the fiction writing exercises in this chapter, it won't be long before you understand what Ron Carlson means when he refers to as exploring for the spark. In his book *Ron Carlson Writes a Story*, the author reminds us that for fiction explorations, we use a "powerful act of the imagination...empathy."

Whether you are starting a new story, revising an older one, or just wondering how fiction writers go about creating memorable stories, the following exercises will help. As an analogy, imagine that you are practicing to become a competitive golfer. Golfers who are serious about improving their game spend time practicing the individual parts of it—the approach shot, hitting out of a sand trap, practicing uphill and downhill lies—because they know that the total game depends on their mastery of the individual elements. That's what these exercises are about—strengthening the individual elements. And, even if you are a strictly nonfiction writer, time spent practicing the elements of good fiction will benefit your writing. Creative nonfiction is enhanced by creating a clear structure, drawing graspable and most probably sympathetic characters, utilizing dialog well, writing in scene, and having a keen ear for tone.

As you write, you will almost certainly veer into territory you are unsure of. Keep going. You can rewrite later and apply the lessons we discuss. Some stories develop one exercise at a time and some take over the pen, and then the writer's job is to bring shape to, but not cut out, the liveliness that arrived and surprised the writer. Not knowing where you are going with an image that occurs to you or some encounter you suddenly visualize can lead you to rich material. If a cougar appears on the dining room table, deal with him. If your main character suddenly decides he or she must watch every single episode of "Friends" on DVD, write about that. You can apply the exercises ahead to help you decide what to use of your meanderings and how to make sure the material you include functions well in your story.

If you are already writing a story, keep pumping out the words and then stop to do the exercises. Or do the exercises in this chapter without having written a draft first. Alternatively, choose a story you've worked on in the past but didn't finish or are not satisfied with and apply these exercises to that story. Using the exercises in any or all of these ways, you will strengthen your storytelling and fiction-writing abilities.

Finding a Story Idea

Story ideas come from what we are passionate about and from the experiences and emotional situations we must work through in life. In *The Writer's Idea Book*, author Jack Heffron advises writers to write down the 10 most momentous occasions in their lives. To help yourself think of those occasions, group them in feeling categories: scariest, happiest, saddest. Perhaps as a young man, you were elected captain of your football team and you learned a great deal about being a man and a leader. Or perhaps as child you met your state senator and formed career goals of being in politics because of it.

Your Turn

After you make a list of your life's most momentous occasions, it's time to do as Ron Carlson does with his ideas—explore them until they are personal right *now*. "How would my leadership abilities have been encouraged or destroyed if I had had to cope with (or as) a girl on an all boys team?" "How would I really feel working amidst a group of people who seemed to me to be continually selling out?"

Write your questions down. You will keep them in mind and heart as you pursue more preliminary work for your story beginning with creating a narrative line.

Creating a Narrative Line

In his book *The Screenwriter's Workbook*, Field describes how he helps his students learn to create narrative lines by teaching them to come up with two- or three-sentence story descriptions of popular films. For the film *Body Heat*, for instance, he writes: "… a careless attorney meets and falls in love with a married woman, then kills her husband so they can be together. But he's been set up for the murder and ends up in prison, while she ends up with a fortune in a tropical paradise." Although novelists and fiction writers traditionally work differently than screenwriters, turning to Field's clear paradigms offers useful guidance in conceiving a story to go along with the question you have centered on.

Here's an example. Field describes one student he worked with who was writing a screenplay concerning a woman who was to sign treatment consent for her acutely depressed mother. Doctors told her there were two choices for treatment—shock therapy or drug therapy—and the daughter must decide what to do. The writer decided that in her story, the woman's daughter would wait and do nothing to see if her mother would respond in time. Field told his student that she had to decide if the story was about a mother recovering or about a daughter taking charge of the health and well being of her mother.

In the end, Field's student couldn't decide and ended up shelving her project. There's a lesson here for us: We must go back to the questions from the occasions on our list. If this writer had witnessed a friend having to care for a mentally ill mother, she may have wondered about what it is like to have such responsibility for a parent. She might decide that not accepting either of the two medical treatments would provide her more of a platform for exploring this question than if she chose a medical treatment. The story's narrative line might be stated like this: A woman's mother is in the hospital needing treatment for mental illness, and all the options are onerous. Instead of listening to doctors, the woman takes her mother into her home with no treatment. In a delusional state, the mother burns the house down and the two take up residence at the mother's childhood farm, where a farmhand falls in love with the daughter and, with lessons from nature, helps her with the responsibility she has taken on.

Author Nancy Lamb lets us know in her comprehensive and accessible instructional book, *The Art and Craft of Storytelling: A Comprehensive Guide to Classic Writing Techniques*, how she turned one momentous occasion from her childhood into a narrative for a children's novel. When Lamb was in grade school, her friend Patty rode her little brother on the back of a bike. When the boy's foot brushed against the wheel, a spoke cut off his big toe. While he was rushed to the hospital, Patty searched for the toe. She packed it in cotton in a matchbox, according to Lamb, and it soon turned black and wrinkled. Patty stored the toe under her bed and took it out for her friends' inspection whenever someone wanted to see it. Lamb co-authored a story with Muff Singer, called *The World's Greatest Toe Show*. In it, a little girl has saved her father's toe in a matchbox and causes trouble as part of a club.

Your Turn

If your momentous occasion was leading an all boy's team with one girl on it or being allowed, as a girl, to play on an all-boy team, your story's narrative line might be: When a talented girl wins a place on the football team, the team captain succeeds in thwarting the team's backlash but sustains his own injury in the process. The girl ends up succeeding in his place and the team makes it to the state championship game, which he watches from his hospital bed.

Choose one of your momentous occasions and the questions that arose for you. Invent a story you want to tell, one that will allow you to explore characters in a situation that propels them to action. Make sure your narrative line has an incident that begins the story, a summary of events, and an outcome.

Figuring Out a Time Frame

Now that you have targeted a momentous occasion, formulated a question, and shaped a narrative line, it's time to figure out a time frame for your story.

In traditional short stories (over 1,000 words but under 9,000) or sudden fiction (under 1,000 words), the part of the story involved is, of course, smaller and probably occurs over less time than a novel takes on (although James Joyce's *Ulysses* and the contemporary novel *The House on Eccles Road* by Judith Kitchen cover only one day in their hundreds of pages).

To illustrate how you might make timeline decisions, let's work with this story idea: Immigrant girl living in the U.S. meets a boy originally from a country at war with her native country. She decides not to follow her family's warnings and elopes with him.

If you are writing a novel, you could write the story from their meeting to their marriage and a future in which the family's fears are or are not realized, perhaps concerning the children of the couple. In a short story, you might concentrate on the part of the story where the girl must take action and leaves home with the boy. In flash fiction, you might write only the thoughts the girl is having as they ride the bus out of town.

Your Turn

Once you have made your choice about the length of the story you are writing, rewrite your narrative line beginning with where your protagonist is at the story's opening, noting points at which things happen to him or her, and finally where he or she is at the story's end.

Focus on the Protagonist, Your Main Character

As much as teachers taught us to think of literature in terms of overarching values and themes, as authors we set out to accomplish something much humbler. As J. Madison Davis puts it in his book *Novelist's Essential Guide to Creating Plot*,

> If you ask a novelist what she is writing about, she will say, "A guy who tries to rob Fort Knox." If you ask someone who isn't a novelist, he will say, "It's about the materialism of the American middle class." The latter person should be writing philosophy or something, but until he learns to love guys who plan to rob Fort Knox, he won't be a novelist.

If we succeed in our effort to keep our eyes on our character, themes and meaning will develop and become accessible to the reader. But by the time professors and critics are explicating the themes they discover, we'll be writing another story, thinking about "a woman whose husband has been leading a double life as a bank robber," rather than the abstractions "betrayal and loyalty."

In *Writing Shapely Fiction*, Jerome Stern suggests we get close to what makes our protagonist tick by having the protagonist tell an anecdote. However, it has to be one in which the protagonist feels compelled to cover up confusion, love, shame, fear, or other strong emotions. People usually don't want to see negative outcomes as their own fault; they don't want to appear uninformed or inadequate. Stern suggests we make our protagonist talk in a way that readers see what it is the protagonist doesn't want to face despite the cover up.

This writing approach may be exactly what led to a whole story for Ron Carlson in "Bigfoot Stole My Wife" (http://bumbleshoot.tripod.com/nuttiness/

bigwife.html). Carlson has his character describe the scene in his house when his wife is gone, so readers believe they see through his improbable explanation to the more likely truth he is denying, that his wife was unhappy.

> In the two and a half years we were married, I often had the feeling that I would come home from the track and something would be funny. Oh, she'd say things: *One of these days I'm not going to be here when you get home*, things like that, things like everybody says. How stupid of me not to see them as omens. When I'd get out of bed in the early afternoon, I'd stand right here at this sink and I could see her working in her garden in her cut-off Levis and bikini top, weeding, planting, watering. I mean it was obvious. I was too busy thinking about the races, weighing the odds, checking the jockey roster to see what I now know: he was watching her too. He'd probably been watching her all summer.

In another example of unreliability, the protagonist in Sarah Rakel Orton's short story "Scars and Scales" in the January, 2010 *The Sun* magazine begins:

> ...and I, ducking into shadows, carry a platter of beef roast, so raw I can smell the blood, to the edge of the backyard swimming pool. Already Dad has reached the shallow end, and my younger twin brothers, Michelangelo and Leonardo—my mother had a passion for art—are not far behind. I coo to them; their tails move from side to side in anticipation. I sit on the cement and carefully—I have learned to be careful—extend the beef into Dad's open, hungry jaws. Michael and Leo scramble over, snapping teeth and hissing.

When we read this opening, we may think we are reading a metaphor for the way an oldest daughter sees the men in her family or we may think we are reading about a family of crocodiles or badgers. We don't really know why the I, who brings the meat, sees her father and brothers as amphibians or water mammals requiring raw meat. Later, we'll learn that the protagonists' mother has died three months earlier, and this "unreliable" description of her family is a sign of the narrator's ensuing mental illness.

Think about the story in which the daughter refuses the treatments doctors advise for her mother, only to have her mother burn their house down. How does she feel—responsible for causing the problem since she took her mother out of the hospital? Afraid of being blamed? How might she excuse or explain her mother's actions? If she were forced to explain what had happened to a sheriff or the doctors, in trying to convince them that it was an accident, she might become an unreliable narrator, completely believing her story. In it, though, she might "accidentally" reveal details and perceptions with clues that her mother was planning this action, and it was not an accident.

Your Turn

Look at the story you've been developing. Think about your protagonist in any of the situations the story might entail and what he or she doesn't want to reveal. To write a monologue from this protagonist's point of view, have the protagonist exaggerate, make excuses, or lie to cover up a feeling or action.

Ron Carlson's character has to explain why his wife is not there in a way that lets him off the hook: I came home, saw my wife was gone, and figured out Bigfoot stole her because I could smell him (not how dirty his house might have been from his own messy ways); then I put a lot of clues (probably faulty, we figure) together that could have warned me this was going to happen, so now I am warning others (rather than admit his wife was sick of their life together).

In his collection, *A Kind of Flying: Selected Stories*, Carlson actually follows this story with one called "I Am Bigfoot," in which Bigfoot explains how easy it is for him to steal wives. But while we are reading "Bigfoot Stole My Wife," we believe we are in the presence of someone refusing to come face-to-face with reality.

What does your protagonist say under the pressure of covering something up? Write this and you will begin to learn secrets about your character's thinking and issues.

Drop Your Protagonist into An Emotional Moment That Will Demand An Action

Pick an emotional moment in the life of your protagonist, one where he or she is unsure, embarrassed, or afraid, and write the action of that moment. For my story of the girl leaving home with her boyfriend, it might be:

> Smita boarded the bus a step behind Zarapet, her sari too thin for the cold Minnesota night. As soon as they found their seats, Zarapet told her he was returning to the terminal for something.

After you have set your character in the tumultuous moment, write on, giving the character something to do as she or he processes emotion.

> Smita stared at Zarapet's back as he walked toward the door of the bus. One passenger pulled his leg quickly out of the aisle. Another's coat swayed a little from where Zarapet had brushed by. Smita placed the basket of food she'd prepared for the trip on the empty seat beside her. Through the window, she could

see the driver talking with a dispatcher. As she stared, she noticed child-sized handprints on the window glass beside her. Feeling as if other people's eyes were on her, she opened the food basket to check on the pot of lentils she'd cooked extra thick so they wouldn't drip as she and Zarapat scooped them with naan. They hadn't spilled over. Smelling them, she realized how much she missed her family, the crackle of seeds popping in hot oil on this rainy day, her uncles' voices as they argued with her father about soccer and politics.

Smita began counting seconds. Was Zarapet coming back? As cold as she felt, she was glad the bus door was open—there was still time for him to return. She could smell the rain. Now it reminded her of *poori*, another food her mother made when it rained. The handprints on the window beside her seemed like the prints of ghosts, of children waving to help her to see something. Clutching her food basket, she rose and walked briskly toward the open door.

In this scene, what Smita can do in terms of action is limited to what is possible from her seat, what she can sense from the seat, and what that makes her think. Writing in scene, you quickly learn that the way characters interact with an environment helps you reveal who they are as well as their dilemmas. But very importantly, it also provides you with tools for creating a world that the reader enters and stays in. In *The Art of Fiction*, John Gardner famously writes,

> The most important single notion in the theory of fiction I have outlined—essentially the traditional theory of our civilization's literature—is that of the vivid and continuous fictional dream. According to this notion, the writer sets up a dramatized action in which we are given the signals that make us "see" the setting, characters, and events.

Your Turn

Use a protagonist from a story you are working on or a character that might become a protagonist and imagine that character having an emotional moment. Give that character a dilemma and an action that is possible to take because of the dilemma. In her teaching, former editor and script supervisor Dickey Nesenger calls this the three D's: dilemma plus discovery plus decision equals action.

Now, take your protagonist from the scene in which he or she is being false, and extend the character's interaction with the environment he or she is in. There will be things to touch, manipulate, look at, listen to, taste, and smell. All of the interactions with what's around the character will be avenues for letting the reader know the character's dilemma, personality, background, and emotional state.

Try this same exercise with the character in a different situation, perhaps one in which he or she is being truthful about the very same thing he or she was not being truthful about before.

On Plot

Having worked on getting to know your protagonist and understanding the necessity of creating a fictional dream for readers, as well as working on narrative line and time frame, we'll turn to developing the plot and arc of a story.

But before we continue with exercises, I want to offer you information about structure and why we need it.

A Short Lecture on Plot

Think about one of your favorite stories. How would you describe the plot? In talking about Charles Dickens' novella *A Christmas Carol*, for instance, I would describe the progression from Marley's ghost's visit to three more visits by spirits as each bringing Scrooge's attention to more and more dire situations caused by his stinginess and uncaring. Ultimately, even Scrooge joins us in feeling the necessity of redeeming himself for fear that no one will care about his death, and that he will be remembered only for unpleasantness and lack of humanity.

What I am remembering and summarizing is both plot and arc of story: In the plot, Scrooge leaves his office alone and full of dislike for the holiday everyone else is enjoying, is visited by ghosts and spirits, learns life lessons, and awakens a new man. As reader, the arc of story takes me on a journey from feeling horrified at his indifference to others to feeling warmed by his reawakened feelings of connection and service to others. I believe once again in the goodness of human beings and the way we matter to one another. The story sticks with its audience because of Scrooge's harshness when he leaves work on Christmas Eve, the eerie visitations of the spirits, and the party at the end when he goes to his nephew's home with gifts and food.

Stories that stay with us have events that escalate in importance and give characters opportunities to act and react, reveal their weaknesses and strengths, and make turnarounds in their outlooks and behavior. But for decades, the term "plot driven" has been used to mean a story that is less than literary, while "character driven" has been used to mean a story is esteemed. The literati often claim that authors should not outline stories, but follow their characters' needs and desires. But, as much as readers don't want to experience characters as manipulated by the writer, writers can't really ignore plot and story arc in favor of totally character driven stories. We must try to figure out where we are going with something and then stay open to receiving surprises along the way, even if it means we must rethink our characters' situations. Your narrative line has already had you take steps in that direction.

J. Madison Davis writes in *Novelists' Essential Guide to Creating Plot*:

> Without a well-built plot, the story is going to sag, lean and fall to the ground. Any fiction that works has a plot, no matter how small or how simple; it's what holds the story up and allows the reader to attach meaning to the events, feelings and thinking in which the characters are involved.

To create plots that work (that allow readers to experience traits we enjoy in a story—criminal to redeemed, hopeless to hopeful, and cowardly to courageous, for instance) writers use story structure first articulated by Aristotle: Exposition, Inciting Incident, Rising Action, Climax, Falling Action, Resolution. Here's how it works in *A Christmas Carol*:

We start with a protagonist in a life context. Scrooge is ornery as his clerk leaves for Christmas Eve and family time. "A poor excuse for picking a man's pocket every twenty-fifth of December!" (Exposition)

An incident ends the exposition and starts the story—the appearance of Scrooge's dead partner Marley. (Inciting Incident)

The incident creates a chain of events in which the character encounters conflict and obstacles—the other ghostly visits. (Rising Action)

Ultimately, an event occurs that turns the tide and things will reverse themselves—Scrooge sees his own tombstone after hearing what his survivors say about him and realizes he wants to avoid his fate. (Climax)

After the climax, the protagonist embarks on another course of action to accomplish what he now sees as his goal—Scrooge laughs, praises a stranger, buys food for Tiny Tim, and raises Bob Cratchit's salary. (Falling Action)

The falling action comes to a close showing that the character has arrived at his outcome—Scrooge's joyous attendance at his family's Christmas dinner. "...and to Tiny Tim, who did NOT die, he was a second father." (Resolution or Denouement)

Many of us have learned Aristotelian story structure informally—we've read lots of fiction in various genres and watched lots of films. Sitting down to study the story structure of the fiction and films we like, we might find it easy to identify Aristotle's elements. However, when we write our own stories, we may find it very difficult to imitate the story structure we so admire. We may not provide our characters with enough obstacles to allow them to grow as people or we might not chose obstacles that cause believable conflict.

But as Anne Perry puts it in her introduction to Donald Maass' *Writing the Breakout Novel*, "Conflict is essential to story. If there is nothing to fight against, nothing to win, nothing to lose...why bother reading it? In the end, who cares? You don't; you have a better book to read or write or both."

Conflict and trouble, peril and obstacles are at the crux of good storytelling. If you make life easy on the characters, readers will not stay tuned. Readers want to find out how people deal with trouble, whether what they've done leads to a happy ending, a mixed ending, or a tragic ending. So, whether you are writing fiction or from life events, think of the worst possible outcomes of events for your character and put those in the story. If your character is in love with a woman who doesn't love him back, rather than merely having her give him the cold shoulder in the lunchroom, let their boss give them a joint assignment. How does he work with her when she is distant and disdainful? If your character lives with this mother and can't develop further in his adult life because of that, have her die and leave him the house. How does he cope?

Another powerful blueprint for a story structure is referred to as the hero's journey. In *The Writer's Journey, Mythic Structure for Writers*, Christopher Vogler sets out to explain the blueprint to prospective storytellers by using Joseph Campbell's famous teachings on myths in his work *A Hero with a Thousand Faces*. Vogler asserts that Campbell, in recognizing that myths are practical models for understanding how to live, had "broken the code of story."

Vogler explains the story code this way: A character leaves the ordinary world for a special world. He or she receives, and at first refuses, a call to adventure. A meeting with a mentor occurs, and the character crosses the first threshold into danger, where there are tests, allies, and enemies. As the character journeys further, he or she arrives at the "Inmost Cave," and after crossing a second threshold, survives an ordeal, and receives a reward. Then the character takes the road back, experiences resurrection, and returns to the ordinary world with a prize.

If you want to map out this paradigm, rent a movie like *Star Wars, The Matrix*, or *Avatar*. Plot out the protagonist's path according to mythic structure. In *Avatar*, a paraplegic ex-marine arrives at the U.S. space station to fulfill his recently deceased brother's role in a special world where he is able to take on the body of an alien being and live in an alien environment. Diagram the journey the protagonist is taking, noting the ordinary and special worlds, the mentors, the allies and enemies, and the moment when the character becomes committed to a new goal.

Thinking about the hero's journey, or even just parts of it, will help you deepen the stories you are going to tell. Your hero doesn't have to be a mythic hero, because mythic structure turns everyday folks into the kind of characters readers want to track. Your story also doesn't have to take on a whole myth. It can take on a slice of it, but knowing the mythic structure will help you understand what part of the story you are writing, especially for short or flash fiction.

So how do we get protagonists from the beginning to the end of a story and how do we motivate changes in their character and show they have changed or at least will have to change? As Aristotle taught, we do this by thinking of events as "causal"—something happens that sets off a chain of events—and by designing the intensity of events to increase until the story's climax. Events and interactions keep the character in trouble and give the character opportunities to at first act in their usual ways and later in more decisive ways.

Structure is a basic tool that the writer uses to tell a story the reader wants to read. It is the framing for the story; it makes the story a house we can enter.

When I asked Nancy Lamb, author of *The Art and Craft of Story Telling: A Comprehensive Guide to Classic Writing Techniques*, for her wisdom on plot, she sent these tenets based on Aristotle's ideas. If you follow them your story will come out well:

1. *Choose one idea, a few characters, and a few incidents*—Don't overburden your story with too many plot lines, obstacles and distractions.

2. *Create defining conflict*—At the beginning, make certain the reader understands what the central conflict of the narrative is.

3. *Use plot to translate character into action*—When the hero confronts an obstacle, the action that follows is a result of the hero's response to the obstacle. Reaction follows action. Action follows reaction.

4. *Remember that choice creates conflict*—Without choice, there is no conflict. In literature, as in life, the torment of deciding between two equally weighted alternatives creates one of the most powerful conflicts a character can confront.

5. *Use obstacles to pull story from beginning to end*—Moving from one obstacle to the next creates steady forward momentum and helps maintain a strong story line.

6. *Write with a consciousness of pacing and tension*—Increase the action ante with each succeeding scene. The initial obstacle the hero overcomes must be smaller than the one that follows.

7. *Create suspense by creating limits*

   Limit **Time**—If the hero must accomplish his goal by a certain time, day, or date, the motivation for continuing to read is automatically built into the story.

   Limit **Revelations**—Parcel out pieces of the plot puzzle one item at a time. Nothing should be solved all at once.

8. *Remember that action springs from character*—The hero's character dictates the response to the action. Action does not dictate character.

9. *Dramatize the resolution*—Make certain to play out your ending in full and on stage. Anything less cheats the reader.

10. *Make certain the hero is the instrument of his own salvation*—Throughout the story, keep in mind that no matter how helpless or hapless the hero is at the beginning of the book, he must ultimately save himself. Otherwise, it's not a complete and satisfying story.

Whether you are crafting an autobiographical story, one entirely from your imagination, or something of a mix, try your hand at growing a plot that utilizes this structure. As you write, create bounty, but remember, Lamb reminds us, "practice tough love—just because you write a scene doesn't mean you have to include it in the book."

Your Turn

Take the work you've created thus far from these exercises or take an older story you've written and not finished. Create a sequence of events that move the protagonist from the start (the inciting moment that causes him or her to enter the suddenly altered world) to the finish (she or he has learned something and/or received a treasure).

Here are questions to ask as you imagine these events:

- Where is my character as the story opens?

- What is the inciting incident that spins his or her life in a new direction?

- How will my character face this conflict? What does he or she develop as a goal and what results from having that goal?

- What happens as a consequence of his or her actions?

- What does he or she do now and what further problems does the new action cause?
- What event and consequences happen next that are of greater intensity or have graver implications?
- What is the event in the sequence that is the event of no return (meaning the character has two choices and both are risky)?
- How does the character fare? For instance, a true love says yes or no, efforts to be free of a family's entanglements succeed or don't succeed, or a jail sentence is served or commuted.

Point of View

Who is telling the story you are writing? It's an important choice because it dictates what kind of information the narrator knows, and it reveals the window through which you must tell your story to your readers.

Will your story be told in the first person? For instance,

> I had a little lamb who followed me to school one day. I didn't have time to take my lamb back home. I thought I could just tie him up between the hedges until recess. Most of the other kids tried to help me keep it a secret from the teachers, but I knew that if Jack Pratt found out, he would try to get me in trouble.

Perhaps you'll tell it in the second person.

> You have a little lamb who followed you to school. You think to tie the lamb up between the hedges until you can take it back home at recess. You see your classmate Jack Pratt sizing things up. You know he's going to make trouble.

Or maybe you will tell the story in the third-person limited where the narrator can tell the story only through one character's eyes.

> Mary had a little lamb who followed her to school one day. Embarrassed, she tried to hide the lamb between the hedges, but the smirk on Jack's face told her that her secret wasn't going to stay secret for long.

There's another choice. You can tell the story in the third-person omniscient. This way, the narrator can see from more than one character's point of view.

> The day that Mary's lamb came to school is a day that everyone in town remembers clearly, but with very different opinions on the matter. For Mary, the incident has always been a source of great embarrassment. She maintains that she had no knowledge that the lamb was following her, but only her mother and her teacher believe her to be innocent.

You can also choose to tell the story in multiple points of view. In section one, you can tell the event as Mary sees it through a third-person limited narrator, in another section the way the lamb sees it, and in a third, the way Jack sees things.

> Chapter One: "It was amazing to discover my lamb had followed me to school," Mary told her classmates, "I know that if my lamb could talk she'd say how much she wants to learn to read and write. She'd ... "

> Chapter Two: Truth be told, I was just kind of on autopilot. I wasn't really thinking about it. I regretted following her as soon as I saw the door to the brick building. I didn't want to go inside. I didn't...

> Chapter Three: The day that Mary's lamb came to school I was already in trouble with my dad. He was missing three dollars from his wallet and he figured I'd taken them. He told me that he'd punish me in the evening when he came home from work. I needed something special for myself, something to make me feel better, and getting Mary in trouble seemed like the perfect thing...

If you've done the preceding exercises, you have already adopted a point of view. It really isn't possible to write without one. However, understanding more about the choices you have in points of view and experimenting with them will lead to understanding which of them will ultimately provide the most opportunity for you in developing your story. And it will help you remain consistent in writing from the point of view you choose. Even if you are convinced that you want to write in the first person, doing a variety of point of view exercises can help you realize more about your characters.

If you are writing personal essays or memoir, experimenting with various points of view in exercises will help you realize more about your situations and your perceptions and you can then figure out how to best evoke them by using the point of view you have adopted. Also, although in memoir we expect the "I" to tell the story, we can accomplish interesting results employing second or third person.

Samples of the Different Points of View

In most first-person fiction, like *The Kite Runner* by Khaled Hosseini, readers believe the "I" speaker who guides them through the world of the story and they want to know how things will turn out for the narrator because they have developed empathy for him.

> One day last summer my friend Rahim Khan called from Pakistan. He asked me to come see him. Standing in the kitchen with the receiver to my ear, I knew it wasn't just Rahim Khan on the line. It was my past of unatoned sins.

A second person point of view, as in Jamaica Kincaid's story "Girl," can create a sense of poignancy and urgency.

> Wash the white clothes on Monday and put them on the stone heap; wash the color clothes on Tuesday and put them on the clothesline to dry; don't walk bare-head in the hot sun; cook pumpkin fritters in very hot sweet oil; soak your little cloths right after you take them off.

The use of the implied "you" in the story makes us feel the frustration of not being able to escape narrow thinking. Kincaid's story evokes the way that the speaker is held prisoner by the cultural opinions of others, and we get a glimpse into the impact on girls of such a way of thinking passed vehemently and without reconsideration from generation to generation. This second person form is thought by writers to be tricky because the "you" command is off putting, but in skillful hands and in short works it is often compelling.

Ernest Hemingway's *The Old Man and the Sea* is an example of the use of a third-person limited narrator who can see through the eyes of one character and tell us the character's attitudes, values, and needs.

> Once there had been a tinted photograph of his wife on the wall but he had taken it down because it made him feel too lonely to see it and it was on the shelf in the corner under his clean shirt.

Seeing the world from the perspective of the old man makes us feel close to him though we remain at a distance looking into his life being described by someone else.

Jane Austen's novels, such as *Pride and Prejudice*, use the third-person omniscient point of view to have us become acquainted "objectively" with many characters. This omniscient narrator knows what all the characters think, feel, and want.

> He addressed himself to Miss Bennet, with a polite congratulation; Mr. Hurst also made her a slight bow, and said he was "very glad;" but diffuseness and warmth remained for Bingley's salutation. He was full of joy and attention. The first half-hour was spent in piling up the fire, lest she should suffer from the change of room; and she removed at his desire to the other side of the fireplace, that she might be further from the door. He then sat down by her, and talked scarcely to anyone else. Elizabeth, at work in the opposite corner, saw it all with great delight.
>
> When tea was over, Mr. Hurst reminded his sister-in-law of the card-table—but in vain. She had obtained private intelligence that Mr. Darcy did not wish for cards; and Mr. Hurst soon found even his open petition rejected. She assured him that no one intended to play, and the silence of the whole party on the subject seemed to justify her. Mr. Hurst had therefore nothing to do, but to stretch himself on one of the sofas and go to sleep. Darcy took up a book; Miss Bingley did the same; and Mrs. Hurst, principally occupied in playing with her bracelets and rings, joined now and then in her brother's conversation with Miss Bennet.

Multiple points of view are used less frequently but can be intriguing when the characters have very different knowledge or perceptions. An example of using multiple points of view is Audrey Nifffenegger's *The Time Traveler's Wife*, in which the author uses alternating first-person narrations to tell the story of a couple in which the husband has a genetic disorder that causes him to time travel unpredictably. Here Clare goes to meet her future husband, whom she has already spent much time with, but Henry, in his lifeline, has not yet met Clare.

> **Clare:** The library is cool and smells like carpet cleaner, although all I can see is marble. I sign the Visitor's Log: Claire Abshire, 11:15 10-26-91. I have never been in the Newberry Library before, and now that I've gotten past the dark foreboding entrance I am excited.

Later in the same chapter, the point of view moves to Claire's husband:

> **Henry:** It's a routine day in October, sunny and crisp. I'm at work in a small windowless humidity-controlled room on the fourth floor of the Newberry, cataloging a collection of marbled papers that has recently been donated.

The third person limited narrator can also employ multiple points of view by alternating various individual's points of view. In this case, the writer must be sure to invent a pattern for the reader to identify that he or she is consciously changing point of view or the book will confuse and lack cohesion. William Faulkner's *The Sound and the Fury* employs third-person limited multiple points of view. Each of the book's four parts is told through the eyes of a different member of a Southern family in decline. The four parts of the novel relate some of the same episodes as seen from a different point of view and thus emphasize different events in those episodes.

In some stories, the narrator, usually in first-person but sometimes in third-person limited, is unreliable. By choosing a narrator who can't or won't view events through a wider lens, the author helps the reader see the irony, humor, or pathos in situations. Mark Twain's Huck Finn (www.PageByPageBooks.com/Mark_Twain/Adventures_of_Huckleberry_Finn/index.html) is one example of an unreliable first person narrator—he doesn't understand the implications of what he views in the people and society around him.

> He kept me with him all the time, and I never got a chance to run off. We lived in that old cabin, and he always locked the door and put the key under his head nights. He had a gun which he had stole, I reckon, and we fished and hunted, and that was what we lived on. Every little while he locked me in and went down to the store, three miles, to the ferry, and traded fish and game for whisky, and fetched it home and got drunk and had a good time, and licked me. The widow she found out where I was by and by, and she sent a man over to try to get hold of me; but pap drove him off with the gun, and it warn't long after that till I was used to being where I was, and liked it—all but the cowhide part.
>
> It was kind of lazy and jolly, laying off comfortable all day, smoking and fishing, and no books nor study. Two months or more run along, and my clothes got to be all rags and dirt, and I didn't see how I'd ever got to like it so well at the widow's, where you had to wash, and eat on a plate, and comb up, and go to bed and get up regular, and be forever bothering over a book, and have old Miss Watson pecking at you all the time. I didn't want to go back no more. I had stopped cussing, because the widow didn't like it; but now I took to it again because pap hadn't no objections. It was pretty good times up in the woods there, take it all around.

The story of the main character in Ambrose Bierce's short story "An Occurrence at Owl Creek Bridge" (www.pagebypagebooks.com/Ambrose_Bierce/An_Occurrence_At_Owl_Creek_Bridge/) provides an example of an unreliable narrator in the third-person limited point of view. Peyton Fahrquhar is being hanged and during this time he believes he has fallen into water, freed his hands of the ropes that bind them, and made his way to his home, his wife, and children.

> He was not conscious of an effort, but a sharp pain in his wrist apprised him that he was trying to free his hands. He gave the struggle his attention, as an idler might observe the feat of a juggler, without interest in the outcome. What

splendid effort!—what magnificent, what superhuman strength! Ah, that was a fine endeavor! Bravo! The cord fell away; his arms parted and floated upward, the hands dimly seen on each side in the growing light. He watched them with a new interest as first one and then the other pounced upon the noose at his neck. They tore it away and thrust it fiercely aside, its undulations resembling those of a water snake. "Put it back, put it back!" He thought he shouted these words to his hands, for the undoing of the noose had been succeeded by the direst pang that he had yet experienced. His neck ached horribly; his brain was on fire, his heart, which had been fluttering faintly, gave a great leap, trying to force itself out at his mouth. His whole body was racked and wrenched with an insupportable anguish! But his disobedient hands gave no heed to the command. They beat the water vigorously with quick, downward strokes, forcing him to the surface. He felt his head emerge; his eyes were blinded by the sunlight; his chest expanded convulsively, and with a supreme and crowning agony his lungs engulfed a great draught of air, which instantly he expelled in a shriek!

In fact, by the story's end, we understand that all of this was going on inside the character's imagination as the rope tightened.

Your Turn

Think of a moment of conflict in a story (or a memoir) you are writing.

1. Write this moment through the protagonist's eyes in first person.

2. Next, try the second person in a series of commands the protagonist is giving readers so they can imagine following or retracing the character's actions during the event.

3. Then write the same scene in third-person limited.

4. Try the third-person omniscient approach with an impartial narrator telling about everyone involved.

5. Then try multiple points of view in which different characters in the scene each alternate telling the story in first person; next, try using third-person limited that switches from one character to another.

6. Finally, if you'd like to do this, try writing the scene as if your narrator is unreliable—maybe he or she isn't always unreliable, but in this particular moment there may be something he or she doesn't know or want to know that makes the way the character sees events unreliable. Think of what might happen next that will let the reader know the problem with the character's way of viewing things.

You might find it challenging to create points of view that really feel different, and you might also find it challenging to stick to the points of view you are experimenting with, but that's part of learning this aspect of fiction writing. The differences can be subtle, but mastering point of view helps you create the right texture for your stories. The use of dialog can help you out here. When you write dialog into your paragraphs, think about whether you are writing inner thoughts and if the narrator you have chosen is privy to those thoughts. Think about whether the words in the dialog are ones the narrator would have said or heard in the point of view you are adopting.

Here's an example from the story I've hijacked from Syd Field's student, the one about the daughter who takes her mother home from the mental hospital, refusing to follow the doctors' treatment suggestions:

First person

I took Mama home that very day. I couldn't stand to think of her naked and wandering the halls after shock treatment like the patient I'd seen wandering the halls before the doctors could close the door to their office. They tried to tell me that the patient had taken her clothes off herself because her skin tingled and she was uncomfortable. Whatever. I believed then that I could offer my mom better help at home. I thought I'd learn about vitamin supplements and nutritious food. I thought together we could beat her depression. I felt certain about that.

Second person

You look past the doctors' open office door and you see a naked middle-aged woman screaming in the hallway. You see she's wearing only her glasses and they're askew from the way she's flailing her arms.

"She's taken off her clothes herself; the staff didn't do that," they tell you. "She's trying to keep her sensitive skin from bothering her too much." You can't believe what you are hearing. You bolt for the waiting room, grab your mother's coat and then her arm. You hope she can run at least half as fast as you remember when she was running five miles a day. You hope there's a cab at the clinic doors. You hope she'll like the guest bed in your apartment, remember the quilt she'd given you when you went to college. You experience a rush of adrenalin you hope will stay with you for months.

Third-person limited

Sally sat in the doctors' office at a small conference table. The two doctors who had been treating her mother for the last six days sat next to one another. With their blue eyes and white coats, they reminded her of albino rabbits she had kept as a child. She wanted to bolt right then, right out the door facing her. What were they going to recommend that she would listen to anyway? She rehearsed her departing lines as they spoke about shock treatment having come a long way in the last five years. And then she heard a sudden scream from the hallway. A woman stood outside the office door, completely naked, arms flailing, glasses askew on her face. That was enough. Sally grabbed her purse and ran toward the waiting area where her mother sat. She was not going to let her mother stay under these doctors' care one moment longer.

Third-person omniscient

Sally was already seated at the round conference table when Dr. Hemmer and Dr. Preen entered the alcove off the waiting room. The two were forced to take seats facing the wall while Sally could see out into the hallway. The doctors didn't like this arrangement; they didn't feel in control. And for good reason. Sally was already thinking of her departure. She would get up, primly bid them, "Good afternoon," and run to her mother, who sat a few yards away in a grey and pink upholstered waiting room chair. Before she got her chance, however, the three of them heard a scream from the hall. Sally saw the naked woman, arms flailing and glasses askew, before the doctors could swivel their heads in her direction and offer their excuses.

Multiple points of view: first person

Sally: I am not staying in this place one more second. But I'm afraid Mama isn't going to be able to walk with me out to the entrance and I don't want to ask for a wheelchair. I'm afraid they won't bring one to me. I'm afraid they'll do everything in their power to make us feel weak, to make us feel we have to stay here.

Mother: Depression hurts. That's what the ads say. It does. It's a killer. I can't lift my legs an inch or two from the floor before they ache. I can't stand the rubbing of my slacks against my skin. What do they give you in here anyway that makes everything hurt more?

I have learned from the passages I wrote that each point of view encourages me to visualize the scene I am writing a little differently. In the end, I must choose a point of view that will best serve the story I want to tell. Since I think I want to tell a story about how this young woman accepts the caregiver responsibility but will not listen to authority and has to find out whether her idea for her mother was a good or a bad idea, I will most likely choose the third-person limited or first person point of view. But I know that I will stop frequently to play with points of view to see what else I can learn about my character and the situation before writing in the point of view I've adopted for the story.

Reread each of the scenes you created in this exercise. Which point of view seems to tell the story in the most appealing and engaging way to you? Write more from that point of view.

On Building Strong Characters

As humans, we are wired for empathy and vicarious living, so we easily put ourselves into stories if we can identify with what the characters are going through in the emotional and physical situations they encounter. Whether we are reading about war heroes who perform godlike acts and save hundreds of people or the girl next door whose life-changing event is moving from her hometown to the big city, we want to consider how humans handle life. To keep us interested in reading, authors must invent characters that have complexity and inconsistencies like we do, characters that are believable and uniquely individual.

In her book *Creating Unforgettable Characters*, Linda Seger identifies six action items for writers to employ in developing characters. Whenever you feel you have not drawn a character well enough, she advises, stop writing and go back to these items. Here are my ideas about each of her six action items:

1. *Base your character on a person you observe or relate to*—Who interests you in the world? A neighbor? A teacher? A boss? A friend? Why do they interest you? Think about how being around them affects you. What in their manner, interests, and topics of conversation resonate or irritate?

2. *Flesh out your character, drawing him or her in broad strokes*—Use your imagination here, as well as ideas for drawing composite characters from those you know. What does this character look like? How does she or he dress? Where does she or he live? Who is in the family? How does she or he demonstrate a culture? How old is the character? What is the character's profession or job? What hobbies does this person have? What knee-jerk phrases does he or she use? What original phrases come to his or her lips?

3. *Find the core values of your character so he or she will behave consistently*—What will she or he fight for? How did she or he learn that value? What makes it so important to have? What does the character fear would happen if life didn't contain the opportunity to demonstrate this value? You might ask what this character most values about him or herself and what others most value about him or her.

4. *Find the paradoxes within the character's outlook to be sure he or she contains complexity*—People are self-contradictory and surprising. Linda Seger writes about a straitlaced religious professor who had been a cowboy and knew how to use a lasso. After you've figured out your character's core values, give your character an inconsistency that will lead to a trait or relationship that conflicts with the character's core values and makes the character interesting. A character might be a complete rationalist, for instance, skeptical of everything yet addicted to buying lotto tickets.

5. *Add emotions and attitudes that will round out your character*—Give your character opinions, fears, things he or she avidly practices and believes in so you'll know what makes your character sad, glad, mad, or scared. Is she afraid of spiders or speaking in public? Is he happy when he's driving an expensive car down a lonely highway? Does she play mahjong in tournaments? Does he despise golf but enjoy bowling? Does she hate packaged food? Is his pet peeve people who move slowly? Is she bent on independence and self-reliance? Is he trying hard to remain in his father's good graces?

When thinking about inconsistencies, attitudes and values, consider also that characters can have unrealistic views of themselves. A character may think she is a perfect parent when in fact she is missing all the cues a good parent would see. A character may think he is the boss of the group when in fact no one listens to him. A young woman may think she is a glamour gal when how she dresses shows she has no idea about glamour as everyone else views it. A person may think she is humble and modest when in fact she is always striving to be the center of attention. A person might be compulsively neat in the office thinking that this makes him the perfect employee, yet he can't keep his schedule straight and misses appointments.

As you write, you'll find more ways to reveal character. As you've already practiced a bit, you'll find out how, when faced with conflict or other challenges, the character covers up. Or you may find that under pressure, the character reveals a nature he or she doesn't display during more normal times. Writers put their characters in places where they will exhibit contradictions between words and actions or words and inner thought. How others respond to the character in their words and actions also helps readers know the character more deeply.

6. *Make the character specific and unique through details*—The idiosyncratic way a character sets food out for a pet or calls to her children or answers the phone is going to make that character memorable. Think about how

your character answers the door or parks her car, how he avoids or moves toward people at a meeting. Visualize this person in the world. Note the idiosyncratic parts of his speech and gestures. These little things build up to flesh out a character.

In addition to the protagonist, another important character is the antagonist, whose actions thwart the desires and needs of the main character. You also need to round out this person and make sure that his or her actions will be coming out of a life filled with goals, feelings, obsessions, and desires. One-dimensional people are not very interesting. Create an antagonist who has surprisingly pleasing traits even though he or she is the reason the protagonist can't get what he or she wants. People may do evil and people may be greedy and thoughtless and tiresome, but all people have something tender and vulnerable about them. I remember hearing a former Alcatraz prisoner who had served a long sentence for murder talk about how he became motivated to turn his life around after he sat handcuffed on a train ride from one prison to another watching a two-year-old boy stare at him. He didn't want to die without redeeming himself if he could. Certainly your antagonist, a mother with nothing good to say to her daughter about the girl's father, can have a moment of hoping that when they do see the father, he will be interested in his daughter.

In his book *The Weekend Novelist*, Robert J. Ray writes about detailing characters this way:

> ...you need to stay *open*...*one* way to stay open is to bring a character onto your novel's stage and see what happens once she gets there. You sketch her first. You give her a past and some dreams and a place to live and a wardrobe that fits her life-style. As she comes on stage, you take notes. Let's say she lights a cigarette. What brand is it? Light falls across the glass-topped table to illuminate a film of dust. What is the source of the light? When she leaves her chair, where is she going? Staying open means not knowing but paying attention to the moment.

Whatever way you look at it, details create the character. Without the details, the character is generic, interchangeable among stories.

Midge Raymond, author of the short story collection *Forgetting English*, says, "All good stories start with great characters—and while they don't necessarily have to be loveable, they do have to be interesting." Developing a new character, Raymond says, is "not unlike meeting a new friend":

> It's a getting-to-know-you process, and it happens gradually. First, you'll see what a person wants you to see (how he looks, what he says, what he does). Later, you learn more (what motivates her, what she fears, what she desires or

avoids). Then you can take a good look into the character's true nature (i.e., what he says and does versus how he feels—and whether these are in synch or in conflict). Once you get going, you'll likely start thinking of your own questions, particularly those that are directly related to other characters and the plot of your story.

Raymond advocates asking the following questions as you develop your character:

> How does your character react to getting cut off in traffic? What sort of gifter is this person around the holidays—generous or stingy? A regifter? What's in the glove compartment of his/her car, and what's in the bedside drawer? Who cleans his/her house? Who is the closest person in the world to your character, and who does he/she battle with the most? (Note: This may be the same person.) What thoughts keep your character up at night, and how does he/she treat insomnia? From here, try creating some of your own questions; then answer them. Once you get going, think of more questions, particularly ones directly related to other characters and the plot of your story.

To help you see your character from different angles, Raymond suggests writing a conversation between two people talking about your character behind his/her back. As a follow-up, you can write another scene in which your character overhears this conversation. How does he/she react?

In *Ron Carlson Writes a Story*, Ron Carlson uses the word "inventory." Give the characters settings and props. "When in doubt include things." He says,

> We may have Doris over the sink trying to get the lid off the espresso maker while not getting water on the sleeves of her silk blouse, and we may not know her state of mind, but at least we have that small appliance, the running water, and her sleeves to help us into the next sentence.

David Reich, author of *The Antiracism Trainings*, sums up the importance of reading E. M. Forster's discussion of writing characters in *Aspects of the Novel*:

> Major characters in fiction ought to be "round" if the fiction is to succeed, with the most important aspects of their roundness being the ability to change and learn and their ability to surprise the reader—either because they have changed in a surprising way or because they reveal an unexpected side of themselves that on first glance seems out of character but in the end makes some kind of sense.

When you write to know your character well, you will learn about the character's ability to grow and how it figures into the story and its outcome.

Beyond Protagonist and Antagonist: Your Secondary Characters

Even secondary characters have to seem as if they've come from life, rather than having being hired from a central casting agency for a short generic performance. Think of some of the people in your main character's life, people from that character's work life, family, gym, or favorite restaurant. Run some of these characters through the six action items Linda Seger suggests. You might not use all of that in the story, but all of it will inform the encounters the main character has with the secondary characters. At the start, you can't know which traits you'll use, but the exercise will keep you focused on making characters stick in the minds of the readers. The characters will add to the fictional dream you are creating, not distract from it by appearing as if they are there only to create opportunities for the main character to have someone to talk with or react to.

When you are dealing with secondary characters, Adrianne Harun, author of *The King of Limbo and Other Stories*, takes a line from Carol Shields' *The Stone Diaries* as her guiding light, "Life is an endless recruiting of witnesses."

Harun notes:

Many beginning fiction writers find it difficult to move from a situation to a story. There are all sorts of reasons for that, of course, some having to do with understanding causality, others having to do with not fully comprehending what the situation means to the characters, what the greater subtext might be.

One route to uncovering a reason and dynamic for the story within a situation is to put the secondary or minor characters to work, and to do that, first you have to get to know everyone a bit better. To see how secondary characters and stories can illuminate a larger story, take a secondary character from a chapter or story and have that character relate a memory tangential to the larger situation.

For example, say your story or chapter introduces two feuding sisters who speak to each other only through their housekeeper, whom they treat like a useful kitchen tool. You might have the housekeeper relate a memory about a sibling of her own, say a story about her deaf younger brother. Perhaps the housekeeper's brother once got into trouble while she was supposed to be watching him, but instead was intent on listening to a new record through her headphones. Or the housekeeper might recall how that same brother saved a girl's life because he was the only one to see a beam breaking in a crowded and extremely noisy nightclub. Or maybe the housekeeper's brother wandered into a bank robbery and foiled it by his seemingly fearless appearance between the robbers and the frightened tellers. This secondary story must contain a dramatic element—that is, *something must happen*. The main characters—in this case, the sisters who employ the housekeeper—must not be mentioned in this anecdote/story.

Additional Advice for Making Engaging Characters

Josip Novakovich writes in his book *Fiction Writer's Workshop* that in good stories, some characters change and some do not; the ones with constancy and unchangeability can make the story, too, Novakovich says. "The part of the character that does not conform builds a conflict and the conflict makes the story." For instance, a father who belittles his son for not having the kind of profession the father enjoys—the son refuses to be ambitious and instead of becoming a doctor makes a living as a paramedic or a fireman—learns the value of his son's job when people like his son save the father's life. The son hasn't changed and his not changing may become productive for developing the story.

Whoever your character, though, never stereotype, Novakovich instructs. We may need gamblers and misers in our stories to tell them, but we must write them not as misers, but as people "who happen to be miserly."

He uses questions like these to sketch out his characters:

Name? Age? Place of birth? Residence? Occupation? Appearance? Dress? Strengths? Weakness? Obsessions? Ambition? Hobbies? Illness? Family? Parents? Kids? Siblings? Pets? Politics? Tics? Diet? Drugs? Favorite kinds of coffee, cigarettes, alcohol? Erotic history? Favorite books, movies, music? Desires? Fears? Most traumatic event? Most wonderful experience? The major struggle, past and present?

Your Turn

To work on developing your characters, pick and choose from among these writers' exercises. If you become stuck in writing your story, you can stop and answer more of the questions or create your own: What holiday is my character's favorite holiday? Why? Where does my character hope to go on vacation? Where does she shop for food?

You get the idea. The aim is to find out enough to have your characters act believably as well as surprisingly in your imagination and in the story you are writing.

An idea for writing a story as you develop a character: Give your character an imaginary Facebook page: What conflict is brewing in his or her soul and what does he or she post because of it? What do others post back? What causes and groups is he or she asked to become a fan of? What Facebook games does the character play? I don't know if this has been done yet in short story or novella form, but I think creating a story this way lends itself to practicing good character development.

If you don't like Facebook, you can develop something similar by using the diary form—choose a character, choose a conflict facing the character, keep a log. For instance, maybe the character has just learned she is diabetic, has to cope with weight loss, and has been told to keep a food journal. What does she write in it? How revealing can you make it about her life?

The April 12, 2010, issue of *The New Yorker* magazine has a short story by Mike Sacks and Scott Rothman, all in tweets. In "Geoff Sarkin Is Using Twitter!" a groom begins updating his followers as he is walking down the aisle to meet his bride and continues through the first night of his honeymoon! Facebook, Twitter, diaries—it isn't hard to find a way to learn what your character is up to and how he or she speaks.

Writing Good Dialog

In real life, spoken language together with body language carries mountains of information and, like many if not most writers, you may find it difficult to convey the richness of this in prose. But you have already started writing dialog by doing writers Adrienne Harun's and Midge Raymond's exercises on character development. In Harun's exercise, a secondary character tells an anecdote of which she is reminded by her current situation vis-á-vis the main characters. In doing Midge Raymond's exercise, you have two characters speaking behind the back of a third character.

Now that you've written some dialog, it's time to consider what makes dialog really good. Writing good dialog means remembering that, in real life, people don't always say what they mean, don't always give the information they are asked for, or answer questions and/or react in a direct manner. ("I'm pregnant," the teen said to her grandmother. "Oh, my dear, I've just made you some snickerdoodles.") Writing good dialog means understanding that dialog is not for telling things to the reader that the author is afraid readers will miss or that the author just wants to get in there out of sense of her own mission.

In *The Art and Craft of Storytelling: A Comprehensive Guide to Classic Writing Techniques*, Nancy Lamb uses this example to show what happens when a writer puts a lesson in a character's mouth: Two people are discussing a third who smokes a lot of dope. One says she doesn't know why he does and the other answers, "I just read a study that says smoking dope changes your chromosomes—not to mention the fact that heavy use impairs your memory." The purpose of dialog is to reveal character, not the author's message, "I'm really worried about him, too."

Dialog creates mood, and it has to be right for the story and the people in it. Characters must sound like themselves, not like the book's narrator or the author or like one another. A believable character is not going to say, "I am asking for this reservation because I want to impress my girlfriend." Depending on his nature, he might say, "Do you have a table for two at 7? How about a table for one knockout beauty queen and the guy who gets to take her to your restaurant?" Or, "Come on; you've gotta have one table free."

When you start listening to people as a writer, you'll find many bright sparks of dialog among the mundane and repetitive words we utter all day long. Listen to how people hide behind their words, knowingly and unknowingly reveal themselves, and say many things without thinking. When you do hear interesting phrasing, make note of it. Some writers keep notebooks of overheard or imagined dialog that strikes them, thinking they might use it in a story. As writers, we usually take out "umms" and "ers," "likes" and "you knows." We don't have characters talk unless they need to—which means only the significant passages of what they say are included. And we are careful that the dialog we write doesn't simplify people and make them sound dull by spelling everything out. "Oh, yes, we will be there by seven on the dot because I am always punctual," is dry and expository, showing the hand of the writer announcing, "I want to be sure my character is noted for such and such." It is our job as writers to make our characters sound like people anyone might have heard, though some of their language is more entertaining or gripping than the words heard around us everyday.

In *Creating Unforgettable Characters*, Linda Seger reminds us that good dialog has a subtext, which indirectly shows what is at stake emotionally for a speaker. When people are together they say a lot of things that reveal the level of their self-esteem and perceived rank vis-á-vis others. They say things they think will be perceived as cool when they feel awkward and anything but cool. As we've practiced, they keep secrets. They may try to be polite when hostility is threatening to leak through at any moment or calm when they are worried. The grandmother doesn't say, "Oh, my, I need time to process this," or "Oh, I must stay calm," or "Oh, this is too surprising for me," but offers snickerdoodles, an action that may allow her time to gather her thoughts and reactions.

When you write dialog, think about who is talking and how what they say reveals their occupation, rank, region of origin, ethnicity, educational level, attitudes, thinking style (logical, impulsive), desires, obsessions, and concerns. Also remember, that in addition to using external dialog—words a character says to others—we can do some of our job using internal dialog—words the character thinks.

Novelist David Reich was inspired by two particular authors in his study of dialog:

> The late George V. Higgins was celebrated for capturing the speech of local Boston hoods. The main way he learned it, he told me when I interviewed him in 1985, was by reading transcripts of wiretaps while he was a prosecutor, and also by noting what people said (and how they said it) on the witness stand, especially when they were nervous and/or lying. *The Friends of Eddie Coyle*, *The Digger's Game*, and *Cogan's Trade* deal with criminals, and in all three much of the story is told in dialogue—past action is revealed in detailed conversations between the characters, essentially one character telling a story to another and the second character interjecting comments. It's a technique that Higgins more or less invented and made good use of throughout his career.
>
> In addition to Higgins, I've looked closely at the Flannery O'Connor short story "The Displaced Person," which features a variety of dialects, including southern black farm worker, southern white farm worker (and even gradations within this group, from less to more respectable yeoman), southern landowner, Catholic priest (apparently Irish in origin but living in the South), and finally eastern-European immigrant.

In studying dialog, I very much enjoy James Baldwin's use of outer and inner dialog in the short story "Sonny's Blues," where Baldwin portrays a main character's sadness and anxiety. In the story, a teacher, who is the older brother of an incarcerated man, has a surprise visit from his brother's ne'er-do-well childhood friend. The main character speaks first here, not really wanting to have this exchange with the visitor:

> "Look. I haven't seen Sonny for over a year, I'm not sure I'm going to do anything. Anyway, what the hell can I do?"
>
> "That's right," he said quickly, "ain't nothing you can do. Can't much help old Sonny no more, I guess."
>
> It was what I was thinking and so it seemed to me he had no right to say it.
>
> "I'm surprised at Sonny, though," he went on—he had a funny way of talking, he looked straight ahead as though he were talking to himself—"I thought Sonny was a smart boy, I thought he was too smart to get hung."
>
> "I guess he thought so too," I said sharply, "and that's how he got hung. And how about you? You're pretty goddamn smart, I bet."
>
> Then he looked directly at me, just for a minute. "I ain't smart," he said. "If I was smart, I'd have reached for a pistol a long time ago."

"Look. Don't tell me your sad story, if it was up to me, I'd give you one." Then I felt guilty—guilty, probably, for never having supposed that the poor bastard had a story of his own, much less a sad one, and I asked, quickly, "What's going to happen to him now?"

He didn't answer this. He was off by himself some place.

"Funny thing," he said, and from his tone we might have been discussing the quickest way to get to Brooklyn, "when I saw the papers this morning, the first thing I asked myself was if I had anything to do with it. I felt sort of responsible."

I began to listen more carefully.

> As readers we assume characters look and move certain ways as they speak. But if the writer points out what they are doing with their bodies, it may contradict what we think and help us understand subtext. A man nervous about meeting a blind date might ring her bell and awkwardly hold flowers obscuring his face while he says, "You look just like Sally said you would." This could indicate his fear about how she'll like his looks.

Your Turn

Using your story characters, try this exercise Lisa L. Owens, author of *Frenemies: Dealing with Friend Drama*, uses to focus her students on getting comfortable using dialogue that they can build into a story:

> Spend five minutes writing a scene or complete short-short story using nothing but dialogue. No narrative or description allowed. Start your dialogue with the statement below and see where it takes you. Imagine that the first speaker is a 12-year-old boy.
>
>   "I don't want to."
>
> Decide who he is talking to and what that person has to say about what he doesn't want to do. Write without stopping. Have fun and try not to overthink the process—just see what comes out. At the end of five minutes, put down your pen/take your hands off the keyboard.
>
> Take a quick moment to think about how different your dialogue might be if you kept the same basic situation but made the first speaker a 12-year-old girl. Who is she talking to and what is that person's response to what she doesn't what to do? Now try that. Write for another five minutes. And remember, no stopping, no editing.

Now using the same characters, try this exercise inspired by Janice Eidus, author of *The Last Jewish Virgin* and *The War of the Rosens*:

> Write a story with two characters, in which much of what they say to one another is a lie. What is the characters' motivation for lying? Do they believe one another's

lies? If so, why? If not, why not? Using italics, write the internal thoughts of the characters as a kind of dialog to let the reader know the answers to these questions. Inner dialog is most interesting when it contradicts the outer dialog.

Try one or more prompts from this list I've created to get your characters speaking:

- It's like this whenever I...
- Come on. Let's...
- What about [those Mariners or the time you...]
- Aren't you going to tell her/him we're going to be....
- I told you I was voted best...
- If I've told you once, I've told you a hundred times...
- Where did you think I was going to get something like that?
- If I had a pink suitcase [tickets to Hawaii, a cigar to smoke], I'd...
- One of these days, I'm going to [or not going to]....
- Hardly anyone knows this about me. Well, I can't say it out loud really, so let me tell you how it happened....
- It isn't really as horrible as it sounds [looks]. I can explain....
- Look, I love you, but....
- I'm tired of you telling me that....

Finally, try your hand at alternating between inner and outer dialog. Put your character in a position of having to convince others in the story to do or buy something. What does he or she say to the others? What does he or she think as she is talking and hearing and seeing the others' responses and expressions?

Don't forget to also give the character something to do. Sip or gulp coffee? Stack and restack papers on a desk? Pace? Count the leaves on the wallpaper?

Evaluating and Fixing Your Dialog

The more practice you give yourself writing dialog, the more natural it will seem to use it in your storytelling. And the more direct speech you have in your fiction, the more immediate the story. If you start writing stilted dialog, finish a scene and then go back and fix the dialog. Finding the places where the character doesn't sound like him or herself, and the places where you the author or your narrator have decided to put message words in the characters' mouths instead of using other story elements, will help you write more fully and engagingly.

As Thaisa Frank and Dorothy Wall write in *Finding Your Writer's Voice*:

> Surrendering to your characters takes a leap of faith: You must believe that their thoughts, words and actions will convey the story adequately, so the reader "gets it." But it's precisely this surrender that gives them a chance to become themselves. At the same time that you find your voice, you relinquish voice to your characters.

Your Turn

If you have questions about when to use dialog, how much dialog to put in a story, and what the general purpose of conversation is in your story, go with what happens naturally as you write. Then show early drafts to trusted readers and ask them where they missed hearing what the characters have to say and learning what they are thinking. Ask where they felt the story slowed down because of too much dialog and inner thinking. Ask them where the dialog kept them reading and where they skipped over the characters' words. Ask them if there are places a character seems out of character and if that was entertaining or places that, although the character added important information, the reader found it distracting.

Using Setting, Building Scenes

François Camoin writes in "The Textures of Fiction," a contribution to *Words Overflown by Stars*, edited by David Jauss:

> Fiction is little bits of action to keep us turning the page, to keep us moving through the landscape that is the point of the enterprise. The events and characters exist for the sake of the place; Madame Bovary is only there so Flaubert's rainy, muddy, depressing provincial town can come into existence...

Setting is the entirety of a story's locations and time periods, which introduce ambiance, and out of that ambiance comes a good part of the emotional message of a story. The "little bits of action" Camoin refers to happen in particular places. Every character speaks and thinks from somewhere. What those somewheres look like and sound like, what textures, tastes, and smells they contain help authors tell stories. Characters inhabit settings through their senses, and they make readers notice what they are noticing, projecting onto, or overlooking. What characters are doing and thinking—whether that takes place on a park bench, in a train compartment, on a cafeteria line, camping in the woods, sitting in a particular room at home, or working in an office cubicle—includes the objects and sensations from the place they inhabit.

In *Practical Tips for Writing Popular Fiction*, Robyn Carr writes:

> Too many writers think of setting as the landscape, the description, and don't use every sense. You are told about dust, but no on chokes on it. You're told about crashing waves, but the water has no temperature; no conversation is obliterated by noise. You're told about a splintered wooden banister, but if no one snags a sleeve, it drifts through your head as meaningless flab....The splintered banister doesn't matter if it has no function in the story...

"Something happens to someone (or with someone) someplace, sometime" is the way Carr summarizes the work of fiction. Setting is woven into every scene—the writer must give readers enough sensory information to answer questions like "Where is this taking place?" "What time of day is it?" "Does the character like or dislike the place he or she inhabits?" Writers have to show readers how a place affects the story's characters, thoughts, and actions.

If the writer doesn't fully imagine the story's scene settings, readers will feel uninformed, confused, or inattentive. The writer must incorporate what the character touches and sees, hears, tastes, and smells in a scene and imagine what in the environment helps or interferes with what characters want and can do. And writers must seek out what in an environment catches or escapes their characters' attention. When a character has a reflective moment, the writer figures out how what the character takes in through the senses becomes part of the character's thinking.

Kinds of Scenes

Now that you've thought about the images you can harness for writing scenes and ways to plunge right into a scene that contains high emotion, consider that most stories have a variety of kinds of scenes that move the story forward.

In *Fiction Writer's Workshop*, Josip Novakovich names three kinds of scenes: (1) summary, (2) silent, and (3) big. Summary scenes and silent scenes lead up to the big scenes, the ones that use the most dialog and/or description, the ones that happen uninterrupted by the author filling in information. That information is delivered in the summary and silent scenes that precede the big scenes.

The summary scene sets up an action we can expect repeats itself over time. For example:

> She talked to her mother every Sunday evening on the dorm floor's one phone; she curled into the cement block wall, her right heel popping out of her untied Clark's desert boot, as she talked and hoped not to be overheard.

The silent scene contains a description of actions that aren't repeated ones but help move the story along. Here is another example I've written:

> I am so close to him that I feel his breath moving my hair. My whole body wants to be his but we do not touch. I hear the bell of the elevator arriving at my floor. I hope he is looking at me as I walk in what I imagine is a sultry fashion through the open doors, glad I've worn the black skirt with the high slit over my calves. As I exit the elevator, I smile at a man holding the door for his office mates who are still down the hall, though I am miffed as I walk ahead to the water fountain; the man I want so desperately will have a harder time seeing me through the doors when I bend over for a sip of water, swiping my hair over my shoulder.

And the big scene, Novakovich tells us, happens when you know your characters and their conflicts and put them in harm's way (whether that's meeting the teacher who is down on them, fighting the bully, walking out on a jealous husband or giving in to intimacy with a peer at work). Here you will write, no matter what point of view you've chosen and what tense, what the action is by having the characters speak and do things in the course of the scene.

Here's a "big" scene I wrote for a short story:

> The lights went up slightly, signaling the last dance. In five minutes homecoming would be over. *Well.* Natalie sucked in her breath. *It's now or never.* As the band began their rendition of *Love Me Tender*, she strode across the gym-turned-dance floor, her heels clicking determinedly along the hardwood floor.
>
> "Steven, this is definitely our dance," she announced to the skinny boy with more than a little dab to do him on the lock hanging heavy over his forehead. The boy she'd hoped all semester would ask her out now met her earnest gaze with a look of terror.
>
> "I don't...can't....not a good...," he stammered, looking around as if to find someone who would agree with him.
>
> She took hold of his hand and yanked him from the metal folding chair, spilling the cup of punch he'd put beside him on the table.
>
> "I don't dance. I mean I can't..." his voice trailed off like the puddle spreading under the table.
>
> Afraid if she let go of his hand he'd flee, Natalie kept her grip and tried to lead him in the waltz. He was the only boy who seemed to notice that she was alive and now that she had his hand, she wasn't going to let go. She ignored the mess on the floor, red as his cheeks had become.

"I....I....I can't," he stammered again, shuffling his foot a couple of inches forward, which turned out to be just far enough for Natalie to waltz onto it full force.

Embarrassed by her clumsiness and her forward behavior, Natalie blurted, "You keep staring at me in biology and in math! Why don't you talk to me? You can take me to a movie or something. Why don't you ask me out?"

Steven's eyelids fluttered. Waiting for an answer, Natalie noticed Brylcreem smudges on his forehead. They looked like fingerprints on her class slides.

In building scenes we learn to use direct dialogue, physical reactions, gestures, sights, smells, sounds, and thoughts. As Jerome Stern writes in *Making Shapely Fiction*:

> When you want to make a scene in your writing, render the sensations fully so that readers cringe at the slap in the face, hear the whimper of pain, see her elbow hit the blue chair, and feel your character's rage and frustration.

Your Turn

Think about the story you are writing and try your hand at least one of each of the three kinds of scenes: summary, silent and big. If you have a draft of a story, look at it and decide which of your scenes is a summary scene, which a silent scene, and which a big scene. Then decide if they should be the kind of scenes you've made them. If not, convert the scenes into the appropriate kind.

Revising: Check Your Scenes for Action, Wants, and Subtlety

Jordan Rosenfeld, author of *Make a Scene: Crafting a Powerful Story One Scene at a Time*, thinks of scenes as using different amounts of the same ingredients, depending on the use of the scene toward the story's goals. One ingredient is what the characters want, both overall in the story and in any particular scene. Another ingredient is action. Something has to happen in a scene. "Scenes function as a bit of a chain reaction; one scene builds upon another, upon another, upon another until we get a full sense of the world" inside the story. A third ingredient is subtlety.

Your Turn

When you are revising what you have written, go through your work and see where you might build longer scenes rather than move through events too quickly for the reader who wants to feel as if he or she is in the scene with your characters. Think about where events lend themselves to slowing time down and moving the reader closer to the emotional core of your story.

Look for places that you have created repetitive scenes when one summary scene can let readers know something about your character's personality or dilemma.

Look to see if you emphasized scenes with dialog when they would serve the larger story better as silent scenes.

Finally, locate the places where protagonist and antagonist face off or where an insight is arising for the protagonist. Practice combining dialog with images from the place the scene is happening to build a long scene that reads as if the action is happening in the now of the story.

Working on Subplots

What is a subplot? It is a smaller story inside a larger story and it illuminates the life, times, personalities, themes, and issues of the main characters, often by introducing peripheral characters and events.

In novels (and in films) subplots are typically the place that readers make their identification with the main character. Writing for the website helium. com, freelance editor Leigha Comer writes about the wildly successful Harry Potter novels:

> How many people reading these books can sit there and understand how it feels to have a crazed, evil wizard try to kill us? Probably not too many. But how many of us know how it feels to lose a loved one, to have a crush, to fight with our best friends, or to despise someone so much that we consider them our greatest rival? Without its subplots, I can guarantee that the Harry Potter books wouldn't be the success that they currently are. While none of us can go to Hogwarts, or pick up a wand and perform magic, we can still identify with Harry and other characters in the books. And with all of these different things going on in Harry's life, and all the day to day problems, it becomes believable and true to real life.

Comer reminds us that in life, we are never confronting a single problem. Even as our boss is making life miserable for us, we also have situations in our personal and social lives. That's what makes life interesting and seeing the main characters in several aspects of their lives makes them believable to us. How they cope in the many aspects of their lives helps us understand them better. Is the person who has the difficult boss, Comer asks, ignoring her children and husband to show she can do the job at work?

I think of the television series *Nurse Jackie* here. The main character's work with patients and co-workers at a hospital is the main plot. Her life with her two daughters and her husband is a subplot. The way she seems always to half-heartedly spend time with them as opposed to her deep involvement in the high stakes world of the ER where she works informs readers about who she is and the risks of doing the kind of work she does. She has many secrets concerning drug and sex addiction, and as she tries to compartmentalize them in the different areas of her life, they threaten to get out. This adds suspense for the viewer.

Even in short fiction, which usually doesn't have well-developed subplots and focuses on one event, thinking about the character's life outside the event pays off. Comer asserts that "when writing your story about a person on a sinking ship, don't concentrate solely on the fact that the person needs to escape. Add some internal dialogue about that distant lover, and make it so that the urge to be together fuels your protagonist's will to live."

Your Turn

Here are two exercises in which you can gain practice with subplots by writing subplots that are missing from stories you know. In addition to gaining practice with subplots using the exercise ideas, you might also find you can develop the exercises into short stories of their own.

1. Do you remember the classic short story "The Lady, or the Tiger" (www.eastoftheweb.com/short-stories/UBooks/LadyTige.shtml) by Frank Stockton? In it, a king has a particular method of dealing with those he doesn't like—they must go into a ring and choose one of two doors— behind one is a beautiful lady and behind the other, a ferocious tiger. When the king discovers that his daughter is in love with a young man who is below her royal station, he wants to get rid of him by putting him in the arena, to either be torn apart by a tiger or married to a beautiful maiden of his station.

   "The ranks of maiden youth and beauty throughout the land were carefully surveyed by competent judges, in order that, the young man might have a fitting bride in case fate did not determine for him a different destiny." We learn that ultimately the maiden chosen is one the princess believes she has seen making flirtatious gestures to the young man. The princess has gotten word to her lover that she will know what is behind which door and signal him which to choose. He assumes she means the one with the maiden. But the author asks us to think about which we think she would choose—one that allows her lover to have a life with someone else or the one that will destroy him because of her jealousy.

In the story of the king's intervention between the lovers, there is to be a search for the beautiful woman who is suitable for the lover, but the search is not written. The princess figures out a way to learn what is behind each door, but we don't learn what that way is. The daughter and the father don't interact about his decree.

For practice with subplot, read "The Lady, or the Tiger" and imagine where you might fill out the story. You could write the story of the men who must search for the maiden who will be behind the door. You could write the feelings and thoughts of the maiden chosen to be behind the door to illustrate her knowledge of and troubles with the princess. You could write interactions between the king and the princess. You might figure out where the queen has gone and what she has to say.

2. Do you know the play *Rosencrantz and Guildenstern Are Dead* by Tom Stoppard? In it, the playwright builds a plot using two of *Hamlet's* minor characters, schoolmates and friends of Prince Hamlet. The action of Stoppard's play is described as taking place "in the wings" of Shakespeare's play, with occasional appearances by *Hamlet's* major characters in fragments of the original play's scenes. Rosencrantz and Guildenstern are, of course, confused by events that they did not participate in during Shakespeare's *Hamlet*. This clever idea for a play helps illustrate subplot because it reverses what we normally view—events involving the play's main characters become a subplot and the minor characters take center stage.

You can borrow this idea for a writing exercise: Find or create a minor character for a story you have read—the kid across the street or a dog-walker who passes by each day, or an unhappy worker, for instance.

Write about an event in the story from this minor character's point of view. What was this character doing at the time of the events? What was happening in his or her own life at the time? Why is talking about this event important to the minor character if at all?

If you'd like, write a scene in which the main character does what he or she always does—writes a book, runs a company, keeps house—and comes up against obstacles you plot—writer's block, a difficult worker, something going wrong with the kids or the plumbing. Write a subplot in which the main character meets the minor character you have expanded or invented. What happens that illuminates the main characters' concerns? What happens that ultimately helps the main character overcome an obstacle? What happens that keeps the main character from overcoming an obstacle? You may have a good story there.

More on Subplots

There are several kinds of subplots. Parallel subplots go on for awhile in parallel, allowing the author to tell a story from more than one point of view. Mark Twain's *The Prince and the Pauper* (http://books.google.com/books?id=0ubs8rj-h1QC&printsec=frontcover&cd=1&source=gbs_ViewAPI#v=onepage&q&f=false) has parallel stories as the boys trade lives and live in the situation they each thought they wished to live in. Hailey Mills's movie *The Parent Trap* has a similar turn of events, as twins meet at summer camp but return to one another's home, unbeknownst to the parents. Of course, the main plot is the story about what happens as a consequence of the trading.

Episodic subplots form a chain of adventures involving the main character; these are stories in and of themselves, and readers follow the character's journey through these adventures to safety and/or home. Stories with episodic subplot structure that we've read in school are *A Thousand One Arabian Nights* (http://books.google.com/books?id=xSIYAAAAYAAJ&dq=A+Thousand+One+Arabian+Nights) and *The Odyssey* (http://books.google.com/books?id=ezJJA AAAYAAJ&printsec=frontcover&dq=The+Odyssey&cd=1#v=onepage&q&f=f alse). Imagine the Harry Potter stories presented in one novel instead of a series; they would be episodic.

Some stories, such as *Catcher in the Rye* by J. D. Salinger, are told entirely in flashback inside a frame of the present. If, however, flashbacks are not the whole story, they can be considered a kind of subplot. Authors warn, though, that using flashbacks is risky because they interrupt action in the now of the story, which can frustrate readers. Still, well-placed flashbacks help readers accumulate knowledge of the character motivations. When post-traumatic stress disorder is a part of the main character's life, for instance, events in the now of the story set off memories from before the story began. Seeing aspects of the character's life in well-placed flashbacks can inform the story, build interest, and set up suspense about what the character will do given the back story.

In the novel *Flash Forward* by Robert J. Sawyer and in the recent television series loosely based on the novel, writers have played with the concept of flashbacks by using flashforwards. In the story, everyone on earth becomes unconscious at the same time and sees themselves in a situation that will occur in the future; it is presumed that those who didn't see themselves in the future will be dead. The stories that come of characters trying to find others who were in their flash forwards, and of characters trying to ward off what will happen to make them lose their lives, create subplots, while the main story is about a core group of FBI agents trying to figure the event out and prevent it from happening again.

Your Turn

Here are exercises to help you play with parallel, episodic, and flashback/flashfoward subplots. Again, the writing you produce will not only help you build subplot writing skills but may also become short fiction of its own. If you choose a character from an old short story written in English around which to develop a subplot, you will probably find that the short story is out of copyright and in the public domain. You could write an original piece inserting your subplots into the main story. Come up with a great title, and you'll have something interesting.

1. *Flashbacks/Flashforwards*—Think of a time in your character's life or in the life of a character from literature that occurred several years before the story starts. What in the character's life today makes him or her remember that time? Write a piece in which the character indulges him or herself in memories of that time. If you take a character from literature, practice putting pieces of the flashback into the action of the published story.

    Think about what the character you've chosen might have a premonition about. Write a piece about that premonition. Fully imagine the scenes in the premonition as well as the character's reactions. Can you put pieces of the premonition into the main story?

    By thinking about how your character deals with the memories and premonitions, you may create a story made of two parts, flashback and flashforward; or you might be writing one that entwines flashbacks or premonitions into a larger story.

2. *Parallel Subplots*—Think of two minor characters from a story you've written or one you've read. Write two parallel subplots concerning their individual lives when they are "off stage" in the story they came from.

For instance, in "The Inn," a tale by Guy de Maupassant, a mother and her daughters hike with a young Swiss man named Ulrich Kunsi to their family's inn in the mountains. Kunsi will be caretaking the inn over the winter along with an older man named Gaspard Hari, while the family remains in the village. Kunsi takes an instant liking to one daughter in the family and spends his winter longing for her. One day, Hari leaves the inn to do chores and doesn't return. Kunsi searches and searches for him, but to no avail. For the rest of the winter, Kunsi believes he hears Hari moaning nearby. In spring, after the roads are clear of snow, the family returns to the inn and finds Kunsi has gone mad.

Choosing characters from this story, you could write parallel subplots that involve the daughter in the village and how she is longing for Kunsi just as he longs for her, or about Hari, who haunts Kunsi. Or you might write two parallel subplots in which each character is, in their own way, as isolated as Kunsi is at the inn—perhaps the daughter is isolated from her family for emotional reasons and Hari is isolated from the inn due to ice and weather or a fall. What do these characters think, see, feel, deal with, and remember? When will you have the characters' lives intersect or become linked and how?

3. *Episodic Subplots*—To practice writing episodic subplots, think of a character on a journey. This character can be on a simple journey that becomes complex. In a children's story, for instance, a mother might tell her child it is time for the child to get into pajamas for bedtime. While the mom is finishing washing the dishes, the child may journey from the kitchen to the bedroom, but have many adventures on the way—feeding goldfish, playing with a dog, completing a puzzle, dreaming about climbing a tree that is outside the house, and so on. Maybe the pajamas are in the laundry basket in the basement of an old house, and the journey involves getting to the pajamas and having spooky adventures on the way. Or maybe the pajamas are on a clothesline outdoors, and the adventures involve noticing the outdoors and creatures in it in a new way.

An adult journey might be something like this: A wife asks her husband if he brought home something he promised to get while on a business trip, and he says he didn't. When she asks "How come?" he can relate a series of adventures that kept him from completing the task, entertaining her and easing her annoyance.

Writing subplots for fun will help you learn to fill out the stories you create, whether they are short or longer fiction.

Setting the Tone of Your Story

What is tone? It can seem a hard element to isolate, but we definitely know it when we read it. Compare these two descriptions of the same event:

> The protest erupted into violence today as police attempted to keep the entrance to the building secure.
> When they reached the building, the police unleashed their forces and the peaceful demonstration gave way to confusion and chaos.

In the first sentence, readers are told violence erupted against police who were doing their job. In the second one, readers are told that the police rushed the demonstrators, an action that created the violence that occurred. As readers, we are given two very different attitudes toward the demonstration and what happened.

Wikepedia popularizes this idea:

> [Tone] encompasses the attitudes toward the subject and toward the audience implied in a literary work. Tone may be formal, informal, intimate, solemn, somber, playful, serious, ironic, condescending, or many other possible attitudes.

In his list of writing devices (http://www.scribd.com/doc/24864456/Literary-Devices), teacher and writer Jay Braiman describes tone this way:

> [Tone is an] apparent emotional state, or "attitude," of the speaker/narrator/ narrative voice, as conveyed through the language of the piece. Tone refers *only* to the narrative voice…
> *The poem has a bitter and sardonic **tone**, revealing the speaker's anger and resentment.*
> *The **tone** of Gulliver's narration is unusually matter-of-fact, as he seems to regard these bizarre and absurd occurrences as ordinary or commonplace.*

Sometimes a story's tone indicates each word is to be taken seriously and sometimes a story's tone is sarcastic or humorous or uses subtleties or under-statement to relate an attitude the story takes: In the last line of "The Story of an Hour" by Kate Chopin (www.pbs.org/katechopin/library/storyofanhour.html), for example, we learn that "the doctors said she died of heart disease, *of joy that kills.*"

Let's compare the attitude towards life in "Are You Drinking?" (www.poemhunter.com/poem/are-you-drinking/), a poem by Charles Bukowski, with the tone of the opening lines from the novel *The Portrait of a Lady* (http://books.google.com/books?id=5haFQgAACAAJ&dq=Portrait+of+a+Lady &cd=2) by Henry James. Here are some of Bukowsi's lines when he writes from bed and imagines a conversation with his doctor:

> "yes, doctor, weak legs, vertigo,
> head-aches and my back hurts."

The doctor, he believes, will ask him if he is drinking and taking his vitamins, and he will answer:

> I think that I am just ill
> with life, the same stale yet
> fluctuating factors.

Henry James writes:

> Under certain circumstances there are a few hours in life more agreeable than the hour dedicated to the ceremony known as afternoon tea. There are circumstances in which, whether you partake of the tea or not—some people of course never do—the situation is in itself delightful. Those that I have in mind in beginning to unfold this simple history offered an admirable setting to an innocent pastime. The implements of the little feast had been disposed upon the lawn of an Old English country-house, in what I should call the perfect middle of a splendid summer afternoon. Part of the afternoon had waned, but much of it was left, and what was left was of the finest and rarest quality. Real dusk would not arrive for many hours...

In Bukowski's poem, the speaker seems to drink because life is stale. James's storyteller, on the other hand, sets up an attitude of innocent pleasure.

It is easy to see tone differences among diverse authors. We must tune our ears to also notice them in our own writing when they creep in unintentionally. Therefore, it is important to examine tone in the reading we do and to get enough distance from our own work to be able to see where our tone is in support of our story and where it needs help, so the storytelling can continue to create the attitude we want readers to feel toward the story.

Novelist David Reich says of his redrafting process:

As Wordsworth points out, poetry (or to my mind, any non-critical literary writing) "takes its origin from emotion recollected in tranquility." As I put together draft 1, I had plenty of emotion but not yet the needed tranquility. The emotion in draft 1 was too raw, and thus the draft was not as entertaining or edifying as it I'd hoped it would be.

Here's how David Reich worked through a revision for tone purposes over the years of writing his novel, *The Antiracism Trainings*. Reich says:

I was angry with my treatment by a former employer and, by way of making lemonade out of lemons, decided to tap the experience in a satirical novel. (Most good fiction comes from bad experiences, I think.) I began an early draft a short time after I left my job with this outfit, but as I went to revise it, a few years later, I saw I had to calm the prose down a lot to make the writing work. That's easier to do several years after the fact, of course. An agent who read an early draft said she could see I was a decent professional writer but "couldn't relate to" my narrator. I thought about this comment when I looked at the book after it had sat in the drawer for a while.

When Reich was ready to address the narrator's tone, he took a lesson from Norman Mailer in *Advertisements for Myself*, where he discusses his revision of the first-person narration of his novel *The Deer Park*, placing early and revised versions of particular passages side by side. Reich notes that he learned how "fairly small changes in word-choice, syntax, and selection of detail can effect larger changes in the way a reader views the narrator."

In revising his book, Reich changed his narrator's personality:

[Mickey Kronenberg changed] from a blunt-spoken skeptic into someone who views the world more favorably and bends over backwards to find the good intentions behind other people's actions. That way, the reader often gets to see what's going on before Mickey does and to have a little joke on him. And it's certainly more fun than being told the obvious, as happened in too much of the original draft.

Here are some passages to illustrate how Reich worked on tone.

Passage 1: Mickey's office described
Old: It was the size of one of those musty closets where they keep a mop and pail, and it could have used a thorough dusting, but it was seven stories up and had a million dollar view of the Boston Common, where at that moment little children of all races and creeds were splashing in the Frog Pond.

Revised: I got up and paced my office floor: two steps forward, then turn, then two steps back. I stopped to look out the window, with its million-dollar view of the Boston Common, where children of every race and creed were splashing in the frog pond. That supplied a needed lift—not the view itself so much as the fact that I had the view, that I'd arrived at a point in my checkered career where I rated such a view, however small the office from which I viewed it.

Reich comments:

Instead of the blunt and somewhat hackneyed comparison with a moldy broom closet, the revised version shows you the size of the office in an understated (and I hope funnier) way, by showing the limits to how far the narrator can move in the space. ("Two steps forward," etc.) Also, the revised narration makes more of the "million dollar view," explaining why Mickey values it and hooking it into his personal story, which in turn makes him more real and more sympathetic. In the old version, it's more of a throwaway detail.

Passage 2: Mickey and his boss Laura critique Don Pulliam's column for the upcoming issue

Old: Once off the phone, Laura looked up at me and said, "How convenient. I was just about to go find you." As far as I knew, she had never even breathed in secondhand smoke let alone smoked a cigarette, but she had somehow acquired one of those great smoky voices. It made a perfect fit with her overall aging sexpot persona. "I wanted to talk about Don's column for September."

"Funny you should say that. I also wanted to talk about Don's column for September." I entered her office and eased into a chair. From this angle I could see her a little better. A well-presented Euro-American person in her upper forties. Her best feature was her bright, amused-looking eyes, the approximate color of lager beer. Such things were left unsaid at the LRC [Liberal Religion Center, the name of Mickey's employer], but I sensed that the older men on staff found her maddeningly attractive.

"What do you think of his lead? A little shaky?"

"I guess I can see why he used it," I said, starting from a place of generosity, in accordance with the First Suggestion of Universal Love and Knowledge. (Yes, I even agreed with the Five Suggestions. G-d forgive me, I still do.) "The family angle makes heartwarming copy," I continued. "Brings him down to ground level. Instant connection to the person in the pews. But I guess I unfortunately see your point. That stuff about Harvard could be read as self-aggrandizing, and the rabbi motif—he's used it before, but what if a rabbi, I mean a bona fide rabbi, or some other Jewish person, saw the column? Would it look good for the church? Would it help promote interfaith cooperation?" I was speaking with more heat that I had intended.

Revised: Once off the phone, she took a moment to compose herself. [She's been on the phone with her divorce lawyer, hence the need to compose.] "Mickey. How convenient," she said at last. "We need to touch base on Don's new column." Though a lifelong nonsmoker, she had somehow acquired one of those great smoky voices.

"Funny you should say that." I eased myself into her leather wing chair. From this angle I could see her better. Her best feature was large, amused-looking eyes the rich, warm brown of English ale. The eyes and her fleshy, curvaceous build and the smoky, aging sexpot voice.... Such things were left unsaid at the LRC, but I sensed that for older men on staff she had a maddening allure. (I exclude myself here, having recently married the exquisite Patty. OK, that's not quite accurate. Laura had a maddening allure for me, too, but I took special pains not to let it show.)

"The column isn't bad, far from it," I said, starting from a place of generosity in conformance with the First Suggestion.

"But?"

I ticked off a dozen reservations. Midway through the list, I found I was speaking with more force than was strictly necessary. I modulated down a notch.

Reich comments:

By the time the reader gets to this episode, she'll have already read Pulliam's (half-insane) column and can judge its merits for herself. Further, Mickey is more likable when we don't have to see him alternately nitpicking and equivocating, as in the original of this scene.

Tone is typically defined as having two components. The first is the narrator's implied attitude toward the subject of the piece of writing, and the other is his attitude toward himself in relation to the subject. In the original version of Passage 2, Mickey notes that some of his older colleagues find themselves attracted, against their will, to the "aging sexpot" Laura. In this version the tone can be read as superior. In the revised version, Mickey places himself among Laura's many acolytes, and the tone can be read as self-effacing.

Passage 3: Shortly before this scene, Mickey and his co-worker Ann-Elise and the rest of the trainees have been pressured by the trainer-in-chief, Alfred Hittenmiller, to agree to a "covenant" to speak their minds fully during the antiracism training. Mickey and Ann-Elise discuss the covenant at the start of the antiracism training:

Old: A cart of late night snacks had been wheeled into the room, and I caught up with her there. "How did you like that covenant?" she said, dipping a piece of raw broccoli into a white substance in a bowl. Ann-Elise had strong opinions—you couldn't be a lesbian theorist without them—and more often than not she stated them bluntly, but she was careful about who she stated them to. She was smallish and thin, with a heart-shaped face and slouchy posture, and I gathered that most LRC staff saw her, incorrectly, as nonthreatening, somewhere on the spectrum between cute and mousy.

"Did you raise your hand?" [Raising one's hand, in this particular context, signifies acceptance of the covenant.]

"Yup," she said. "Did you?"

"Halfway." Both of us laughed unhappily.

Revised: A cart of late night snacks had been wheeled into the room. I caught up with Ann-Elise while she waited to get at the assortment of chips and cut-up salad vegetables. "So what did you think of that covenant?" Ann-Elise said when she noticed me. She fluffed her hair, a dark brown permanent. Ann-Elise had strong opinions—you couldn't be a lesbian theorist without them—and more often than not she stated them bluntly, but she was careful about who she stated them to. She was smallish and thin then, back before the start of her weight training program, with a heart-shaped face and slouchy posture and a tinny little voice, and I gathered that co-workers tended to view her, incorrectly, as non-threatening, somewhere on the spectrum between cute and mousy.

I started from a place of generosity, wanting to give the trainings a chance and not let myself be swayed by Laura's irrational dislike of Mal Bond. [Mal Bond, the LRC's "antiracism czar," oversees the training.] "The covenant," I mused. "On the surface, it felt a little coercive, but I think it serves a purpose by reminding us we need to participate. What good is a training, after all, if the people being trained are too scared to talk, or if they end up saying things they don't truly believe?"

"I did one of these trainings at the *Gay Gazette*, and another at the place where I worked before that. With everyone saying what they truly believe, these things can turn nasty before you know it."

"I doubt this one will," I said hopefully. "Not with Mal in charge. You may not have gotten to know the guy yet, but he has such a sweet nature. If someone at the training, even Al Hittenmiller, looks like he might get out of line, Mal will jump in and shut him right down, and he'll do it with a velvet glove, so you'll barely even notice."

Reich comments:

In the revised version, Mickey is striving mightily to view the covenant (and train-ing) as benign. He eventually realizes they're not that benign, but it takes him much longer to realize (or admit) this than it should take most readers—or than it takes Ann-Elise, who in the revised version of this scene assumes a bit of Mick-ey's former role as blunt-spoken skeptic.

Passage 4: Mickey and Ann-Elise discuss the vacant job of editor-in-chief.

Old: "So is Sykes the heir apparent?" I said to Ann-Elise then, sitting back down in my ergo-chair.

Ann-Elise was applying for the job herself but only out of stubbornness—that was how I saw it, anyway. John Rain had told us that Pulliam was insisting on a Uni, or Yoonie, as adherents of the faith liked to call themselves, which was pretty much the same as saying no Jews (or Christians) need apply. I knew enough to take the hint, but then I didn't really want the job. That is, I wanted the title and the salary but not the inside politics that went along with them— the squabbles with unhappy readers, the tension-filled powwows with Pulliam and his many vice presidents, the periodic run-ins with the Rev. Mal Bond and his committee.

Revised: "So is Sykes the heir apparent?" I said to Ann-Elise then, leisurely resum-ing my ergo-seat.

It was something I probably shouldn't have raised. Ann-Elise was applying for the job herself, even after John Rain had told us both "in confidence" that Pulliam was insisting on a Uni, or Yoonie, as adherents of the faith liked to call themselves. John Rain's news had been easy enough to believe. Pulliam never missed a chance to point out that the magazine had turned into a bastion of irreligion. Unlike Ann-Elise, I had taken the institutional hint, but then again, I didn't want the job. Or I wanted the title and the salary but not the internal poli-tics that went along with them—he constant squabbles with readers, the tension-filled powwows with Pulliam and his many vice presidents, the periodic run-ins with the Rev. Mal Bond and COPA, Mal's committee for promoting antiracist thought, a rising new group at the LRC.

Reich comments:

On at least three occasions in this short passage, the old version tells the reader something he/she can figure out without Mickey's help. The revision, which lets the reader draw the inference without help from Mickey, makes the narration, and

Mickey, seem less overbearing. In addition, the new version provides some perspective (Mickey's belated realization that he should have avoided discussing the topic with Ann-Elise, given its sensitivity) that was missing in the original version, making Mickey a little more sympathetic.

On the matter of making Mickey more sympathetic to the reader, Reich has a caveat:

> It's fine, and sometimes crucial, for a first person narrator to strike the reader as a fool, an ass, a boor, or even a dangerous criminal, but not in a piece of fiction like mine, where there clearly isn't that much space between the writer and the narrator.

Writing well is a continual process of 1) getting your words on the page, 2) stepping back and evaluating how they sound, 3) entrusting others to help because, as authors, we can be too close to the writing we have created to see how it impacts others differently than we intended, and 4) revising based on our opinion of others' responses and our feelings in rereading what we wrote.

Your Turn

Take a piece of writing you've come across, published or unpublished, that you don't like. See if you can make it into something you do like by changing the tone. You'll do this by making choices about changing wording, changing diction, deleting sentences, changing tense, changing point of view, and/or making scenes vivid where before they were abstract. All of this work is what will contribute to creating a tone that you admire and enjoy or allows you to become involved in what you are reading.

You might enjoy taking a letter to the editor that is written as a barb against another's opinion and/or action and changing it into an offer of friendly help; or try rewriting an objective news article as a love letter.

It's a little harder to practice these moves on your own writing, but with some time and distance (and the practice) it can be done. In fact, I think that most of the time when their tone is off, writers can hear and feel it somewhere inside, but they don't listen to the little voice or the body response that signals them something is off. It's pretty easy for the ego to take over when we are writing and tell us we sound good to protect us from having to get into unknown territory as we work to polish our writing. Always pay attention to what your ear is telling you, and use the tools Reich reviews to make good tone choices.

Endings

Novelist Bharti Kirchner wrote a useful discussion of how to approach endings in the July, 2007, issue of *The Writer* magazine. In "Step by Step: Write an ending your readers will savor," she reminds us to bring the protagonist on stage by asking:

> Where is she? Is she alone or with somebody? What is her emotional state, her hopes (if any)? Who has become the most important person in her life? How is she different at these closing moments than she was in the beginning? What important lessons has she learned?

She recounts how Jane Hamilton ends *When Madeline Was Young*, a multigenerational family story:

> When we finished our sandwiches, we turned for the north, leaving the two of them at their places on the deck. The sun was moving beyond the trees and houses, no place in my old town to see it finally slip over the filmy city horizon. Madeline and my father would sit there together until the fireflies appeared and the street lights came on, waiting for the ghostly mothers to ring their bells and sing out the names of their children from the back porches—time, at long last, to come inside.

"Dazzle with a snapshot of the physical surroundings," Kirchner says. "The image should say something about the person or the situation, or should provide a vision of things to come."

In her novel *Pastries: A Novel of Desserts and Discoveries*, Kirchner planned on showing her protagonist Sunya alone, assessing how her trip to Japan and studies had transformed her life. She wrote, "As I lock the door to my bakery, I give a glance to the signboard above." She realized, though, that the main character's lover, Andrew, had to be there too at the ending because her relationship to him had affected her transformation. So she switched the locale of the ending to Andrew's apartment. As Sunya waits for him she thinks:

> How different the space appears, how remote it feels. The bed, bereft of its sheets, seems somber and cold. ... Open suitcases are not only ugly, but also malevolent obstacles that trip you up no matter which way you turn.
>   A man on the move. A man who does what he wants, yesterday's promises forgotten.

Thematically, the author says, Sunya realizes in Andrew's physical absence that he is absent from her new sense of purpose.

Bharti Kirchner Helps You Take Your Turn

Here is Kirchner's instruction:

> Do some free writing on the last few moments of your story to blow up each moment. You can, for example, begin with such phrases as: "It was time to...." "She looked up and..." or "He ran toward..."
>
> Write for five minutes without stopping. When you are done, select the best sentences or paragraphs and you will be zeroing in on your ending.

*****

Now that you have practiced with the elements of fiction, select a short story, film, or novel and pay close attention to how the writer handled all of these elements. Go back and forth working on your own project and reading another's work. Compare what you are doing in your writing to the techniques the author you admire uses.

Share your work with trusted first readers and see if they are responding to your work as you are responding to the work you admire. If they are not, can you see why? If they are, can you see what you have done that is encouraging this response?

Writing fiction is as intricate as building and furnishing a house. But everything is done in stages, from laying the foundation and building the framing to painting and furnishing the rooms. With a house, you don't have walls to paint until the framing is done, the roof on, and the drywall installed. In writing, it is easy to slip from framework to painting. Go ahead, it's okay. But when you look into revising to complete your story, try to see the work as something you build. Check out the foundation (narrative line and time frame); look at the framing (plot and arc of story); take a look at the walls (point of view, character development, and dialog), and at the paint job (scenes and tone). When you open the door, is the story a place you want to enter? When you exit the house, have you had a complete experience of the place you left behind?

As in everything you write, does a door click shut, leaving you satisfied and another door open, haunting you to stretch in your thinking and feeling as a consequence of what you read?

A Juncture! More Travel Ahead!

Now that you've finished the journey you began with me in an attempt to demystify creative writing, I'm certain you realize that mysteries will continually crop up along the way in your creative writing journey. But just like tourists who are familiar with travel but not necessarily with particular spots, always feel free to ask questions of those you think may have answers. There is so much to discover and experience in the writing life. Here are some of my favorite questions from students and other teachers of writing:

Question: What should I do about writing about my family, friends, or colleagues when I worry that they will be angry at me for writing about them?

Answer: You should write what it is you have to write. If it helps you to change the names of people in your writing, go ahead. If you are worried about legalities, know that when you are done you can seek legal advice. You must not stop your process even if you are worried about what you will do in the end about publication. Should you decide not to publish something because it will upset someone or produce trouble, you will have cleared yourself of the topic and be better prepared to go on to write on other topics.

It is very important to remember that when you finish a piece of writing, you will have come to see things more fully; those who you thought would be upset with you might be interested in your truths. You may be worrying about what they will say, rather than facing your worry that you might not be able to write well enough to do your topic justice. You must use your energy to work on your writing. After it is completed, you can decide what to do about showing it to those who might dislike it. Many writers share their manuscripts and ask if there are parts someone named would like to see deleted. Carolyn See once told a bookstore audience that she showed her manuscript of the memoir *Dreaming* to the three ex-husbands she wrote about, expecting them to disagree with some of what she said. The only reported problem, she said, was that one of the husbands was upset that she had described him as balding.

While you are writing, writing groups are very valuable because they are made up of people who understand the dilemma writers face in writing from their life experience, and they are very supportive, providing an audience that will approve of the fact that you are working something out through your writing and want, with the help of your peers, to find what it is you have to say.

Question: Is there not only writer's block but writer's guilt, as well? My husband supports my staying home and focusing on creative work. There's the rub! I am finally getting our lives organized enough to have a few extra hours each day. Yet they are still easily drained away with triviality. In order to get my first book written, I had to stay behind while he took a year sabbatical. It is now one year later and my book needs a major reworking before being truly ready. I had several years at home before even beginning to make that bit of progress. I feel stymied every time I sit down. I've climbed this huge mountain, and have more huge ones ahead. How can I set up a way to measure progress and focus on what use I can make of the time I do have, instead of feeling so beaten down?

Answer: First of all, you made a major commitment and stuck to it by staying home while your husband went on sabbatical. In a sense, you were on a sabbatical, too, one devoted to writing your book. But books don't always get finished in one year. My memoir took me seven years, many of them after I had written my way from a beginning to an ending. I think if you produce a work plan for revision and development you will feel that you are focused. I am not sure how much of the reworking you are already clear on, or if the reworking is something you are just now figuring out, but here are some ideas of what that part of your process might entail:

1. Might you hire an editor to work with you on five pages? You can learn a lot from having a professional copyeditor point things out about the prose,

and then you can apply those lessons to the whole book in your revising efforts.

2. Might you submit the manuscript for developmental help if you haven't already done so? The Author-Editor Clinic (http://www. authoreditorclinic.com/) in Seattle does good work. I also evaluate manuscripts (http://www.writingitreal.com/page.php?p=one_on_one_help).

3. If you have already done things similar to 1 and 2, here are some milestones you can set for a writing schedule that allows you to feel you are making progress on the reworking: You can find trusted readers to read the revisions and give you response. You can begin sending excerpts out for publication in venues appropriate for the content. You can learn how to write a book proposal, and in doing so you will find out more about the reworking you must do to match what you are pitching. You can also tighten sample chapters to go along with the proposal. You can learn about query letters (*The Writers' Market* from Writers' Digest Books is a good source) and how to write them and send them to find editors and agents interested in reading the book proposal. They won't expect you to have the whole book done unless you are a first time fiction writer.

4. Most of all, realize that if you wrote from beginning to end in a year, you have done an enormous amount of work and accomplished an important goal. Now you deserve to take mini retreats where you can concentrate on the work ahead in chunks of uninterrupted time.

Question: How do you know when you're really done with a piece?

Answer: I often feel that a piece of work is finished because I have gotten insight or peace of mind from what I wrote, or I feel I have figured out how to provide a lesson in the case of instructional writing. Then I show the work to an editor or writing group and, lo and behold, they have questions—and I realize that there is more I have to do to allow my thinking and feeling to make full contact with someone outside of my mind and heart. I have to fill in the gaps I'd left on the page because I didn't need them or I leap too quickly from one moment to another. Sometimes, it is a matter of just getting the reader there with me, but sometimes it is a matter of realizing that I was doing a little jerry rigging and have to really mine my experience for all of the truth.

So, how to know when you are done—when you feel the ah-ha moment? Not really. When others do? Probably. When an editor has trimmed and the piece is even better? Very likely.

Is there a final way to know? No, I don't think so. I think writers just continue until they don't know what else to do or until they feel excited by where the writing brought them. Then it is the others who help the writer make the piece one that reaches many because the connections it is making ring true.

Question: In reading prize-winning poetry, I find some of it full of imagery *AND* the meaning is clear and understandable. Other poetry leaves me scratching my head; though the words might be beautiful, they seem a jumble of random words. Is it me? Obviously someone thinks those poems are great.

Answer: Many people find a lot of the poetry out there to be unpoetic or unintelligible. It's hard to have an answer for this question without having examples of the poems that read like "a jumble of random words." Sometimes, allowing ourselves to get the message from poems means suspending our logical brains and allowing ourselves to go with the metaphors and make leaps of association. Still, there will be an emotional logic to it all that should keep the poem from reading like a random jumble.

There are so many fine poets out there and so many fine poems, that my advice is not to worry about why the poem isn't working for you and find poems that do work for you. And then read everything you can by that poet. And look to see where that poet's work appeared before it was collected in a book and read those literary journals—the same editor must have collected other poems you will appreciate. Also, you might read some interviews with the poet you like and find out who that poet loves to read. In this way you will create a line of poetry you do enjoy.

You might bring the poems that you have trouble liking or understanding to a study group with other poets and see what their reactions are. There's certainly enough poetry to go around, but stretching one's own appreciation by seeing how others absorb a poem can be eye- (ear-? heart-?) opening. Or it may affirm just what you thought— "random jumble of words." Poetry 180 (www.loc.gov/poetry/180/), the website Billy Collins started, is a great place to start for poems that are accessible and moving. Then you can move onto the PoetryFoundation.org (www.poetryfoundation.org/) archives. I know you'll find poems you love on these sites. If there are some that are unintelligible, don't worry—go on to read more of the ones you like and that carry you away. But do find out what others think, and if they like a poem you don't, why they like it.

Question: What is your advice about writing contests?

Answer: Contest judges have so many entries that they are looking for reasons not to have to read so much, and if your entry comes in without following the guidelines, that is a reason not to read it. Follow the stated submission guidelines.

Big name contests may be "good for your career," but they might not be winnable; there are so very many writers out there, and so many of them are in a group that knows one another on a national level. There are stories of how this influences the judges despite entries coming in without names. Also since screening judges are employed, the big name final judge doesn't see the overwhelming number of entries. What is good for your morale and your local presence are local contests: arts commissions, local magazines, colleges with literary magazines, and local presses; all hold contests and I think they are worth entering. Winning them is a step up on the ladder and does bring you to the attention of your local community, which can be incredibly supportive and help you become a rising star.

Question: Why is it so hard to keep a regular practice of writing when it feels so good to do it?

Answer: I think it is a question of inertia—we get so used to being one way with ourselves, our minds, our time, that it is hard to move into an altered state, which I believe writing is. Also, to write well, we have to give up control and allow the words to come through us without judgment, at least in starting the material and writing until there is enough down on the page to make good use of our editing and shaping skills. We don't like to give up control, to be surprised by what we say, even to try at times to make sense of what the words are telling us. And sometimes they tell us things we want to ignore.

But once we have moved beyond the inertia and our brain is in flow, we get such a high. Still, the next time we have to move once more beyond the fear of not knowing what we will have to say, as well as the fear that our words are not up to the challenge of saying what we have to say.

Writing isn't built in one session, though, and as writers we need to look for the words and phrases we put down that we want to continue writing from and then continue, rather than get stuck in harshly judging our first drafts and freewrites as inadequate.

And guess where we learned such judging ways? In school, when we weren't taught that writing is a process and where we had to write without sounding like we'd written what we wrote if teachers demanded "objectivity."

Question: I have an idea for a novel. I think it will make a great story, and I've written several scenes. However, I don't know where to start to organize the whole thing and create the structure that makes a good novel, such as a strong beginning, middle and end, and a strong plot. Where do I start?

Answer: I have valued reading accounts of the writing process by many who write novels, short fiction, and screenplays. Each author has their own way of organizing their work and their approach and so of course do I—after reading so many people on the topic, I have put together exercises to do in an order that I believe will get you writing well and continually without too much worry about how to do it and more emphasis on doing it! Go back and read the fiction part of this book—it wouldn't hurt to review the exercises every time you start a piece—they are something tangible to hold onto as you swim into new waters.

Question: Where does creative writing end and uncreative writing begin?

Answer: This is most likely in the eye of the beholder, whether that is the reader or the writer, but there are attributes of creative writing that set it apart from technical, research, journalistic, and scientific writing. I would say that the most definitive of the attributes is the desire creative writers have to create a mood in their reader—nostalgic, sentimental, joyous, awestruck, and sorrowful among them—by shaping their experience for the page. Another distinguishing attribute is that creative writers don't fully know what they are writing about until they have written it. In the other written forms, the writer already knows what information to impart and writes to impart it. That's not to say that writing information you already know doesn't always also deliver surprises and help you see things in a new way. So, where does noncreative writing stop and creative writing start? Along a spectrum, I would say. A most important question for me when I am writing on a topic to impart information is, "What is in this for me? What will I learn by writing what I am about to write?" Seeking something turns all writing into creative writing for me.

Question: What compels us to record our thoughts, our imaginative leaps and stretches, and our insights?

Answer: We are meaning-making by nature and it takes leaps and associations to find meaning and to think things through. Research shows we don't make decisions with our minds only. We use our hearts and intuition. We are wired for it all and like to use it!

Question: What resources are there out there for me as a new writer?

Answer: Plenty of them. I'll list some more of my favorites, ones that are chock full of listings and useful information:

Five More Books on General Creative Writing

Writing in a New Convertible with the Top Down, Sheila Bender and Christie Killien, www.Libertary.com

A Year in the Life: Journaling for Self-Discovery, by Sheila Bender, International Association for Journal Writers, www.iajw.com

Writing Brave & Free: Encouraging Words for People Who Want to Start Writing, Ted Kooser and Steve Cox, University of Nebraska Press, Lincoln, NE, 2006.

The Muses Among Us: Eloquent Listening and Other Pleasures of the Writer's Craft, Kim Stafford, The University of Georgia Press, Athens, GA, 2003.

The Power of Story: Write to Shape Experience, Gabriele Lusser Rico, Absey & Company, Spring, TX, 2009.

Five More Books for Poets

Poem, Revised: 54 Poems, Revisions, Discussions, edited by Robert Hartwell Riske and Laura Cherry, Marion Street Press, Portland, OR, 2008.

Ordinary Genius: A Guide for the Poet Within, Kim Addonizio, W. W. Norton & Company, NY, 2009.

The Poetry Home Repair Manual, Ted Kooser, Bison Books, University of Nebraska Press, Lincoln, NE, 2007.

The Shape of Poetry: A Practical Guide to Writing Poetry, Peter Meinke, Jefferson Press, Chattanooga, TN, 2008.

Triggering Towns: Lectures and Essays on Poetry and Writing, Richard Hugo, W. W. Norton & Company, NY, 1992.

Five More Books for Creative Nonfiction Writers

In Pieces: An Anthology of Fragmentary Writing, edited by Olivia Dresher, Impassio Press, Seattle, WA, 2006.

Word Painting: A Guide to Writing More Descriptively, Rebecca McClanahan, Writer's Digest Books, Cincinnati, OH, 2000.

Inventing The Truth: The Art and Craft of Memoir, edited by William Zinsser, Houghton Mifflin, NY, 1995.

Writing the Natural Way, Gabrielle Rico, Tarcher, NY, 2000.

A Walk Between Heaven and Earth: A Personal Journal on Writing and the Creative Process, Durghild Nina Holzer, Bell Tower, NY, 1994.

Five More Books for Fiction Writers

A Piece of Work: Five Writers Discuss Their Revisions, edited by Jay Woodruff, University of Iowa Press, Iowa City, IA, 1993.

The Story Behind the Story, edited by Andrea Barrett and Peter Turchi, Norton, NY, 2004.

The Art of Subtext, Charles Baxter, Graywolf Press Series, St. Paul, MN, 2007.

A Story is a Promise, Bill Johnson, Blue Heron Publishing, Portland, OR, 2000.

What If? Writing Exercises for Fiction Writers, Anne Bernays and Pamela Painter, Harper Collins, 1990.

Five More Resources for Learning More About the Writing Life

Writer's Digest magazine (www.writersdigest.com) has electronic as well as in-print resources ranging from how-to columns, author interviews, conference information, and website listings, to market information for writers. The magazine offers a free electronic newsletter as well as online classes. The website also features writing prompts and responses to them.

The Writer magazine (www.writermag.com) also offers a free electronic newsletter, a print magazine, articles both online and in print on the writers' craft, conference listings, and market information. The website also features blogs on the craft of writing.

The Associated Writing Programs (www.awpwriter.org) maintains a listing of all undergraduate and graduate accredited writing programs in the United States; it publishes *The Writer's Chronicle*, a rich and full resource about writers and their work, and maintains conference listings among other useful information.

Poets & Writers magazine (www.pw.org/magazine) offers articles and interviews about writing and writers, contest listings, conference listings, and publication information including an interesting section on manuscripts wanted—often about themed anthologies. Visit the website for daily news of interest to writers.

Facebook is a rich source for writers, from fans of pages for books and writing organizations to sources of help and prompts. Do a search using the keywords "writing" and "writing organizations," and you'll find many pages full of resources, camaraderie, and help.

* * * * *

Go forth and wander the world of your experience, your memories, and your imagination. You have tools now that will help, and, I believe, the understanding that only you can give yourself the go-ahead to travel the pathways of this strange/familiar, large/small, public/private engrossing terrain.

Contributors

I write to find out... what I didn't know I knew... until I wrote about it.

Caroline Arnold is the author of more than 140 books for children, many of them illustrated with her own art. She conducts author presentations and workshops at schools and libraries nationwide and teaches in the Writer's Program at UCLA Extension. *A Walrus' World* and *A Killer Whale's World* are in her series *Caroline Arnold's Animals* published by Picture Window Books. Her website is www.carolinearnold.com.

Kellie Van Atta packed her bags and moved to Malibu to attend Pepperdine in 2000. She enjoyed her stay at Pepperdine and was privileged to study overseas in Heidelberg. Upon her return, she became serious about pursuing a teaching career and got a job teaching 9th and 10th grade English at Oaks Christian High School. This is Kellie's sixth year teaching. She is still learning about grammar, teaching, and teenagers, and passionately loves her job.

Kit Bakke's bio-memoir, *Miss Alcott's E-mail: Yours for Reforms of All Kinds*, imagines the author and Louisa May Alcott exchanging e-mails across time and includes historical essays about Alcott's life and Bakke's own politically radical past. She won Honorable Mention in the Pacific Northwest Writer's Association's Mainstream Novel category contest and has delivered the University of Washington's Blom Endowed Lecture. She has been a resident at the Ragdale Foundation and has taught at writer's conferences such as Edmonds Write on the Sound, Fields' End, and A Book for All Seasons. She coordinated Seattle's Hugo House's InPrint speakers series in 2006–2007. She is a founding member of Seattle7Writers, a group of published authors supporting local literacy efforts.

Lori Brack graduated from Western Washington University with an MA in poetry. Now in Kansas, she leads poetry workshops at a high school and teaches advanced composition at a community college, as well as writes for a history museum and an art museum. Three of her poems appear in *The Packingtown Review*. Other work appears in *The North American Review, The Midwest Quarterly*, and *Rosebud*. Her chapbook manuscript, *Another Case for the Dead Letter Detective*, was a finalist in the Pilot Books call for manuscripts.

Jefferson Carter has won a Tucson/Pima Arts Council Literary Arts Fellowship, and his poems have appeared in such journals as *Carolina Quarterly, Cutthroat*, and *Barrow Street*. His chapbook *Tough Love* won the Riverstone Poetry Press Award. *Sentimental Blue*, published by Chax Press in 2007, was nominated for a Pushcart Prize. His eighth collection of poems, *My Kind of Animal*, is now available from Chax Press. He is a volunteer with the Tucson, AZ, environmental organization Sky Island Alliance.

Janice Eidus' latest novel is *The Last Jewish Virgin*. Two-time winner of the O. Henry Prize for Short Fiction, she's published five other books, including the novel *The War of the Rosens* and the story collection, *The Celibacy Club*. She frequently writes about Jewish identity, popular culture, sex and gender, and being a writer/parent. She teaches Fiction Writing and Creative Nonfiction Writing for the Low Residency MFA Program in Creative Writing at Carlow University and is a private writing coach. She divides her time between Brooklyn, NY and San Miguel de Allende, Mexico.

Elizabeth Evans' two story collections are *Suicide's Girlfriend* and *Locomotion*. Her novels are *The Blue Hour, Rowing in Eden*, and *Carter Clay*, which was selected by *The Los Angeles Times* for "The Best Books of 1999." She is the recipient of numerous awards, including a National Endowment for the Arts Fellowship, a James Michener Fellowship from the University of Iowa, a Lila Wallace Award, and The Four Corners Award; she has been a fellow at MacDowell, Yaddo, and Hawthornden International Retreat in Scotland, among other foundations. She is Full Professor in the Creative Writing Program at the University of Arizona.

Meg Files is the author of *Meridian 144*, a novel; *Home Is the Hunter*, a collection of stories; *Write from Life*, a book about using personal experience and taking risks in writing; *The Love Hunter and Other Poems*; and *A Hollow, Muscular Organ*, a forthcoming novella/story collection. She is the editor of *Lasting: Poems on Aging*. Her poems and stories have appeared in many publications, including *Fiction* and *Crazyhorse*. Her awards include a Bread Loaf fellowship.

She was the James Thurber Writer-in-Residence at Ohio State University. She teaches creative writing in Tucson.

Deborah Gaal is a former entrepreneur and corporate executive and a student of the craft of writing. Her first work, a novel with the working title, *The Synchronicity of Noah Friedman*, won an "Editor's Choice Award" at the San Diego Writer's Conference. She is working on her second manuscript.

Raul Gallardo was born on December 22, 1982 in Leon, Mexico. He tried to fit in with the novelists, short story writers, and screenwriters in every possible genre until he discovered poets were the only club in which he felt authentic and unique. A finalist for the Wergle Flomp humor contest, his poems have appeared in online magazines such as *Pens on Fire* and *Neon Magazine*.

Dorothy Randall Gray has appeared with the Nuyorican Poets Café, and at the United Nations, The Kitchen, Museum of Natural History, International Center for Cultural Studies, Huntington Women's Studies Association, PEN America, Columbia University, Carnegie-Mellon Institute, Pitzer, The Open Center, UNESCO, and the Center for Policy Studies. Author of *Soul Between the Lines: Freeing Your Creative Spirit Through Writing*, her work appears in many other publications as well, including *Muse Blues, Woman, Fierce with Reality, Family, The Passion Collection*, and *A Taste of Tamarinda*. She has contributed to *Personal Journaling, Heart&Soul*, the *NY Times, Drum Voices, SisterFire, HealthQuest*, and *Conditions*. Her website is www.DorothyRandallGray.com.

Adrianne Harun's first short story collection, *The King of Limbo*, was a Sewanee Writing Series selection and a Washington State Book Award finalist and included award-winning stories originally published in *Story* and the *Chicago Tribune*. Stories from an upcoming collection have been short listed in both *Best American Mystery Stories* and *Best American Short Stories*. She teaches in the Rainier Writing Workshops, an MFA program at Pacific Lutheran University.

Jack Heffron is editorial director of Clerisy Press and has been a professional editor for more than 18 years. The books he has edited have garnered publication prizes such as the James Beard Award (cooking), CEO Reads' All-Time Top 100 (business), and the Agatha Award (women's mystery). He is the author of three books for writers *The Writer's Idea Book, The Writer's Guide to Places*, and *The Writer's Idea Workshop*. A founding editor of *Story* magazine, he is a two-time winner of the National Magazine Award for Fiction and editor for the critically acclaimed *Best Writing on Writing* series. He is currently a contributing editor to *Cincinnati* magazine and is developing a series for the History Channel.

Holly Hughes is the editor of *Beyond Forgetting: Poetry and Prose about Alzheimer's Disease*, published by Kent State University Press as part of their Literature and Medicine Series in spring 2009. Her award-winning chapbook *Boxing the Compass* was published by Floating Bridge Press in 2007. Her poems have been nominated for Pushcart and Arts & Letters prizes. A graduate of the Rainier Writing Workshop low-residency MFA program, she teaches writing at Edmonds Community College, where she co-directs the Convergence Writers Series and the Sustainability Initiative. She divides her time between Indianola and Chimacum, Washington.

Bharti Kirchner is the author of four cookbooks and four novels. *Publisher's Weekly* has said Kirchner "proves a sensitive observer of India and the dilemmas of bicultural heritage." Her fourth novel, *Pastries: A Novel of Desserts and Discoveries*, was selected for the Washington Reads program. Her latest publication is a short story that appears in *Seattle Noir* (Akashic Books), an anthology of mystery short stories. Her work has been translated into German, Dutch, Spanish, Thai, and other languages.

Judith Kitchen is the author of two books of essays, *Only the Dance* and *Distance and Direction*. Her novel is *The House on Eccles Road*. She is editor of three anthologies of short nonfiction pieces, *In Short*, *In Brief*, and *Short Takes*, all published by W. W. Norton. She teaches in the Rainier Writing Workshop, a low-residency MFA program at Pacific Lutheran University in Tacoma, WA.

Nancy Lamb is the author of 43 fiction and non-fiction books for adults and children. She is also the author of *The Art and Craft of Storytelling* and *The Writer's Guide to Crafting Stories for Children*. Lamb serves on the faculty of the Big Sur Writing Workshop and the Big Sur Children's Writing Workshop. She taught at the Hariette Austin Writing Program at the University of Georgia, and recently taught a master class in Singapore for the Media Development Authority. An editor and story strategist, she has joined the faculty of a new online learning site for writers, www.ScribblersUniversity.com.

Holly Lisle has won the Compton Crook Award for Best First Novel, was a finalist twice for the John W. Campbell Award for Best New Writer, and has had a number of books hit the Locus Bestseller List. *Diplomacy of Wolves* also spent two months on the Waldenbooks Bestseller List. Visit her website at http://hollylisle.com/ for more information about her scores of books and recent work on behalf of writers.

Kathy Lockwood is pursuing a master's degree at Alaska Pacific University where she is studying poetry. She earned a bachelor's degree at Vermont College,

Norwich University, with an emphasis in nonfiction creative writing. She teaches creative writing and knitting workshops in the Anchorage, Alaska, area, where she finds inspiration in the majestic mountains and wilderness nearby. She enjoys yoga, camping, canoeing, and long walks with her cairn terrier and Labrador.

Rebecca McClanahan is the author of nine books, most recently *Deep Light: New and Selected Poems 1987–2007* and *The Riddle Song and Other Rememberings*, which won the Glasgow Prize in Nonfiction, *Write Your Heart Out: Exploring and Expressing What Matters to You*, and *Word Painting: A Guide to Writing More Descriptively*. Her poems, essays, and stories have appeared in *Ms. Magazine, The Georgia Review, The Gettysburg Review, Southern Review, Kenyon Review, Boulevard, Seventeen*, and numerous literary magazines and anthologies throughout the country. McClanahan has received a Pushcart Prize in fiction, the Wood Prize from *Poetry* magazine, and the Carter prize for the essay from *Shenandoah*. Her work appears in *The Best American Essays 2001, The Best American Poetry 1998*, and has been aired on NPR's "The Writer's Almanac," "The Sound of Writing," and "Living on Earth." McClanahan, currently teaches in the MFA programs of Queens University (Charlotte, NC) and Pacific Lutheran University, the Kenyon Review Writers' Workshop, and the Hudson Valley Writers' Center.

Margaret D. McGee's book *Sacred Attention: A Spiritual Practice for Finding God in the Moment*, published in fall 2007 by SkyLight Paths Publishing, uses personal stories and practices to show how a moment of close attention can be a prayer to God. *Stumbling Toward God: A Prodigal's Return*, published in 2001, tells the story of the author's journey from atheism to a new faith with the help of both the Episcopal parish and Unitarian Universalist fellowship in her small town. At her website, IntheCourtyard.com, she shares her further adventures along the spiritual path through prayers, meditations, and other writings that spring from her relationship with the Episcopal Church.

Cheryl Merrill's poems have appeared in *Paintbrush, Northwest Review, Willow Springs*, and others, and have been anthologized in *A Gift of Tongues: 25 Years of Poetry from Copper Canyon Press* and a chapbook of poems, *Cheat Grass*, from Copper Canyon Press; parts of her photo-essay series about elephants appear in *Iron Horse Literary Review, South Loop Review, Isotope, Alaska Quarterly Review*, and in *The Drexel Online Journal*. Other elephant essays have also appeared in *Brevity, Fourth Genre, Pilgrimage, Creative Nonfiction* "Best of Brevity," *Ghoti*, and *Seems*. Her essay "Trunk" received special mention in the Pushcart Prize anthology of 2008 and "Singing Like Yma Sumac" was reprinted in *Short Takes: Model Essay for Composition*.

Dinty W. Moore is Professor of English at Ohio University and a low-residency instructor for the University of New Orleans' San Miguel de Allende Summer Writing Workshops. He has published three books of creative nonfiction, *Between Panic and Desire, The Accidental Buddhist,* and *The Emperor's Virtual Clothes;* a short story collection, *Toothpick Men;* and the textbook, *The Truth of the Matter: Art and Craft in Creative Nonfiction.* His essays and stories appear in *The Southern Review, The Georgia Review, Harpers, The New York Times Sunday Magazine, Utne Reader, Arts & Letters,* and *Crazyhorse,* among others. He edits *Brevity,* the online journal of concise creative nonfiction. He is a recipient of grants from the National Endowment for the Arts and the Pennsylvania Council on the Arts and is currently president of the Associated Writing Programs.

William Mawhinney has led monthly poetry circles at a local library, volunteered as a poet in elementary school classrooms, and offered poetry workshops and readings throughout the Southwest. Chased from the woods by a wildfire, he and his wife, Wanda, an abstract painter, now live in Port Ludlow, WA. He organizes and hosts Port Townsend's Northwind Reading Series, performs poetry in local retirement homes, and tends his Japanese garden. His books of poems, *Songs in My Begging Bowl* and *Cairns Along the Road,* are available through him; email mawhinneyw_w@msn.com.

Josip Novakovich is a Croatian-American writer whose fiction and nonfiction have won many awards including a Whiting Writer's Award, a National Endowment for the Arts fellowship, and a Guggenheim fellowship. His major works include *Infidelities: Stories of War and Lust, April Fool's Day, Yolk, Salvation and Other Disasters,* and *Apricots from Chernobyl.* He has also been anthologized in *Best American Poetry* (1997).

Lisa Owens is a writer and editor working in children's publishing. Since 1993 she has put her stamp on thousands of works for kids and educators. As children's author, she has published more than 70 books and stories. Recent titles include *Frenemies: Dealing with Friend Drama* and *The Great Chicago Fire.* Find her online at LLOwens.com and OwensEditorialInk.com.

Midge Raymond's short-story collection, *Forgetting English,* received the Spokane Prize for Short Fiction. Her work has appeared in *TriQuarterly, American Literary Review, Ontario Review, Indiana Review, North American Review, Los Angeles Times,* and other publications. Midge has taught communication and creative writing at Boston University, Boston's Grub Street Writers, San Diego Writers Ink, and Seattle's Richard Hugo House. She is the recipient of a 2009 Artist Trust/Washington State Arts Commission Fellowship (www.artisttrust.org).

Nahid Rachlin's publications include a memoir, *Persian Girls*; four novels, *Jumping Over Fire, Foreigner, Married to a Stranger* and *The Heart's Desire;* as well as *Veils*, a short story collection. Her individual short stories have appeared in about fifty magazines, including *The Virginia Quarterly Review, Prairie Schooner, Redbook*, and *Shenandoah*. Her reviews and essays have appeared in the *New York Times, Newsday, Washington Post*, and *Los Angeles Times*. She has held the Doubleday-Columbia Fellowship and a Wallace Stegner Fellowship, and received the Bennet Cerf Award, PEN Syndicated Fiction Project Award, and a National Endowment for the Arts grant. She teaches at the New School University and is an Associate Fellow at Yale. Her website is www.nahidrachlin.com.

David Reich is a novelist, short fiction, and nonfiction writer who received his MFA from the University of Arkansas. His new novel is *The Antiracism Trainings*; his shorter works have appeared in *North American Review, Transatlantic Review, Beyond Baroque, The Smith*, and other journals. An earlier novel, *The Path of Bowling*, was nominated for the Editor's Book Award. As a journalist for more than 20 years, Reich has published profiles and interviews of major figures in politics, the arts, law, law enforcement, and economics.

Susan Rich is the author of three books of poetry from White Pine Press: *The Cartographer's Tongue: Poems of the World, Cures Include Travels*, and *The Alchemist's Kitchen*. She has received awards from the Academy of American Poets, PEN USA, and Artist Trust. Her poems have appeared in *The Antioch Review, Harvard Review*, and *the New England Review*. She teaches English and Film Studies at Highline Community College in Washington State.

Peggy Shumaker's newest book is *Just Breathe Normally* (University of Nebraska Press, 2007). Her most recent collection of poems is *Blaze*, a collaboration with the painter Kesler Woodward (Red Hen Press). She teaches in the low-residency MFA Rainier Writing Workshop. Please visit her website at www.peggyshumaker.com.

Michael Dylan Welch founded the Tanka Society of America in 2000, serving as its president for five years. He has also served as vice president of the Haiku Society of America for many years, and co-founded both the Haiku North America conference (1991) and the American Haiku Archives (1996). He has won first place in numerous haiku, senryu, and tanka contests, and his poetry has been published in hundreds of journals and anthologies in more than a dozen languages. He has also published numerous books of his poetry, including translations. He lives with his wife and two children in Sammamish, Washington.

Steven Winn is an award-winning journalist and fiction writer who spent many years as a staff writer at the *San Francisco Chronicle*. His family memoir, *Come Back, Como: Winning the Heart of a Reluctant Dog,* was published in 2009 by HarperCollins. A Philadelphia native and founding staff member of the *Seattle Weekly,* he held a Wallace Stegner Fellowship in fiction at Stanford University. His work has appeared in *Good Housekeeping, National Lampoon,* the *New York Times, Parenting, Prairie Schooner, Sports Illustrated,* and *Utne Reader.* He lives with his family in San Francisco.

Linda C. Wisniewski is a librarian and writer in Bucks County, PA, where she teaches memoir workshops at senior centers and retirement homes and for Bucks County Community College. Her work has been published in anthologies and literary journals, both print and online. Her memoir, *Off Kilter: A Woman's Journey to Peace with Scoliosis, Her Mother and Her Polish Heritage,* was published in 2008 by Pearlsong Press. Linda speaks to groups on the healing power of writing.

Index